*Joseph Smith
Fought Polygamy*

"What a thing it is for a man to be accused of committing adultery, and having seven wives, when I can only find one."—Joseph Smith

Joseph Smith Fought Polygamy

How Men Nearest the Prophet Attached
Polygamy to His Name in Order to Justify
Their Own Polygamous Crimes

Richard and Pamela Price

Volume 1

Price Publishing Company
Independence, Missouri

Copyright © 2000
Price Publishing Company
915 E. 23rd Street
Independence, MO 64055

Phone (816) 461-5659
FAX (816) 461-5565

Printed in the United States of America

Library of Congress Cataloging-in-Publication Data

Price, Richard, 1924–
    Joseph Smith fought polygamy : how men nearest the prophet attached polygamy to his name in order to justify their own polygamous crimes / by Richard and Pamela Price.
        p.   cm.
    Includes bibliographical references and index.
    ISBN 1-891353-06-3 hardcover (alk. paper)
    ISBN 1-891353-05-5 paperback (alk. paper)
    1. Polygamy--Religious aspects--Mormon Church--History of doctrines. 2. Mormon Church--Doctrines--History. 3. Smith, Joseph, 1805–1844--Contributions in doctrine of marriage. 4. Marriage--Religious aspects--Mormon Church--History of doctrines. I. Price, Pamela, 1926–   . II. Title.
BX8641.P87   2000
289.3--dc21   99-41763
                                                                          CIP

Contents

Maps, Illustrations, and Pictures vii
Preface ix

Chapter   Page

1. Cochranism: The Origin of Utah Mormon Polygamy 1
2. Other Accounts of Cochranism 9
3. Church Missionaries Converted Cochranites 19
4. Brigham Young: The Father of Mormon Polygamy 31
5. The Apostles Brought Polygamy into the Church 41
6. Early Efforts to Eradicate Polygamy 49
7. Dr. Bennett Laid the Foundation of Polygamy at Nauvoo 63
8. Dr. Bennett and Eliza R. Snow 77
9. Eliza Snow Was Not Pushed down the Mansion House Stairs 89
10. More Evidence Concerning Eliza Snow 101
11. Bennett and Francis Higbee's Polygamous Activities Discovered in 1841 111
12. Chauncey L. Higbee Expelled for Polygamous Activities 133
13. Joseph Sued Chauncey L. Higbee in Court at Carthage 143
14. Dr. Bennett Expelled from the Church 161
15. Dr. Bennett Persecuted Joseph and the Church 173
16. Bennett's Polygamy Charges and the Saints' Responses 189
17. Isaac Sheen Was Not a Credible Witness Concerning Polygamy 207

Chapter	Page
18. The Book of Mormon Condemns Polygamy (A Study of the "Righteous Seed" Theory)	219
19. Joseph's Sermon against Polygamy	231
Bibliography	239
Index	247

Maps and Illustrations

Map of Cochranite Area	20
Map of Kirtland and Vicinity	62
Diagram of Mansion House Stairs	88
Eight Color Pages	119–126
Robinson's Transcript	149
Joseph's Subpoena	152

Pictures

Joseph and Emma Smith	119
Portraits of Prominent Persons	120–121
Nauvoo as Seen from Montrose	122
Nauvoo as Painted by David H. Smith	122
Joseph Smith's Red Brick Store	123
Upper Room in Red Brick Store	123
Homestead House	124
Nauvoo Mansion House	124
William Marks' Home	125
Brigham Young's Home	125
Mansion House Stairs	126

Preface

Our study of polygamy among the Mormons began in the early 1950s when we decided to make a serious effort to discover the roots of the doctrine of polygamy in the Church. Polygamy was a subject of natural interest to both of us because of our Church backgrounds. Pamela's great-grandfather, James Robert Dale, went to Utah during Brigham Young's lifetime. James was baptized in Salt Lake City in 1870, and was married and endowed in the Endowment House in the same year. Pamela often heard her grandmother, Mary Dale Sanders, tell how her father, James Dale, fled from Utah to escape polygamy and Brigham Young's tyranny.

Richard was reared in Idaho and Nevada where Momonism was the dominant religion. His father died when Richard was two, and he had two Mormon stepfathers. The first stepfather joined the RLDS Church, but that marriage ended in divorce. His mother, a third-generation RLDS member, later married a staunch Mormon elder, a widower who had gone to the Mormon temple in Salt Lake City where he was endowed, married, and sealed to his first wife and their children for time and eternity.

In our research on this subject, we were encouraged by letters to Pamela from the Prophet Israel A. Smith, president of the Reorganized Church of Jesus Christ of Latter Day Saints. Over the years our endeavors turned into an exhaustive research project as we gathered information by travel and correspondence from many libraries throughout the United States and England. In these studies it was discovered that polygamy as it is known among the Mormons did not begin with Joseph, but was brought into the Church by missionaries and their converts.

This was particularly true of those who were converted from a sect called Cochranites, which was started by Jacob Cochran about 1816. When Cochran's church disintegrated, Latter Day Saint missionaries, including Brigham Young and Orson Hyde, converted some of its adherents, and these people brought their polygamous beliefs with them when they came into the Church. Later some of the Latter Day Saint apostles took plural wives, including women who had known of, or had been connected with, Jacob Cochran's church and its teachings. Cochran's polygamy was well-known throughout New England before the Church was organized. Some of the apostles and their close friends, who had ministered in Cochran's area, began secretly practicing polygamy at Nauvoo at least two years before Joseph's death.

Joseph fought against this doctrine from the time he was married to Emma in 1827 (even before the Church was organized) until the time of his death. He did not practice polygamy nor teach it to others.

Years later his sons went to Utah and proclaimed against polygamy. In order to counteract their efforts, the leaders of the Mormon Church, such as Brigham Young, John Taylor, and Heber C. Kimball, had some of their wives and other women make affidavits that stated they had been Joseph's wives in Nauvoo. The fact that Joseph and Hyrum had no children born of polygamous wives, and that the testimonies of the alleged wives can be proven false, is only a part of the vast amount of evidence which indicates that Joseph was innocent.

It can be proven that men nearest the Prophet entered into a conspiracy against Joseph and Hyrum and attached polygamy to Joseph's name in order to justify their own crimes of practicing it. The polygamous doctrines promoted by this conspiracy are still the basis of the Mormon Church's theology.

Chapter 1

Cochranism
The Origin of Utah Mormon Polygamy

For over a century and a half, the leaders of the Church of Jesus Christ of Latter-day Saints with headquarters in Salt Lake City, Utah, have claimed that the Prophet Joseph Smith, Jr., received a revelation in July 1843, which commanded the Saints to practice polygamy. The truth is, however, that polygamy in the Church had its beginnings, not with Joseph, but with a man named Jacob Cochran. About 1816 Cochran started a denomination in the area of Saco, Maine, in which he introduced polygamy. Some of his polygamous practices were later adopted by Apostles Brigham Young, John Taylor, Heber C. Kimball, Parley P. Pratt, Orson Hyde, and others. These Church leaders secretly practiced polygamy in Nauvoo before Joseph's death, without his approval.

The astounding story of Jacob Cochran's polygamy is told by G. T. Ridlon, Sr., who was related to some of the "Cochranites," as they were called. He spent twenty-five years writing a book, published in 1895, entitled *Saco Valley Settlements and Families*. Excerpts from his book are printed below to acquaint the reader with polygamy as it was being practiced prior to the organization of the Church in 1830. Titles have been inserted in brackets into Ridlon's account in order to lay a foundation for later discussions of the various subjects in his book:

—The Cochran Delusion—

He [Jacob Cochran] must have been a unique and very remarkable character. His intellectual, mesmeric, and physical powers were certainly extraordinary. Whatever view we may entertain regarding the soundness of his doctrines, the methods employed by him, or the character of the man, we have no warrant for believing that he was an illiterate, impulsive ranter, who carried forward his work like a cloud driven by a tempest. On the other hand, he was cool, calculating, and deliberate. . . .

In the towns bordering on the Saco [River] several hundred professed conversion under his preaching, and the influence of the "revival" extended from this locality into other towns in western Maine, until, within a year from the inauguration of the movement, about a thousand persons made a profession of religion. Many of these were sincere believers in the New Testament and were never involved in the ridiculous practices encouraged by the leader.

When Cochran first began to preach in Scarborough and Saco, his commanding appearance, evident learning, matchless oratory, and the uncertainty existing regarding his creed opened to him the churches, and some of the settled pastors listened to him with amazement. . . .

[Revelations to Practice "Spiritual Wifery"]

When Cochran had secured a firm foot-hold in the community, his creed evolved a new and startling phase. He preached against the legal marriage bond, and in the ideal state pictured by him the inhabitants were neither married nor given in marriage; this should begin on earth, being God's standard for society, and be as nearly approximated as mortal conditions would admit of. The affinities were to be all spiritual and were infinitely superior to any relations formed by natural affection. He admonished all who had been united in the bonds of matrimony according to the laws of the land to hold themselves in readiness to dissolve such union and renounce their vows. All revelations to this end were to come through Cochran, of course, and in the allotment of the spoils the leader, by virtue of his rank, was sure to get the "lion's share." Tradition assumes that he received frequent consignments of spiritual consorts, and that such were invariably the most robust and attractive women in the community.

[Cochran Taught the Exchanging of Wives]

As we have intimated, he had a sort of permanent wife, locally known as "Mrs. Cochran"; but his loyalty to her was subject to such revelations as he might receive anent his duty (?) to others. Some who were conversant with these affairs, now living, relate that on one of Cochran's professional visitations he informed one of his male followers that he had, while at prayer in his house that morning, received a communication direct from Him who dwells above the stars that embodied, *inter alia*, a requirement of a peculiar character, namely, that he and the brother addressed should, for the time being, *exchange wives* (italics added). To this, as from the Lord, via Cochran, his medium, the layman consented, and leaving Cochran to assume the government of his family, he immediately went to pay his respects to Mrs. Cochran. Now this woman was somewhat skeptical in regard to her husband's doctrines and practices, and when she responded to the knock at her door and inquired about the nature of the man's errand; when he told her about her husband's new revelation, with clenched fist and flashing eyes she replied: "You go straight back and tell Jake Cochran his God is a liar."

[The Origin of the Garden of Eden Temple Ceremony]

In place of figure-drawings upon a black-board to illustrate scriptural incidents, he employed the more impressive mediums of flesh and blood. One of the favorite tableaux introduced by these fanatics was the personification of our first parents, as they were supposed to have appeared before fig-leaf aprons were in fashion. We have not found a description of the stage scenery used as accessory to this performance, but a part of the programme was for the disciples present, both male and female, to sit upon the floor in a circle while the ideal Adam, in the person of Cochran, and Eve, in the person of some chosen female, came into this extemporized "Garden of Eden". . . .

But disintegrating elements were now beginning to disturb the system. The fact that the preaching of Cochran had the effect to destroy domestic peace, and ruined the home life of many who had become identified with the movement, produced a more healthy reaction than the leader had anticipated. Married men embraced the doctrines promulgated, while their more virtuous or level-headed wives would have no part or lot in the matter. On the other hand, women who had hitherto lived consistent and respectable lives became infatuated with Cochran and his preaching, while their husbands were decidedly averse to both.

These conflicting elements in the home were stimulated rather than conciliated by the leader, and hatred was eventually engendered between heads of families which culminated in separation. . . .

But as the people became acquainted with his style, and the prejudice that preceded his coming wore away, he would excite curiosity and stimulate sensation by introducing some novel ceremony or by making startling statements in his sermons. . . .

At Limington, meetings were held at the dwelling of a native of Buxton, who once lived on Woodsum's hill, below Salmon Falls. Runners were sent down to Buxton and Hollis to advise Cochran's disciples that "Brother Jacob" would hold meetings on such a day and evening. To avoid suspicion, the Cochranites went from home at night and followed a circuitous route to Limington. One of these was a brother of the man at whose house Cochran was to preach. Sister Mercy [a beautiful young "medium"], the one who alternated between the terrestrial and celestial worlds, was there, ready to soar away or to remain in the body, as the leader of ceremonies might wish; if it was deemed best for the success of the service that Mercy depart, Cochran gave the signal and away she went—upon the floor. On this occasion, however, she did not go beyond recall, for when the services had closed and the time for rest came, the owner of the house placed a candle in Cochran's hand, opened a sleeping-room door, and with a significant gesture bade Brother Cochran and Sister Mercy "goodnight". . . .

The matter embodied in this chapter was not culled from dim traditions, that had been handed down from generations enfeebled by age, but has been received from the lips of venerable persons, of unimpaired mental faculties, who had listened to the preaching and witnessed the peculiar practices of Jacob Cochran while he held such a mighty sway in the towns on the Saco [River]. I could have supplemented these statements by quotations from a bundle of yellow documents that were formulated by a magistrate who lived in Buxton at the time these things occurred, but some of these affidavits would be of too sensational and personal a character for my purpose. I have not torn the veil asunder from the top to the bottom, by any means, and have left out enough of tradition and documentary evidence, relating to this remarkable delusion, to fill a volume. . . .

The result of this wide-spread religious epidemic was far-reaching and ruinous. For nearly three-score years this corroding wave of influence has been creeping downward, keeping pace with the three generations of descendants of those who were involved in the original delusive excitement inaugurated by the villainous destroyer of homes and human happiness, who, though dead, speaks still through the instrumentality of his influence and by the soul-blight of their posterity, born out of wedlock.

Some of the scenes witnessed in the domestic circles in the Saco river towns were heart-rending. Young wives who had refused to prostitute their principles of virtue, by submitting to the demoralizing practices of the Cochranites, were bereft of their children and forsaken. Such were left in sorrow and poverty, and all their remaining days refused to be comforted because those they had loved "were not." An aged and saintly woman was recently visited whose father, once an industrious farmer with a pleasant home, became a public advocate of the Cochran creed, and who, after long neglect of his farm and family to follow what, in his delusion, he called duty, visited foreign lands and eventually died, a stranger among strangers, thousands of miles from home and kindred. As this venerable woman adverted to her childhood days and her father's expatriation, she groaned in spirit and wept; a far-off echo of a voice that had preached pernicious doctrines, but long ago silenced by the paralyzing hand of death.

We know of a sea captain who lived on the west side of the Saco. He had married a beautiful daughter of respectable parentage, and to them two pretty boys had been given. Before Jacob Cochran appeared in that community peace and contentment reigned in that home-circle. But the father, a man of speculative and unstable mind, was swept from his moorings by the sophistry of this imposter and spent the time that should have been devoted to the interests of his family with the followers of the "New Apostle to the Gentiles," as some called him. He had a "spiritual wife" assigned to him, said farewell to Hannah, tore her children from her bosom, and left for the westward, where a community of primitive Mormons had congregated. . . .

[Restoration Missionaries Labored among the Cochranites]

The Cochran craze paved the way for a Mormon invasion in the Saco valley. A full-blooded Cochranite made a first-class Mormon saint.* Jake Cochran was a John the Baptist for the Mormon apostles, who appeared on his old battle-ground and gathered up the spoils. The inhabitants of the river towns, as well as some in the interior, were afflicted with Cochranite grasshoppers, followed by Mormon locusts. Scions cut from the decaying trunk of the old Cochran tree were readily engrafted into Mormon branches, but the fruit was not the same; when these had become firmly united, they were transplanted bodily to new soil, considered more congenial to their development, in the state of New York.

Some of the old people, now living, confound the two movements, and we have found insuperable difficulty in sifting the chaff of error from the wheat of truth. It seems to have been a most remarkable coincidence, which has the appearance of concerted action between Cochran and his successors. Almost as soon as he vacated the field, the founders of the Mormon hierarchy invested it. The history of the Mormon church makes Brigham Young come to Maine in 1832 or 1833. The doctrine preached by [Samuel] Smith, Pratt, and Young, in York county, was not of an offensive nature; it was, properly speaking, Millenarianism.

The excitement was immense. The inhabitants went twenty miles to hear these earnest missionaries preach. A change from Cochranism was wanted, and this new

---

*This statement by Ridlon was printed in 1895 when the controversy over polygamy in Utah was receiving national attention and was at its zenith. It applies to the Mormon Church in Utah at the time, and not the Latter Day Saints during the lifetime of Joseph Smith, Jr.

gospel seemed to be an improvement. Old wine was put into new bottles, and many drank to their fill. *At this time polygamy had not been mentioned* [among the Mormons] (italics added). No attempt was made to form an organized church; Cochran had preached against such, and Brigham found these disciples averse to any ecclesiastical government, and waited until he had transported his converts to Manchester, N. Y., before enforcing this part of his creed. . . .

The Mormon excitement spread into every town where Cochran had made converts; these had been washed from their moral and rational moorings by the tidal-wave let loose upon the community by Jacob, and the Mormon inundation landed them high—if not dry—in New York state.

The Mormon elders were unwearied in their efforts to enlarge the circle of their influence and to drum up recruits for their semi-religious community. Like flaming heralds, they traveled from town to town, and their evident sincerity and unbounded enthusiasm drew thousands to hear them. . . .

James Townsend went from Buxton with his family, consisting of a wife and four children. He proved loyal to the end; went westward by stages, and built the first hotel in Utah. Only a few years ago he visited the East and called upon his relatives and early acquaintances. He returned to his home in Salt Lake City and soon died, leaving a vast estate.

Some who joined the westward Mormon tide became preachers and traveled extensively on our continent and in foreign lands to promulgate the faith held by the church of the Latter Day Saints. Many who removed to the New York settlement went west as far as Ohio, and some of them, after their brethren went to Nauvoo, purchased land and became successful farmers there. (G. T. Ridlon, Sr., *Saco Valley Settlements and Families*, 269–283)

Ridlon's 1895 Account Illustrates the Cochran Connection

The information taken from Historian Ridlon's book, in his chapter entitled "The Cochran Delusion," reveals some definite likenesses between Cochranism and the Mormon Church's polygamy, including:

1. Cochran used the term "spiritual wives" just as the Utah polygamists did;
2. Cochran claimed that permission to practice polygamy must come through revelation to the leader, just as in the Mormon Church's theology;
3. The leader's permission was required before spiritual wifery could be practiced;
4. "Assigning of wives" was practiced in both systems;
5. Exchanging of wives was sometimes practiced by both;
6. Oaths of secrecy were a requirement of Cochranism, and are still a part of the LDS temple ordinances;
7. The "Garden of Eden" ceremony was practiced by Cochran and is also a part of the Mormon Church's temple ceremonies.

Chapter 2

Other Accounts of Cochranism

In addition to Ridlon's account of the story of Jacob Cochran and his polygamous practices and theology, other writers added their testimonies.

Among them are a number of histories of counties and towns in southern Maine where Jacob Cochran lived—from which the following excerpts are gleaned.

Ephraim Stinchfield's Account Was Written during the Cochranite Craze

A minister named Ephraim Stinchfield, who called himself "A Watchman," published a twenty-two-page booklet in 1819, detailing the activities of the Cochranites at the time that Jacob Cochran was at the height of his fame. His book is entitled *Cochranism Delineated: or, a Description of, and Specific for a Religious Hydrophobia, Which Has Spread, and Is Still Spreading, in a Number of the Towns in the Counties of York and Cumberland: District of Maine.* Stinchfield's book was published in Boston. The following is extracted from it:

> While passing through the town of Scarborough [Maine], in the month of February, 1817, I . . . [was] informed . . . of a stranger, who had lately moved into the neighborhood, by the name of JACOB COCHRAN, who called himself a preacher . . . he had lately moved his family into the place, from Conway, in the State of New Hampshire. . . . [T]he report I received from this family respecting Cochran, sounded like that of an impostor. . . . I was then about to take my leave of them, when they informed me this same singular man was expected to preach at their house the fol-

lowing evening. They urged me hard to tarry . . . I at length consented. I heard him through. . . . I still retained my suspicion that he was an impostor. . . . I heard no more from this stranger, until the summer following when a report was in circulation, that large numbers (some said more than one thousand) had been converted under his ministry. As I was passing through Kennebunk, in the winter of 1818, I was informed . . . that the reformation, under the said Cochran, was marvellous—such as was never known in those parts before. . . . [A]s I was passing through Kennebunk, and hearing of a meeting of this society, I thought I would once more go and hear for myself. . . .

They had *private*, sometimes *dark*, meetings; in which none, but such as were bound by oath, to the most inviolable secrecy, not to divulge what was transacted in the meeting, upon penalty of eternal damnation, or of having their names blotted out of the book of life, were admitted. That each brother and sister in this fraternity has a spiritual husband, wife, mate, or yoke fellow, such as they choose, or their leaders choose for them. These spiritual mates, dissolve, or disannul, all former marriage connexions; and many of them bed and board together, to the exclusion of all former vows . . . .

Cochran pretends to have the power of life and death in his hands, and frightens his pupils into a compliance with any of his injunctions, by threatening to stop their breath in a moment; by which means he takes females from their parents, and carries them to his brothel. He declares that he has the keys of the kingdom of heaven, and pretends to open it for, or shut it against, whom he sees fit, by stretching out, and making a violent twist with his arm, one way or the other.

He has introduced among his followers a feast, which he calls the *passover*; at which they all partake, at one table, provided for the purpose, at which, large quantities of mutton, lamb, bread and wine, &c. are expended. At this feast, he has a method of marching in a double file, consisting of a male and female, as far as the number of the males will admit, or hold out. But they pretend to have *seven women to one man* (italics added), in the society, alluding, as they told me, to a prophecy, in Isaiah—*On that day, shall seven women take hold of one man.* . . . [H]is [Cochran's] dwelling-house, in Saco . . . is on the road leading from Saco falls to Buxton corner. . . .

The general family consists of twelve females, besides those who visit the house occasionally. Some of these are widows, who, with the rest of the females, have surrendered their persons, character and property into the common stock; and remain in this place, as those declare who have left them, destitute, to all appearance. . . . [H]is original purpose of having *all things common*. . . . [He] tells of more than *two thousand people*, now under him. . . .Those, who are in close communion with him, are bound to obey him, without gainsaying; and this will account for his ruining the character of so many innocent females. . . .

Another young man, in presence of Judge Woodman, of Buxton, and myself, with several others, declared, that when he was admitted a member of Cochran's fraternity, he had to hold a Bible in his hand, while Cochran administered a solemn oath, or what was called so. The amount of which was, that if ever he divulged what took place in their private meetings, his name was to be blotted out of the book of life, and he suffer eternal damnation. He then pointed to, and named this young man's spiritual wife, and said he was willing they should lodge together, which they did, a number of nights, though he declared himself innocent of any sinful conduct. He testified, that Jacob Cochran lodged two nights, to his certain knowledge, while he was there, with a woman not his wife. Five couple[s] more lodged in the same house, who were not husband and wife; one of which, had a wife at home at her father's house at the same time. ("A Watchman" [Ephraim Stinchfield], *Cochranism Delineated*, 3–19)

Cochran Established a Community

Historian Edward E. Bourne stated:

> He [Cochran] must have a place which would be abiding, where the community of his disciples could enjoy a common home and have all things common. He accordingly found an impressible disciple in a neighboring town, owning a large house, who was willing to open his doors and receive the brethren and sisters under his roof. To make the home fit for

more complete freedom, some of the partition walls were taken away, converting the rooms into one, so that day and night they could enjoy all the communion and fellowship which they desired. *Here he broached the new doctrine that spiritual men should have spiritual wives. . . . Some females from Kennebunk became associates and part of the great family* (italics added). Here, under his own roof, Cockran and his disciples preached, and carried out this religion. How large his community was, we have not learned. But, while here, in the exercise and enjoyment of his spiritual freedom, violated law took hold of him, and he soon found himself an inmate of the State's prison. (Edward E. Bourne, *The History of Wells and Kennebunk*, 635)

The Testimony of Daniel Remich

Maine Historian Daniel Remich recorded:

One Jacob Cochrane, who started on his career from Fryeburg, Maine, about 1815, succeeded in creating a wonderful excitement and in gaining great numbers of proselytes in several towns in Oxford, Cumberland and York Counties during the years 1816, 1817 and 1818. . . .

Cochrane soon gained a prominence and fame which at the outset he had neither sought nor expected. The superstitious notion that led him to become a religious teacher had no basis of sound morality, no affinity with pure Christian faith. Surrounded and fawned upon, as he was, by females of all ages, it was easy for him to cast aside the modicum of spirituality that had influenced his action—if, indeed, he had ever been moved by such an influence—and to yield to the "lusts of the flesh," to devote his unexplainable gift to the basest purposes, to become an impostor and a scourge. There were among his followers pure-minded, truly-excellent men and women, who would not participate in the unhallowed practices of their leader. Some of these had sufficient intelligence and firmness to enable them to abandon the cause altogether. Others, weak-minded, credulous and superstitious, disapproved and lamented the gross corruption of their chief, but could not subdue the feeling that such power as had been imparted to him must be from above. . . .

The *Newburyport Herald* (May or June, 1819) says: "We have seen a pamphlet, published by a Baptist minister of regular standing in New Gloucester [Maine], giving an account of Cochrane and his deluded followers. It appears that under the guise of religion they have committed the most indecent and abominable acts of adultery. . . . One of their leading tenets was to dissolve the ties of matrimony as suited their convenience, and a promiscuous sexual intercourse was tolerated by each male, being allowed to take *seven wives*! It seems Cochrane, the high priest of iniquity, had had nearly half his female followers for wives in the course of his ministration, which has been two years standing."

The principal places of resort of the disciples of Cochrane, so far as we can learn, were New Gloucester, Buxton, Saco and Kennebunk. At the last-named place meetings were frequently held in Washington Hall, and there were in the village three private dwelling-houses in some one of which a meeting was held every evening when the hall was not occupied for that purpose. In the largest and best of the three from ten to twenty of the brothers and sisters were accustomed to take up their abode from two to four weeks at a time, perhaps quarterly. . . .

The time came when it was believed by the lovers of good order that these flagrant offenses against the best interests of society should be met by the fiat, "No farther." In February, 1819, Cochrane was brought before Justice Granger, of Saco, on a complaint of gross lewdness, lascivious behavior and adultery, filed against him by Mr. Ichabod Jordan. On examination, the allegations of the complainant were so well sustained by the evidence produced that the Justice ordered the accused to recognize in the sum of eighteen hundred dollars for his appearance before the Supreme Judicial Court, at York, on the third Tuesday in May following. This he did.

At the commencement of the May term of the Supreme Judicial Court the grand jury found a bill against Cochrane and "he was arraigned on the third day of the term on five several indictments for adultery and open and gross lewdness," to each of which he pleaded "not guilty." On the trial for the offenses charged in the second bill of indictment the jury brought in a verdict of "guilty." It was found that the prisoner was not in court when the jury rendered its verdict, and farther inquiries disclosed the fact that he had absconded . . . .*

We learn from the court records that at the November (1819) term of the Supreme Judicial Court "the said Cochrane is brought into court and set to the bar" and sentenced,—on the first count, to solitary imprisonment for the term of five days and that afterward he be confined to hard labor for eighteen months; on the second count a like sentence is imposed; on the third count, three days solitary confinement and one year hard labor; sentence to be executed at the state prison in Charlestown, Mass. Warrant for removal to the prison issued November 3, 1819. (Daniel Remich, *History of Kennebunk from Its Earliest Settlement to 1890*, 268–274)

"The Cochran Fanaticism in York County"

A Maine Historical Society document states:

> The history of fanaticism in this State can never be fully written, without a record of the rise, spread, character, and influence of Cochranism. It dates from 1817 or 1818 and onward. It's range was in York County [Maine], with a few converts in other places. It's centre and fullest development was in the upper part of the town of Saco, Buxton, Hollis, North Kennebunkport and Scarborough. It's chief instigator, teacher, "head centre" and actor was Jacob Cochran—hence it's name. . . .The place where he won his greatest popularity and perpetrated his most infamous impostures lay between the Orthodox meeting houses of Saco, Buxton and Scarborough . . . .
>
> Cochran commenced his public labors; and with a great show of sympathy, earnestness and deep religious feeling he took well with that people. He did not claim to belong to any existing sect; nor avow any design of forming a new one; but with a great show of sanctity strove to raise all believers to a greater degree of devotion;—to the state of primitive piety, and if that was accomplished he said they would secure the privileges of the primitive Christians, the working of

---

*See also Gamaliel E. Smith, Esq., *Report of the Trial of Jacob Cochrane* [Kennebunk, Maine; Printed by James K. Remich, 1819], 40; New York City Public Library.

miracles and apostolic gifts. He said but little of these points of difference and dwelt largely on those already believed by his hearers. Considering his attractions as a public speaker, and remembering his unparalleled, artful, cunning and deep penetration into human nature, it is not strange that the masses were drawn after him. . . .

In the vicinity of the Heath Meeting House in Saco he still made his headquarters; and there in the Summer of 1818 there was an extensive and powerful revival. . . . There was great excitement, loud responses, shouts, and various outbursts of emotion, but no grievous departures from rapturous religious feeling. It was for a while considered by many as a good work; and to some extent so it proved. Two thousand were thought to be converted. . . .

In this noted revival Cochran rose to the highest crest of his popular wave, and in consequence of it precipitated himself to his deepest disgrace. He could not modestly and temperately bear such unexpected popularity. He did not exalt the Devine Power and realize his own mere instrumentality. His most sanguine admirers became mentally intoxicated, and did not repress indecent adulation. *Females in the craze of their fanaticism would embrace him in public meeting and unblushingly kiss him, and he found apology for it in "the holy kiss" of Scripture* (italics added). Previous to this he had not broached any of his corrupt and damnable heresies. He had intimated innovations, but had not pressed them; had aspired to leadership, but moved towards it in an adroit and modest way. He now felt that Cochranism had become rooted, and he proceeded to give it a distinct form. . . .

His fame spread, and other wandering stars scented from afar their disgusting idiosyncrasies, and were drawn to his aid. For in other parts audacious heresies had been preached, and vile free love abominations practiced by the Osgoodites, and others, under the sacred garb of Christianity; and it is said that notorious adepts of this sort—pre-historic Mormons— came to Cochran's aid and helped sink him to his worst behavior. . . .

His next, and worst of all his devices, was his assault upon the sacred bonds of matrimony for the most corrupt purposes, and by the most revolting machinations he attempted to demolish this devine and all prevalent institution. Given in Eden for the virtuous propagation of the race; as the guardian of the most precious social enjoyments, it has kept pace with the descending ages, defying barbarism, ignorance, heathenism and lust; and yet this besotted fanatic, in the sacred name of religion thrust a dagger into it's vitals.

He taught a spiritual matrimony sanctioned by a ceremony of his own, into which any man or woman, already married or unmarried, might enter choosing at pleasure a spiritual wife or a spiritual husband, with all the privileges of a legitimate marriage. Existing vows were violated, connubial happiness tortured often with the forsaken party, and hitherto happy families severed. And soon it did not wait for any ceremony, but liberty was taken to practice unbridled licentiousness, of which Cochran himself was the most noted example (italics added)....

But many still adhered to him; many who had been hitherto modest and virtuous, but now having no other rule of action but his word, no confidence in any persons which he did not approve, no other worship than that which he prescribed. Some connected themselves, their families, their property entirely to his dictation, and he was verily King in his realm....

With the means contributed by his followers he purchased a house a little retired from the river-road running from Saco Village to Buxton, and in this his wife and children resided, and several others of his deluded followers. Here too he had a regular harem, consisting of several unmarried females . . . now subjects of his seduction and nothing else than his concubines.

Nor were his vile practices confined to himself, nor to these concubines, but wherever he went he corrupted any wife, mother or maiden that he could seduce, and his devoted followers generally walked in the same steps. With true fanatical zeal he pressed on in propagating his actions and corrupting views....

Calling one day upon a certain family, the husband found it necessary to step out for a short absence, and upon returning caught him [Jacob Cochran] in criminal connection with his wife. This was too much for his principles or patience. He did not however settle the abuse as another husband did a similar offence, by seizing his ox-goad and giving him a smart drubbing, but went to a magistrate and had him legally arrested. . . .

But by this Cochranism was death struck, a steady depletion from his counted ranks followed. Heretical spiritual matrimony tottered and fell; its entangled victims returned to their former homes and wives, and silently sought to keep out of harm's way. . . .

The jury convicted him, but sentence could not be pronounced in the absence of the prisoner [for he had escaped]. At the next term of the Court he was arraigned and sentenced to the State's Prison in Charlestown for a term of four years . . . .

Cochranism had now received its death blow. It had been well given. It fell upon the Head of the Beast. Others were guilty, and were pestilent in their influence and deeds, but he was the leader, the corrupter, the most guilty.

After he was thus removed it dwindled away, and stayed it's poison. Many of his victims discovered their folly and shame, and deeply repented of it; but a few were so thoroughly taken captive that they still adhered to it, aiding and encouraging each other, and occasionally meeting in some private house, and waiting their leader's enlargement.

After his liberation from prison he gathered his family, and such as cast in their lot with him, and, by the aid of friends, purchased a small farm in a remote part of Hollis . . . .

Sometime about 1829 the clan removed from this place and left the State, and their resting place is not sufficiently well known to state it. At length death overtook him. . . . After his death his wife, and such as still survived of his attachees came back to Saco, from New York State. ("The Cochran Fanaticism in York County" [typed manuscript, dated August 3, 1867; compiler quotes "From the manuscript letter of P. Huntoon, Esq., . . . of Enfield, N. H. . . . July, 1866"], 1–19; this reference is also cited in *Saints' Herald* 109 [May 1, 1962]: 22)

Cochranism Continued after the Founder's Death

Historian G. T. Ridlon explains how Jacob Cochran's denomination continued:

> But Cochranism was not extinguished with the death of its founder; the doctrines promulgated by him had taken too deep root. Long before Cochran had left the Saco valley he had anticipated what ultimately came to pass and had prepared for the extension of his empire. He saw the importance of introducing a missionary spirit into his system, and preached special sermons calculated to stimulate the zeal of his supporters on this line. With the same sagacious perception which had been so prominent a factor of his success in all his undertakings, he discovered those who had been gifted with natural fluency of speech and encouraged them to go forth and preach the doctrines they had embraced. This many did, absenting themselves from their homes and neglecting to provide for their dependent families and the cultivation of their farms until the inevitable results of poverty, hunger, and cold followed. (Ridlon, *Saco Valley Settlements*, 279)

Latter Day Saint missionaries arrived in southern Maine in 1832, only three years after Jacob Cochran moved from Maine to New York State. The Church missionaries visited the Cochranite communities, stayed in their homes, taught them the gospel, baptized some, and urged them to gather to Zion. As a result, many of his followers joined the Church and moved to Kirtland and Nauvoo. Some took their polygamous beliefs with them. They and their influence caused the "church of Christ . . . [to be] reproached with the crime of . . . polygamy" (see Doctrine and Covenants [1835 Edition] 101:4; RLDS Doctrine and Covenants [1950 Edition] 111:4b) and assisted in bringing about the untimely deaths of two innocent men, Joseph the Prophet and Hyrum the Presiding Patriarch.

Chapter 3

Church Missionaries Converted Cochranites

Jacob Cochran established his small denomination in the area between Boston, Massachusetts, and Portland, Maine. By 1830 Cochran had gone into hiding to escape imprisonment due to his practice of polygamy; and his denomination was struggling to continue under the leadership of John Dennett and others. Shortly after the Book of Mormon was published in March 1830, Latter Day Saint missionaries began to make their way into the Boston area, where they found that making converts among the Cochranites was fruitful. So successful were they that a Church conference was held in Saco, Maine (the heart of the Cochranite area), August 21, 1835, at which nine of the newly ordained apostles were in attendance (RLDS *History of the Church* 1:583; *Latter Day Saints' Messenger and Advocate* 2 [October 1835]: 204–207; LDS *History of the Church* 2:252). The LDS reference states that seven of the Twelve met in conference at Saco, Maine.

But the converting of the Cochranites and their gathering to Church headquarters at Kirtland, Ohio, and later to Nauvoo, Illinois, brought the Church more than just increased numbers. It also brought the plague of polygamy—for some of the Cochranites brought their doctrines with them. This was a natural consequence of the fact that these people had lived in polygamy for years. They were men who had practiced polygamy, women who had been plural wives, and children born of polygamy. They had been indoctrinated with the belief that polygamy was a sacred doctrine.

An even more devastating result of missionary work among the Cochranites was that some of the Latter Day Saint missionaries, including Apostles Orson Hyde and Brigham Young,

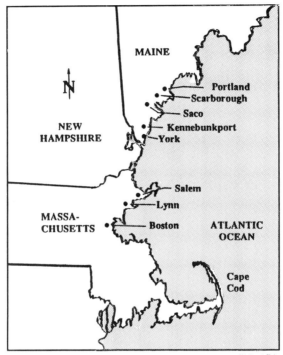

The area where Church missionaries converted many Cochranites in the early 1830s.

accepted the doctrine of polygamy and began practicing it at Nauvoo before Joseph Smith's death. Joseph moved to bring these men before the High Council for trial, but was martyred before he accomplished the task.

Two of the first missionaries assigned to take the gospel to this area, which included the states of Massachusetts, New Hampshire, and Maine, were twenty-six-year-old Orson Hyde, and the Prophet Joseph's younger brother, Samuel Smith, who was twenty-two. They left Kirtland, Ohio, on February 1, 1832, for their mission. Each kept a journal in which he recorded his daily experiences as they traveled through this area, preaching at every opportunity. The original *Journal of Orson Hyde* and the *Missionary Journal of Samuel Harrison Smith—1832* are now in the archives of the LDS Church Historical Department in Salt Lake City, Utah. Typescripts of the two journals, which tell of their work among the Cochranites, were obtained by Richard and Pamela Price. Below are extracts taken from Orson and Samuel's journals.

Orson wrote on June 29, 1832, at Boston:

> Preached in the evening ... two ladies confessed their faith in the work, and a Miss and Mrs. [Augusta Adams] Cobb.

Samuel penned on the same day:

> Baptized three: Augusta Cobb, Elizabeth Harendeen and _____ Porter.

Orson recorded on July 1, while still in Boston:

> attended to Sacrament, considerably disturbed by false spirits in a man and woman that believed in the Cochranite Doctrine. We cried against them and after a little got them considerably quelled. ... Not a very good time because of disturbance.

Samuel wrote of that meeting:

> Somewhat interrupted this day in the meeting by a man and woman that taught the doctrine of the devil, such as ... having spiritual wives. ... They came to our meeting. The woman arose and began to preach and we requested her to stop and

> she would not, and we cried against her spirit, for we knew that it was an unclean spirit, and we cried against it that it was of the devil, and it made considerable stir. The man that had the same spirit tempted us, saying: "Cast the Devil out," crying amen to the words of the woman. After considerable muttering and grumbling and shaking of her frame, she stopped and we proceeded with our meeting.

This was the first time that Orson and Samuel mentioned Cochranism in their journals. Note that Augusta Cobb, one of the baptismal candidates, was in the meeting where Cochranites were present. She later became a plural wife of Brigham Young (*The Utah Genealogical and Historical Magazine* 2 [April 1920]: 54).

Orson and Samuel continued their walking and preaching journey from Massachusetts, through New Hampshire, and into Maine, staying a part of the time in polygamous homes. On September 25 they were in the village of York, Maine, where they again came in contact with the Cochranite woman who had disrupted the Sacrament service in Boston on July 1. Samuel explained concerning her:

> a large congregation came together and Brother Orson preached to them. . . . We then were invited to go home with a young man by the name of Ludgkins and stayed overnight with him. His stepmother we had seen before. We had seen her in Boston, the woman that came into our meeting and we had cried against her spirit.

On September 28 Orson and Samuel were in Kennebunkport, Maine, another Cochranite stronghold. Orson wrote:

> attended a Cochranite meeting, and they said, "if any one had a message from God there was liberty to give it unto the people." And I commenced by prayer, but thought I would not tell them about the work then, but would get their confidence in the first place.

Samuel added to the story on that same day:

> we went to a meeting in the evening and the people were called

Cockrinites because the man that first preached their faith, his name was Cockrin. They gave liberty for anyone to speak .... Brother Orson spoke to them and exhorted them to faithfulness to the Lord and to humility and to stand in the Councul of the Lord, that they might know the voice of the Good Shepherd, that they might when the voice came "behold the Bridegroom Cometh" go out to meet him. And they said "Amen." When meeting closed, we spake that we would like to preach to the people. . . . They would not let us.

On October 10 Samuel and Orson were still among the Cochranites. Orson wrote:

> Visited three families but without much hope of doing anything to profit them because of the "Cochranite's," a deluded sect of people, by whom many had been deceived, and the people were afraid of the truth, and for this cause the way of truth was evil spoken of. . . . [B]ut few came out to meeting.

Samuel's journal for October 10 contains this revealment:

> a less number came together in the evening than before, but we declared unto them that they must repent and go up to Zion.

On the following day, October 11, they walked only three miles to Ogunquit and found another Cochranite congregation, in which they were allowed to preach. Orson's journal states:

> preached to a congregation of Cochranites who gave liberty; *told them again to repent and go up to Zion*, and we lifted our cry in the Spirit, and I hope some of them will go; but they had a wonderful lustful spirit, because they believe in a "Plurality of wives" which they call spiritual wives, knowing them not after the flesh but after the spirit, but by the appearance they knew one another after the flesh. (italics added)

Samuel gave his opinion about the Cochranites. He recorded:

> the people in these parts were under a delusion and such a spirit of confusion had seized them that it appeared to be impossible to teach them, to get them to hear and understand

by the right Spirit.

The astounding thing about Orson's preaching (for he nearly always took the lead) was the fact that he preached the doctrine of the gathering to the Cochranites, and urged them to gather without weighing the terrible consequences of polygamy entering the Church.

On October 15 Orson and Samuel were in the town of Newburyport, Maine. Orson wrote:

> called on Mr. Goodrich and Stimpson; tried to persuade them to go to Zion, and they seemed to have some little disposition to go, but could not bring them to repentance before God. Came up about two miles farther to Mr. [Timothy] Hams and tarried all night; found him an enthusiastic man,—a Cochranite—Not much hopes of going to Zion or embracing.

On October 16 Orson and Samuel remained at Mr. Ham's. Historian G. T. Ridlon, Sr., wrote that Ham was "among the more notable who went out to plant Cochran's standard" (Ridlon, *Saco Valley Settlements*, 279). The two ministers helped Ham dig his potatoes and Samuel says, "Got them [members of Ham's family] to wash some clothes." That evening Samuel and Orson had a meeting with the Cochranites.

On October 17 Orson recorded:

> Visited three families and talked a good deal; some hopes of their going to Zion some time.

In commenting upon Orson's sermon, Samuel said:

> Brother Orson preached to them. . . . Spake upon the Covenant. Declared unto them that they must repent, all of them and be baptized and go to Zion. But they were hard and unbelieving and we had not much hope of them.

But by the next evening, October 18, Samuel had more hopes for some of the Cochranites, for he and Orson had moved to the home of still another Cochranite, Captain Andrews. Samuel was encouraged. Not only had Captain Andrews subscribed to the Church's periodical, *The Evening and the Morning*

Star, but there were hopes that some of the Cochranites would "gather." Samuel declared:

> visited some of the neighborhood and found some that we thought would go to Zion.

On October 20 and 21 they were guests of a polygamous Cochranite and his plural wife. Orson reported:

> Tarried all night at Mr. McKinney's, who lived with what he called a spiritual wife.

On October 22 they left Kennebunkport and traveled to a neighboring Cochranite settlement. Since they were walking from one Cochranite group to another, it appears that friendly Cochranites were directing them in making new contacts. The journals of both men verify that before preaching on October 24, near Hollis, Maine, they visited with Samuel Hill and a Mr. Burrell [who were evidently Cochranites]. Some, who were opposed to Cochranism, were suspicious of Orson and Samuel because they were fraternizing with those polygamists who had caused so much sorrow among the people of that area. On the evening of October 24, after Orson had preached, a man questioned the two missionaries about their Cochranite connections:

> One man arose and said the people would not be likely to receive it [the doctrines brought by Orson and Samuel] if it were true because of Cochran's description. He then mentioned the names of two Cochranites, and said if we had any fellowship for them he wished us to depart out of their coast. I then told them that our message was from God, and it was as much to Cochranites as Free Will Baptists, and that I should rejoice as much to see a Cochranite redeemed from his errors as a Free Will Baptist. But I told them I had no fellowship with error nor iniquity. They did not request us to hold another meeting; but a man three miles from the place was there, a Cochranite, and he invited us to go there; and we gave out an appointment for the next evening.

Samuel told the same story in these words:

> one man arose and said that there had been a deceiver through that country and had deceived the people and the people were

afraid and ... if we had fellowship with that people that had been deceived (Kockranites) he should desire us to depart out of their coast, that the people would not desire to hear us any more. We told him our mission was unto all people and we did not believe in the doctrine of the Kockranites. ... Hill [one of the two men they had been visiting] was some believing, but rather stupid ... yet we had hopes that he and his family would go to Zion.

On October 25 Orson and Samuel were in the town of Limon, Maine, guests of Simeon Weymouth, a Cochranite. They helped Weymouth husk corn that day and the next, and he allowed them to preach evenings in his home. On the twenty-seventh, Orson and Samuel again visited Timothy Ham, a Cochranite, and the Dennett family, whose daughter was very ill. On the twenty-eighth the missionaries preached twice.

Orson wrote:

Samuel preached in the spirit; people paid good attention, and some, I think will go to Zion.

By October 30 Orson and Samuel were guests at the George Dennett home, and were helping him dig potatoes by day and having meetings "at the School House" at night. They had a good attendance. On November 1 they returned to visit their Cochranite friend, Simeon Weymouth, and again spent the night. On November 2 they returned to Dennett's and preached the funeral sermon of the Dennett girl, whom they had visited earlier. This show of concern by Orson and Samuel, as well as their having helped with the harvest, and staying in their homes, caused the Cochranites to show so much interest in the Restored Gospel that the missionaries had a prayer meeting with members of the polygamous sect.

On Sunday, November 4, the two men attended a Methodist meeting, but were not persistent in making contact with the Methodists, and were soon back with the more obliging Cochranites. Orson revealed:

Went to Methodist meeting in the forenoon, hoping to give out an appointment for evening, but the Minister gave out an appointment before me, and we arose disappointed, but I spoke to them about 15 minutes, and bore a strong testimony upon the "gathering." Held a meeting in the evening at Mr. Dennit's; cried against one unclean spirit, and had a very good time and meeting.

Samuel confirmed:

> Went to a meeting expecting to give out an appointment for the evening, but the preacher gave out one for himself. We returned to Dennet's and Timothy Ham and others that were in the doctrine that was called Cochranites and some of them desired us to come into their quarter and preach. Ham began to pray as he called it and went into a wonderful spirit of distraction and confusion, yea, it was an evil spirit and we bore testimony against his spirit. Stayed overnight at Dennet's. Held a meeting in the evening.

The missionaries spent November 6 at Simeon Weymouth's, and then returned to Dennett's. On the eighth they traveled to Weymouth's, where they baptized Simeon Weymouth and his wife Esther, Sally Taylor, and Lovey Dennett. Under the date of November 9 Orson's journal states:

> Went up three miles to S. [Simeon] Waymouth's and baptized him [George Dennett], and in the evening had prayer, and a very good time; and the Lord was with us; and Satan also came in—a crazy sort of a female; we cried against her, and after a short time got her still. Tarried [stayed that night] at the same place.

Upon reading Orson's description of the woman who disrupted the meeting, one is left to wonder if she were a plural wife; and if so, was her mental derangement a result of the baptism of one of the Cochranite men? Elders Hyde and Smith never addressed the problems of the polygamous wives and children in their journals. Their fate has been a well-kept secret for over 160 years.

Now the mysterious puzzle begins to fit together. The shelves of many libraries still hold heart-wrenching stories, such as the following example:

> We know of a sea captain who lived on the west side of the Saco [River]. He had married a beautiful daughter of respectable parentage, and to them two pretty boys had been given. Before Jacob Cochran appeared in that community peace and contentment reigned in that home-circle. But the father, a man of speculative and unstable mind, was swept from his moorings by the sophistry of this imposter and spent the time that should have been devoted to the interests of his family with the followers of the "New Apostle to the Gentiles," as some called him. He had a "spiritual wife" assigned to him, said farewell to Hannah [his legal wife], tore her children from her bosom, and left for the westward, where a community of primitive Mormons had congregated. When these sons had grown to manhood they retained a faint recollection of a mother, and refused to call one by that dear name who had taken her rightful place. They instituted a searching inquiry for their mother's family, came east and visited the old homestead, but, alas! too late to see her who had found a premature grave in consequence of the great sorrow that had fallen upon her heart. (Ridlon, *Saco Valley Settlements*, 280)

On November 12 Orson and Samuel were guests at the home of John Dennett. This may have been the notorious John Dennett previously mentioned—the leader of the Cochranites, who took Jacob Cochran's place at the head of that sect when Cochran fled.

On the thirteenth Orson and Samuel preached and stayed all night with a neighbor. Orson summed up his thoughts with these words:

> I think some of them will go to Zion.

The above selections from the journals of Orson and Samuel are sufficient to show that the Church's missionaries labored extensively among the Cochranites. A vast amount of information is available in libraries in many states, including the LDS Church and RLDS Church archives, which shows beyond a shadow of a doubt that polygamy entered the Church through the Cochranite religion!

There were other polygamous societies in America and England during the Kirtland-Nauvoo period, and they too contributed toward polygamy entering the Church. But Cochranism was the polygamists' primary mainspring into the Church. However, many who joined the Church in Cochranite areas were not polygamists, but stalwart Christians with excellent morals. Among those faithful ones were two young women, Mary Bailey and Agnes Coolbrith, who were baptized as a result of Orson and Samuel's preaching. Samuel Smith, the Prophet's brother, married Mary Bailey, and Don Carlos Smith, another brother, married Agnes Coolbrith. Also from the midst of the Cochranites came Arthur Milliken, who married Lucy Smith, Joseph's youngest sister. Neither Mary nor Agnes embraced polygamy, and Arthur Milliken was a faithful member of the Church during the presidencies of Joseph the Martyr and his son, Joseph III. Arthur and Lucy bitterly opposed polygamy.

Orson Hyde and Samuel Smith were not the only missionaries who journeyed through the Cochranite areas. Other Church ministers traveled and preached throughout the region with great success during the Kirtland and Nauvoo eras. But Saco, Maine, a Cochranite stronghold, was one of the most fruitful fields for missionary work—so much so that a conference was held in Saco on June 13, 1834 (*The Evening and the Morning Star* 2 [August 1834]: 181; RLDS *History of the Church* 1:521). The following year, "On August 21, 1835, nine of the Twelve [apostles] met in conference at Saco, Maine" (*Messenger and Advocate* 2 [October 1835]: 204–207; RLDS *History of the Church* 1:583). With nine of the twelve apostles making their appearance in Saco, there is no doubt that each one of them became well acquainted with the doctrines of Cochranism, for at that time it was a popular secular and religious news topic. Those evil dogmas must have made a deep impression on the apostles, for of the twelve who were in the apostolic quorum at the time of Joseph's death, at least eleven became polygamists!

Chapter 4

Brigham Young
The Father of Mormon Polygamy

The LDS Church, which has its headquarters in Utah, has taught for over a century that Joseph Smith was the author of Mormon polygamy—and the religious public has been eager to believe the story. But the truth is that Brigham Young and his family and friends were the ones who brought polygamy into the Church of Jesus Christ of Latter Day Saints and made it a cardinal doctrine. All of the writings of Joseph Smith (published during his lifetime) condemn polygamy, but after his death Brigham and the other polygamous apostles published polygamist documents which they ascribed to Joseph. As evidence of Joseph's innocence, he had no children by polygamous wives (even though the purpose of practicing polygamy—according to LDS authorities—was to have many children born of polygamy). Brigham had a total of fifty-six children (John J. Stewart, *Brigham Young and His Wives: And the True Story of Plural Marriage*, 82).

It would take volumes to tell the complete story of Brigham's involvement in polygamy and how he was instrumental in bringing it into the Church. Part of that story is the account of how he requested to travel alone on missions, met a married woman, Augusta Cobb, who was acquainted with members of the Cochranite sect and their teachings, and later took her to Nauvoo and married her as his polygamous wife—before Joseph's death. When Joseph discovered the polygamous practices of Brigham Young and others, he sought to bring them to trial, but was assassinated before he could do so. The polygamist party under Brigham Young then took control of the Church, which assured the success of polygamy as a doctrine among the Utah Saints.

Brigham's Cochranite Connections

Brigham Young had a thorough knowledge of Cochranism, for he made several missionary journeys through the "Cochranite territory" from Boston to Saco, and later married Augusta Cobb as previously noted. He attended the 1835 Church conference in Saco. Brigham chose to travel alone in Cochranite territory instead of going with another elder, "two by two" as the Scriptures direct (see RLDS DC 52:3c; 60:3a; 61:6b; and 75:5c–d; also LDS DC 52:10; 60:8; 61:35; 75:30–36).

The High Council met at Kirtland on February 20, 1834, and its record states:

> The council also decided that Elder Brigham Young should travel alone it being his own choice . . . and that there should be a general conference held in Saco, in the state of Maine, on the 13th day of June, 1834. (*Times and Seasons* 6 [November 1, 1845]: 1022–1023; RLDS *History of the Church* 1:434–435)

Why did Brigham insist upon traveling alone in an area where adulterous temptations were sure to befall any lonely elder?

The report for the June 1834 Church conference at Saco stated that "a numerous concourse had assembled" (*Evening and Morning Star* 2 [August 1834]: 181). Although Brigham did not go to the 1834 conference, he was on a mission to the eastern states from May to September 1835 (Leonard J. Arrington, *Brigham Young: American Moses*, Appendix A, 413).

Brigham continued to work in that area and he reported that he also had been to a conference in Maine on August 12, 13, and 14, 1836, where fifty-two members of the Saco Branch attended (*Messenger and Advocate* 2 [September 1836]: 381–382). Brigham's presence in and around Saco during the Cochranite era is another evidence that he was very familiar with Cochranite polygamy.

Brigham's Polygamous Revelations in England

The Church opened its mission in England in 1837 by sending apostles and elders to conduct missionary work there. The brethren were there for long periods of time without their wives. The mission was very successful and thousands joined the Church. The apostles were idolized by their new followers, and temptations naturally followed. To make matters worse, polygamy was a common topic of discussion in both England and America at the time, and was being practiced in both countries. Under these circumstances, Brigham declared "the doctrine" of polygamy was revealed to him in a vision and revelations while in England:

> While we were in England, (in 1839 and 40), I think the Lord manifested to me by vision and his Spirit things [concerning polygamy] that I did not then understand. I never opened my mouth to any one concerning them, until I returned to Nauvoo; Joseph had never mentioned this; there had never been a thought of it in the Church that I ever knew anything about at that time, but I *had this* for myself, and I kept it to myself. And when I returned home, and Joseph revealed those things to me, then I understood the reflections that were upon my mind while in England. But this (communication with Joseph on the subject) was not until after I had told him what I understood—this was in 1841. The revelation [Section 132 in the Utah Doctrine and Covenants] was given in 1843, but the doctrine was *revealed* before this. (*The Messenger of the Reorganized Church of Jesus Christ of Latter Day Saints* 1 [June 1875]: 29; *Deseret News*, July 1, 1874)

This statement by Brigham is very important because:

    1. He admits that polygamy was not a doctrine of the Church before 1839 or 1840: "There had never been a thought of it in the Church." This destroys the LDS Church's teachings that polygamy was even thought of as a Church doctrine as early as 1832 in Kirtland;

    2. According to Brigham, Joseph had never even mentioned polygamy as a doctrine before 1841;

    3. It was Brigham Young who first developed the dogma of polygamy—and that he claimed he did so by Divine mani-

festations and by a vision.

Apostle Jason Briggs of the Reorganized Church, editor of the *Messenger*, made the following observations concerning Brigham's statement quoted above:

> This is lifting one of the early disguises,—an uncovering of *his* [Brigham's] *trail* so long obscured. Here is an acknowledgment that the doctrine of polygamy was first revealed to him. He "had it for himself" before "Joseph or the Church" even thought of it. Well done, Brigham! Why didn't you tell the people this in the start, that polygamy was introduced through your revelation? The only answer to this is, it was thought essential to the success of this doctrine, that it should have the sanction of Joseph. (ibid., 29)

Stafford's Testimony Concerning Brigham's Adulterous Activities

Seventy Thomas Stafford, who knew Brigham Young in both England and Nauvoo, testified that he had personal knowledge of Brigham's misconduct. Stafford's family lived in England in 1837 in the city of Stockport, when they first heard the gospel preached and became acquainted with Apostle Brigham Young (*Autumn Leaves* 1 [June 1888]: 245). They joined the Church, moved to Manchester, and sailed for America on May 1, 1841 (ibid. [July 1888]: 299). The family arrived at Nauvoo in the summer of 1842 (ibid. [August 1888]: 354). At Nauvoo, Thomas and his brother, Edwin, were "schoolmates" and friends of Joseph Smith III (*The Saints' Herald* 81 [December 4, 1934]: 1545; ibid. 82 [December 10, 1935]: 1588). Both Thomas and Edwin later became ministers in the Reorganized Church of Jesus Christ of Latter Day Saints.

On August 24, 1891, Seventy Thomas Stafford wrote a letter to Seventy Gomer R. Wells telling of improper conduct which he had witnessed on the part of Brigham Young, both in England and in Nauvoo. Stafford wrote:

But I am fully convinced, as I was then, that Brigham (Young), was in adultery in Manchester, England, in the fall, winter and spring of 1840 and 1841. Elizabeth Mayer is the person with whom Brigham was then committing adultery. My reasons are these: We lived next door to her, under the same roof.... This Elizabeth Mayer had a father and a brother who were gardners; they took their dinners, as they worked a long piece from home. After they had left for work, Brigham would step into the house, she would then lock the door and pull down the blinds and curtains, which to me was strange. He never came to see our folks, although not five steps apart; and when he left he was always in a hurry, and she never came to the door with him when he was leaving.

This same thing occurred in Nauvoo with a woman and Brigham. Her name was Greenough; her son was about my age, was always driven out when Brigham came, the door was shut and the curtains lowered. I was puzzled to know why he acted so, if he had a good heart, and was engaged in the business of teaching the truth, why drive the boy out? Why not come also and see my mother, only a few steps apart?

I am now, and was then, satisfied that he was in adultery, in Manchester, England. The seeds of polygamy was sown, and Brigham the sower.... I was present at a meeting in a grove [at Nauvoo], about three weeks before Joseph and Hyrum were murdered, when Joseph made a public statement in the presence of three thousand people, that polygamy was being practiced secretly by some; that it had crept into the church secretly and must be put down speedily or the church would be driven from Nauvoo.

I am satisfied that Joseph was not in favor of it (polygamy) at all. Would swear to all I have stated. (R. C. Evans, *Autobiography of Elder R. C. Evans*, 334–335)

Brigham Married a Woman Who Was Acquainted with Cochranism

Between 1834 and 1844, Brigham Young made a number of journeys into the Boston area, where the Cochranite doctrine was prevalent. During this time he met Augusta Adams Cobb. Augusta was baptized on June 29, 1832, by Samuel Smith, as noted in a previous chapter (see *Missionary Journal of Samuel*

Harrison Smith—1832, and *Journal of Orson Hyde*). Both journals show that Augusta Cobb requested baptism at a meeting where at least two Cochranites were present. This establishes the fact that Augusta was familiar with the doctrines of the polygamous Cochranites when she met Apostle Young. Augusta was an educated woman from a well-known Boston family, married and living in luxury with her husband of twenty-one years—Henry Cobb. According to Augusta's great granddaughter, Mary Cable, Augusta and Henry were the parents of seven children (*American Heritage* 16 [February 1965]: 50). In the fall of 1843 Augusta deserted her husband and all of her children but the two younger ones—Charlotte, six, and Brigham, only a few months—and went with Brigham Young to Nauvoo to become his plural wife (ibid., 52).

While on the journey to Nauvoo the infant, Brigham, became ill and died at Cincinnati, Ohio. "She [Augusta] had it put in a tin box and took it with her" to Nauvoo (ibid., 54). A Nauvoo newspaper, the *Nauvoo Neighbor* of November 8, 1843, announced the death of Brigham Cobb, age five months and twenty days. By this time Brigham and Augusta were secretly married.

Brigham Young was already a polygamist at the time he married Augusta on November 2, 1843 (Stewart, *Brigham Young and His Wives*, 86; *Saints' Herald* 105 [August 11, 1958]: 16). He took his first plural wife in June 1842, when he married twenty-year-old Lucy Decker Seely, wife of William Seely. Lucy had borne Mr. Seely three children (Stewart, *Brigham Young and His Wives*, 85; Kate B. Carter, *Our Pioneer Heritage* 16 [1973]: 187–189). In spite of the fact that some of the LDS Church's historical references state that Lucy was a widow, she was not. Official church archive records in the Genealogical Society Library in the LDS Church's headquarters building in Salt Lake City show that William Seely did not die until May 20, 1851. Further, references in the dozens of records give no concrete evidence that Lucy and William Seely were ever divorced. Therefore, Brigham was guilty of polygamy and Augusta and Lucy were both guilty of polyandry—the having of plural husbands.

Henry Cobb Sued Augusta for a Divorce

In 1847 Henry Cobb sued Augusta for a divorce. This action and her polygamous marriage to Brigham received nationwide publicity through the newspapers.

High Priest George J. Adams, a popular missionary during the lifetime of Joseph the Prophet, was a witness for Henry Cobb. Adams was a noted preacher in the eastern states, including the Boston area. He had been a close consultant and advisor to Joseph Smith during the last few months of Joseph's life, and had labored fervently to free Joseph and Hyrum from the last legal charges against them before they were assassinated. Adams had served as a missionary in England and other European countries, along with members of the Twelve. Although Adams became entangled in the web of polygamy himself, he asserted that Brigham Young, and not Joseph Smith, brought that doctrine into the Church. He testified under oath as a witness for Henry Cobb that Joseph "did not teach the doctrine of spiritual wives."

The following account of the Cobb divorce case was printed in the *Boston Post* and reprinted in the *Quincy* (Illinois) *Whig* for December 22, 1847, page 2:

> Supreme J. Court—Boston. [Cobb Divorce Case]
> *Divorced from a Woman who had become the "Spiritual Wife" of a Mormon Leader.*—Henry Cobb vs. Augusta Cobb. This was a libel alleging crim con on the part of the respondent [Augusta Adams Cobb] with Brigham Young, in Nauvoo, in August, 1844, and December, 1845. After living 21 years in good repute with her lawful husband, the respondent became led away with Mormonism, leaving her husband, went to Nauvoo, and joined the church there. After a year's trial of the system she returned to Boston, but not being able to content herself here, she made another trip to Nauvoo; returned to Boston again, and again went off, and she is now supposed to be in California [Utah Territory] with Young.
>
> Her conduct in Nauvoo was fully described in the deposition of George J. Adams, better known under the name of "Elder Adams," who testified that he knew Mrs. Cobb, when she lived in the house of Brigham Young, at Nauvoo. We give the follow-

ing extracts from the deposition:

"In the fall of 1844 after her return from Nauvoo to Boston, Mrs. Cobb said she loved Brigham Young better than she did Mr. Cobb, and, live or die, she was going to live with him at all hazards. This was in the course of a conversation in which she used extravagant language in favor of Mr. Young and against Mr. Cobb. Mrs. Cobb went out again to Nauvoo, the second time, and lived with Mr. Young, and their living together, and their conduct, was the subject of conversation in the society [of the Church] and out of the society. The subject of conversation, to which I have alluded, was that persons had a right to live together in unlawful intercourse [polygamy], and Mrs. Cobb avowed her belief in this doctrine, and said it was right.

"In conversation with Mrs. Cobb on the subject of spiritual wives, I [Adams] told her such doctrines would lead to the devil; and she said if it did she would go there with Brigham Young. The Mormons were so incensed with me for my opposition to this doctrine that they attempted to take my life in various ways. I think Mrs. Cobb was originally a woman of good feelings and good principles, but I do not think so of her now. I think she was led away by religious frenzy.

"She said, I never will forsake brother Young, come life or come death. She said that the doctrine taught by Brigham Young was a glorious doctrine; for if she did not love her husband [Cobb], it gave her a man she did love."

In the cross examination, Mr. Adams stated that he performed on the stage when he was a young man; that he was a merchant tailor in extensive business before he joined the Mormons; that he has, since he withdrew, performed at the National Theatre in this city, *that Joseph Smith the founder of Mormonism, did not teach the doctrine of spiritual wives* (italics added); that Brigham Young, in assuming to be president of the church, had usurped authority, and that he, Mr. Adams, opposed the usurpation.

The testimony of Mr. Adams was corroborated by a widow lady, who had been to Nauvoo. . . . Judge Wilde decreed a full divorce from the bonds of matrimony.

The LDS Church in Utah has taught throughout the world that it was Joseph Smith who brought the doctrine of polygamy into the Church, but there is an abundance of evidence that

Joseph and Hyrum did not teach nor practice it. Instead, it was Brigham Young and his large family and loyal friends who secretly began the practice even before Joseph's death. Catharine V. Waite best described the power of the elite group surrounding Brigham Young, which made the polygamy doctrine succeed. Mrs. Waite was a lawyer and the wife of Judge Charles B. Waite, a justice appointed by the Federal Government to the Territory of Utah. She had an excellent opportunity to observe the inner workings of this elite polygamous hierarchy while she lived in Salt Lake City during the 1860s. She wrote:

> It is worthy of remark, that all of Brigham's family became Mormons. . . . His brothers are all at Salt Lake, and are the devoted followers and satellites of the Prophet [Brigham].
>
> Through the plurality system, the Youngs have formed connections so numerous, that almost half the people at Salt Lake are in some way related to the ruling dynasty. This is striking evidence of Brigham's ingenuity in consolidating and perpetuating his power. (Mrs. C. V. Waite, *The Mormon Prophet and His Harem; or, An Authentic History of Brigham Young, His Numerous Wives and Children*, 2)

Joseph and Hyrum fought a losing battle against the doctrine of polygamy because of Brigham's influence and power in Nauvoo. Brigham, and not Joseph, was the father of Mormon polygamy.

Chapter 5

The Apostles Brought Polygamy into the Church

Cochranism was not the only source of polygamy. Indeed, polygamy was a common subject of discussion in America during the 1830s. Over a hundred different religious colonies or communes in America were practicing some form of polygamy during the years that the Church was being formed. In 1868 William Hepworth Dixon wrote two volumes entitled *Spiritual Wives,* which gave much information about the various forms of polygamy, spiritual wifery, and like practices during that time.

Dixon was a distinguished English writer and the editor of the *Athenaeum*, a literary magazine published in London. He traveled extensively in America gathering facts about polygamous groups, and even visited Salt Lake City where he interviewed Brigham Young. Dixon wrote:

> A few words dropt by Brigham Young, in the course of a long reply to questions of mine on another point, told me that the Mormon Pope knew more than could be found in books about that doctrine of the Spiritual wife, which, in our own day, in the midst of our churches, and chiefly, if not wholly, among men of Teutonic race, has flowered out into so many new and surprising domestic facts: at Salt Lake City into Polygamy; among the New England spiritual circles into Affinities; at Mount Lebanon into Celibate Love; at Wallingford and Oneida Creek [New York] into Complex Marriage, and in a hundred American cities into some more or less open form of Free Love. (William Hepworth Dixon, *Spiritual Wives* 1:79)

Dixon's statement that some form of spiritual wifery was being practiced "in a hundred American cities" will no doubt be surprising to many. However, other writers confirm his findings. Of interest also is his statement on the subject of polygamy—that Brigham Young knew more about the "doctrine of the Spiritual wife" than could be found in books. This meant that Brigham Young was intimately familiar with other religious societies which were practicing polygamy. In a sermon in 1860, Brigham Young confirmed that he had a knowledge of many other religions. He said:

> I used to go to meetings—was well acquainted with the Episcopalians, Presbyterians, New Lights, Baptists, Freewill Baptists, Wesleyan and Reformed Methodists,—lived from my youth where I was acquainted with the Quakers as well as the other denominations, and was more or less acquainted with almost every other religious ism. (*Journal of Discourses* 8 [1861]: 38)

It has already been shown in an earlier chapter that Brigham had a firsthand knowledge of Cochranism, having been in attendance at the Church's conference in Saco, Maine, in 1836, and having married Augusta Cobb who was well acquainted with Cochranism.

America was not the only nation in which polygamy was a popular subject of discussion in the 1830s and 1840s. It was a matter of interest and speculation in England and other parts of Europe during the time that the first Church missionaries were there. It seems that whenever God moves to start something as marvelous as the restoring of the New Testament Church, which was officially organized in 1830, that Satan also starts a new surge of evil to destroy it. One of Satan's major efforts in this direction during the time that the Church was being formed was a revival of interest in polygamy—which occurred in three different countries simultaneously, but independently. Dixon recorded:

> It has not, I think, been noticed by any writer that three of the most singular movements in the churches of our generation seem to have been connected, more or less closely, with the state of mind produced by revivals; one in Germany, one in England, and one in the United States. . . .

These three movements, which have a great deal in common, began without concert, in distant parts of the world, under separate church rules, and in widely different social circumstances. The first movement was in Ost Preussen [Germany]; the second in England; the third, and most important, in Massachusetts and New York. They had these chief things in common; they began in colleges, they affected the form of family life, and they were carried on by clergymen; each movement in a place of learning and of theological study; that in Germany at the Luther-Kirch of Königsberg, that in England at St. David's College, that in the United States at Yale College. (Dixon, *Spiritual Wives* 1:84–85)

It is significant that these three manifestations of the polygamous spirit all occurred in religious and intellectual circles—at leading universities in each country. This made polygamy more acceptable than if the practice had occurred in small, unknown, radical groups.

Books published in England attest to the fact that polygamy had long been a subject of discussion in that country before the Church's missionaries arrived in 1837. They include:

T. T. Payen, *The Cases of Polygamy, Concubinage, Adultery, Divorce, etc., Seriously and Learnedly Discussed* (London: 1732);
James Cookson, *Thoughts on Polygamy Including Remarks on Theolyphtora and Its Scheme* (Winchester, England: J. Wilkes for the author, 1782);
Delany Patrick, *Reflections on Polygamy* (London: 1739);
Johannes Lyser, *Polygamia Triumphtrix* (Europe: 1682);
John Towers, *Polygamy Unscriptural* (London: 1780);
William Hepworth Dixon, *Spiritual Wives*, 2 vols., 1868.

Some of the Apostles Increased Their Interest in Polygamy While in England

It was shown in the previous chapter that Brigham Young testified that he had polygamous manifestations while serving as a missionary apostle in England. Elder Edwin Stafford testified that he was satisfied that Brigham Young was in adultery while there. It should be remembered that the missionaries who went to the English Mission were idolized by many of their converts, which had a tendency to increase polygamous desires. An example of their popularity is revealed in the following account:

> Elder Kimball, accompanied by Elder Fielding, walked to Chatburn and Downham for a last farewell. In Chatburn, the people left their work and flocked to the streets to greet them. Children followed them from place to place, singing. "Some of them said that if they could but touch us they seem better. They evidently believe there is Virtue in Brother Kimball's Cloake," Elder Fielding wrote. (*The Ensign of the Church of Jesus Christ of Latter Day Saints* 17 [July 1987]: 26)

In this setting, in a country where polygamy was a subject of discussion, as it was in America, it was natural for the apostles and the other missionaries to develop theories to justify their polygamous desires. There is evidence that these brethren added to their desires for polygamy, and belief in it, as a result of their experiences in England.

As mentioned previously, Brigham Young stated that "While we were in England, (in 1839 and 40), I think the Lord manifested to me by vision and his Spirit things [concerning polygamy] that I did not then understand. . . .[T]here had never been a thought of it in the Church that I ever knew anything about at that time" (*Messenger* 1 [June 1875]: 29; *Deseret News*, July 1, 1874). Lorenzo Snow, also a missionary to England and a brother to Eliza Snow (who became a plural wife of Brigham), stated:

> There is no man that lives that had a more perfect knowledge of the principle of plural marriage, its holiness and divinity, than what I had. *It was revealed to me before the Prophet Joseph Smith explained it to me.* I had been on a mission to England between two and three years, *and before I left England* I was perfectly satisfied in regard to something connected with plural marriage. (*Deseret Semi-Weekly News*, June 6, 1899; italics added)

A Book Promoting Polygamy Was Published in England

In addition to these two admissions of polygamous tendencies, there were other indications that the English Mission was a factor in bringing "a thing which is had in secret chambers" into the Church during the Nauvoo period. One was a book which prominent English priesthood members promoted, that told of Jacob (of the Old Testament) and his twelve sons.

Some of the more prominent priesthood members in England showed an unusual interest in polygamy and the "patriarchal order" (which was their terminology for those ancient patriarchs of the Old Testament who practiced plural marriage and concubinage). Part of their interest was generated by this book entitled *The Testament of the Twelve Patriarchs, the Sons of Jacob*. It was published by Elder Samuel Downes of the Church at Manchester, England, in 1843. Note in the statement below that Downes showed the book to many of the brethren and they urged him to publish it. His preface states:

> Beloved Brother, In sending forth unto the nations of the world the following pages, in a form whereby the humblest of our Brethren may possess themselves of it, I shall not know how truly thankful to feel to Almighty God, if, upon a perusal of its contents, it may meet with that approbation which it is the wish of your humble brother it should do. . . . Having shewn it to many of my brethren, and it having met with their approbation, they are wishful to possess themselves of it also. I now at their solicitation for the church, and for mankind in general, send it forth unto the world; and my heart's desire to God is, that the sublime truths contained in it may cause the hearts of the saints to rejoice and the wicked to see. . . . Art thou a Bishop, a Minister...? Look upon Jacob, O ye parents, peruse the twelve godly fathers in time and order. Learn of him and his to pray aright. (Preface to *The Testament of the Twelve Patriarchs, the Sons of Jacob*)

The books were sold from the Church's *Millennial Star* office and it was advertised in that publication. Editor Thomas Ward published:

> We have received a hundred copies of a reprint of a translation from an ancient Greek manuscript, entitled *The Testament of the Twelve Patriarchs, the Sons of Jacob*. We have to remark that this publication is not at all connected with the Church of Latter-day Saints, but merely printed by a brother, elder Samuel Downes, as a relic of antiquity, containing many portions of truth, and as a general curiosity. (*The Latter-Day Saints' Millennial Star* 4 [October 1843]: 96)

Elder Downes dedicated the book to a patriarch in the English Mission with these words:

> *The Testament of the Twelve Patriarchs, the Sons of Jacob,* Is Most Respectfully Dedicated to My Well-Beloved Brother, John Albitson, Patriarch in the Church of Latter-Day Saints. As a token of respect and esteem for his services and unwearied zeal in the cause of God in this the Evening of Time. By his Brother in Christ, Samuel Downes.

The *Millennial Star* 3 [June 1842]: 30, refers to "Elder Albiston, the patriarch," who was present at a general conference held in Manchester, England, on May 15, 1842. Apostle Parley Pratt presided over that conference.

The book did not condemn polygamy as do all the Three Standard Books of Scripture. That book presented Jacob's plural marriage and concubinage as a godly way of life. It was not a book which edified the reader with true spiritual values. Neither could its claims be substantiated by the Bible, Book of Mormon, or Doctrine and Covenants. For instance, it stated, "Then an angel of the Lord appeared unto Jacob, and said that Rachel should bear but two sons, because she had forsaken the company of her husband, and chosen continency" (Elder Samuel Downes, *The Testament of the Twelve Patriarchs, the Sons of Jacob*, 48). The Bible proves this claim false, for Rachel bore Jacob's last son—Benjamin, and died in childbirth as a result (Genesis 35:16–19). In other words, Rachel did not forsake "the company of her husband."

Downes' book on the twelve patriarchs emphasized the patriarchal order of life in the Old Testament. The same theme was adopted and amplified in the LDS Church's theology—even to this day (see Bruce R. McConkie, *Mormon Doctrine*, 559).

At the meeting in which Brigham introduced the polygamy document (Section 132) to the public in 1852, with Joseph's name falsely attached, Apostle Orson Pratt gave a stirring sermon citing polygamous practices of the patriarchs of the Old Testament as the reason for having polygamy in modern times (*Journal of Discourses* 1 [1854]: 53–66). Orson became the husband of ten wives. Four were from the British Isles (*Utah Genealogical Magazine* 27 [1936]: 113–114).

One of Orson Pratt's biographers explained:

> The Saints soon found that this discourse would mark a fateful turning point for the entire Church. Orson began to talk about the ancient biblical patriarchs Abraham, Isaac, and Jacob and the privileges and blessings they enjoyed. He asked the congregation why the Lord had permitted these former worthies to take more than one wife. The answer, according to Orson, was that this was the most efficient way for the Lord to raise up a righteous and numerous people. (Breck England, *The Life and Thought of Orson Pratt*, 175)

The promotion of the book about the twelve patriarchs and the emphasis upon the patriarchal order are further evidences of the direct connection between the polygamous tendencies among the English missionaries and their converts, and Mormon theology.

Some Plural Wives of the Apostles Were from the British Isles

It is more than coincidence that many of the women who later became plural wives of the missionaries to England were women from the British Isles. This is another evidence that the English avenue helped bring polygamy into the Church. A list of a few of the missionaries sent to England and their first plural wives demonstrates this connection:

Apostle Parley P. Pratt married a total of twelve wives. His first plural wife and four other plurals were from the British Isles (see Parley P. Pratt, *Autobiography of Parley Parker Pratt*, 462–464);

Apostle Heber C. Kimball married forty-three wives, eight of whom were from the British Isles (see Stanley B. Kimball, *Heber C. Kimball—Mormon Patriarch and Pioneer*, 307–316);

Apostle Orson Hyde married a total of six wives, and his first plural wife was of English birth (see Howard H. Barron, *Orson Hyde—Missionary, Apostle, Colonizer*, 323);

Apostle John Taylor married fifteen wives (Richard S. Van Wagoner and Steven C. Walker, *A Book of Mormons*, 354). His first plural wife's birthplace was the Isle of Man, England (*see Utah Genealogical Magazine* 21 [1930]: 105).

Thousands of devoted English Saints joined the Church, and it is tragic that the American missionaries, who should have been godly shepherds over the flock, ensnared some of them in the evil net of polygamy. Later, many of the English Saints became aware of the apostasy and refused to follow the polygamous leaders. Numerous English converts, such as Charles Derry, became faithful workers in the Reorganization. After coming to America, he made great sacrifices to take the Reorganization's message back to the Saints in England.

Perhaps Brother Derry best summed up the destruction which polygamy caused throughout the Church when he stated, "The curse of polygamy has cast the darkest shadow over the church. The world is powerless to bring real discredit upon the church, but this vile system coming forth in the name of the church has given cause for reproach wherever the name of Mormonism is known" (*Journal of History* 8 [January 1915]: 174).

Chapter 6

Early Efforts to Eradicate Polygamy

From the very beginning, the Lord gave warnings against the invasion of polygamy into the Church. As early as 1831 He warned the Saints:

> *And now I show unto you a mystery, a thing which is had in secret chambers, to bring to pass even your destruction, in process of time*, and ye knew it not, but now I tell it unto you . . . . And again I say unto you, that the enemy in the secret chambers seeketh your lives. . . . And that ye might escape the power of the enemy, and be gathered unto me a righteous people, without spot and blameless: wherefore, for this cause I gave unto you the commandment, that you should go to the Ohio; and there I will give unto you my law. (RLDS DC 38:4, 6–7; LDS DC 38:13–14, 28, 31–32; italics added)

Polygamy was the "thing" about which the Lord warned the Saints. It was "had in secret chambers" among the Cochranites at the time of the Church's beginnings. Also, it almost brought the Church to "destruction, in process of time." No other factor nor problem has been so devastating to the Lord's work in these latter days. Some of the apostles and their friends began to practice it secretly in the early 1840s (in "secret chambers"), and they knew it had to be denied and covered with falsehoods. Therefore, the polygamists banded together and conspired more and more to cover their secret acts.

In 1831 the Lord commanded the Saints to leave New York State and move to Ohio, promising that there He would give them the law by which the Church and Zion would be governed. There Joseph Smith received the revelation of February 9, 1831, which is known as the "Law of the Church." And what was the law of the Church concerning polygamy? The revelation included the commandment:

> Thou shalt love thy wife with all thy heart, and shall cleave unto her and none else; and he that looketh upon a [another] woman to lust after her, shall deny the faith, and shall not have the Spirit; and if he repents not, he shall be cast out. (RLDS DC 42:7d; see also verses 20a–c, 22a–e; LDS DC 42:22–23)

In August 1831 God warned the Saints further:

> I, the Lord, am not pleased . . . I gave commandments and many have turned away from my commandments and have not kept them. *There were among you adulterers and adulteresses; some of whom have turned away from you, and others remain with you. . . . And verily I say unto you, as I have said before, He that looketh on a woman to lust after her, or if any shall commit adultery in their hearts, they shall not have the Spirit, but shall deny the faith.* (RLDS DC 63:4–5; LDS DC 63:12–16; italics added)

So God prohibited polygamy and like practices as early as 1831.

There has never been a greater "mystery" in the Church than the mystery of polygamy. During Joseph's lifetime writers of books and reporters throughout the civilized world gave space to the question of whether or not polygamy was practiced in the Church. At Nauvoo Joseph stood firmly with his brother, Hyrum, against polygamy. In contrast, Brigham Young and his brothers, other relatives and loyal friends, practiced polygamy secretly until it became deeply rooted in the Church at Nauvoo.

When the extent of the polygamous practices of these brethren became known to Joseph, he went to Stake President William Marks and explained to him that charges must be brought against the offenders so they could be tried before the Standing High Council, over which Marks presided. But Joseph was martyred before these trials could take place.

The Article on Marriage Was Adopted at Kirtland to Thwart Polygamy

Though most polygamous activities occurred at Nauvoo, a few cases had happened earlier at Kirtland. That was one reason why Joseph and the committee which published the Doctrine and Covenants at Kirtland in 1835 included the article on "Marriage," which said: "Inasmuch as this church of Christ has been reproached with the crime of fornication, and polygamy: we declare that we believe, that one man should have one wife; and one woman, but one husband" (DC [1835 Kirtland Edition] CI [101]: 4). In the 1844 Nauvoo Edition the "Marriage" article is CIX (109), and in the Liverpool Edition, published by Brigham Young, Jr., it is CIX (109). The "Marriage" article is Section 111 in the 1950 printing of the RLDS Doctrine and Covenants. Under Brigham Young's administration in Utah, it was deleted from that church's Doctrine and Covenants at the time the document commanding the practice of polygamy (Section 132) was inserted.

At Kirtland the Seventies Took Action against Polygamy

Polygamy in the Church prompted the Quorums of Seventy at Kirtland to publish a statement against that doctrine. The seventies adopted a resolution which stated, "That we will have no fellowship whatever with any Elder belonging to the quorums of the Seventies who is guilty of polygamy or any offence of the kind, and who does not in all things conform to the laws of the church" (*Messenger and Advocate* 3 [May 1837]: 511).

The Solomon Freeman Case at Kirtland

There are several examples of a person leaving his or her spouse when gathering to Church headquarters, and marrying again without a bill of divorcement. On November 29, 1837, the Quorum of Elders met at Kirtland and charged Elder Solomon Freeman with the crime of polygamy. Freeman, who was living with a wife at Kirtland at the time, denied that he had two wives until he was confronted by witnesses. He then admitted that he had left a wife in Massachusetts without divorcing her, and had married another woman (*Kirtland Elders' Quorum Record* [January 15, 1836–October 5, 1841], 35).

The Strange Case of High Priest Aaron Lyon at Far West

The separation of husbands and wives gave rise to some strange events, as is shown in the case of High Priest Aaron Lyon and Sarah Jackson. Mrs. Jackson and her husband planned to gather to the Far West area while the Church was headquartered there. Brother Jackson was detained at Alton, Illinois, but sent his wife to be with the Saints, after promising that he would join her as soon as possible. Sister Jackson made her home in the area of Salemtown, a newly organized community between Far West and Haun's Mill. It was located on Log Creek, a tributary of Shoal Creek, two and one-half miles southeast of the present town of Kingston, Missouri. Prominent in this settlement were three brothers—Aaron, Charles, and Windsor Lyon, who, after having been driven from Jackson County in 1833, had founded the village. They had built three cabins, a blacksmith shop, and a water mill. Soon other Saints moved to the "Lyon settlement." First it was named Jerusalem; then the name was shortened to Salem or Salemtown.

Sarah Jackson attended the local branch of the Church where High Priest Aaron Lyon was pastor. Soon Lyon, whose wife was deceased, decided that Sister Jackson should be his wife. Therefore, he gave false revelations to her, which declared that her husband was dead, that it was God's will for Sarah to marry him, and that she would be miserable if she did not. Brother Jackson arrived before the wedding date, however, and the irate husband, upon finding what had happened, preferred charges against Lyon before the High Council. The record shows:

Lyon . . . was their Presiding High Priest, and had gained

to himself great influence in and over that Branch; and it also appears that this man had great possessions, and . . . was in want of a wife . . . consequently he set his wits to work to get one. He commenced, (as he said), by getting a revelation from God that he must marry Mrs. Jackson, or that she was the woman to make his wife; and it appeared that these revelations were frequently received by him, and shortly introduced to Mrs. Jackson. It was also manifested that the old man had sagacity enough to know that unless he used his Priestly office to assist him in accomplishing his designs, he would fail in the attempt; he therefore told Mrs. Jackson that he had had a revelation from God that her husband was dead . . . and that she must consent to marry him, or she would be for ever miserable; for he had seen her future state of existence, and that she must remember that whomsoever he blessed would be blessed, and whomsoever he cursed would be cursed, influencing her mind, if possible, to believe his power was sufficient to make her for ever miserable, provided she complied not with his request, &c. Accordingly they came to an agreement, and were soon to be married; but, fortunately or unfortunately for both parties, previous to the arrival of the nuptial-day, behold, to the astonishment of our defendant, the husband of Mrs. Jackson arrived at home, and consequently disannulled the preceding contract. . . .

[The High Council decided, that . . . he should give up his license as High Priest, and stand as a member in the Church; and this in consequence of his being considered incapable of magnifying that office. (*Millennial Star* 16 [March 11, 1854]: 148–149; *Journal of History* 15 [July 1922]: 336–338)

This is an example of how men like High Priest Aaron Lyon practiced priestcraft—they used their priesthood offices and power to claim they had revelations from God, in order to lead trusting, undiscerning Saints such as Sarah Jackson into unlawful marriages.

Joseph Published That the Church Did Not Believe in Polygamy

There were so many different groups practicing polygamy

in America and so much speculation about the doctrine, that nonmembers assumed that the newly organized Church over which Joseph Smith presided also practiced it. While Joseph and other Church leaders were journeying from Kirtland to Far West in the fall of 1837, they were continually asked by nonmembers if the Church believed in polygamy. Joseph listed twenty "questions which are daily and hourly asked by all classes of people whilst we are traveling." One question was, "Do the Mormons believe in having more wives than one?" (*Elders' Journal* 1 [November 1837]: 28). Joseph answered, "No, not at the same time. But they believe, that if their companion dies, they have a right to marry again" (ibid. [July 1838]: 43). Joseph was the editor of the *Elders' Journal*, so this statement came directly from him in 1838.

Joseph Denounced Polygamy
While Imprisoned in Liberty Jail

While Joseph was imprisoned in jail at Liberty, Missouri, reports were circulated by his enemies that he and other imprisoned Church leaders were polygamists. From the prison dungeon Joseph wrote a letter on December 16, 1839, "To the church of Jesus Christ of Latter Day Saints in Caldwell county," in which he denied the polygamy charges. Joseph wrote:

> Know assuredly Dear brethren, that it is for the testimony of Jesus, that we are in *bonds* and in *prison*. . . .
>
> Was it for committing adultery? We are aware that false and slanderous reports have gone abroad, which have reached our ears, respecting this thing, which have been started by renagadoes, and spread by the dissenters, who are extremely active in spreading foul and libilous reports concerning us; thinking thereby to gain the fellowship of the world. . . . Some have reported that we not only dedicated our property, but likewise our families to the Lord, and Satan taking advantage of this has transfigured it into lasciviousness, a community of wives [polygamy], which things are an abomination in the sight of God.
>
> When we consecrate our property to the Lord, it is to

administer to the wants of the poor and needy according to the laws of God, and when a man consecrates or dedecates his wife and children to the Lord, he does not give them to his brother or to his neighbor; which is contrary to the law of God, which says, "Thou shalt not commit adultery, Thou shalt not covet thy neighbors wife." "He that looketh upon a woman to lust after her has committed adultery already in his heart."—Now for a man to consecrate his property, his wife and children to the Lord is nothing more nor less than to feed the hungry, cloth the naked, visit the widows and fatherless, the sick and afflicted; and do all he can to administer to their relief in their afflictions, and for himself and his house to serve the Lord. In order to do this he and all his house must be virtuous and shun every appearance of evil. Now if any person, has represented any thing otherwise than what we now write they have willfully misrepresented us. (*Times and Seasons* 1 [April 1840]: 82–85)

Joseph and Hyrum Forbade the Separating of Spouses When Gathering

The problems occurring as a result of husbands and wives separating from one another when one of them gathered, continued to plague the Church. The problem escalated at Nauvoo where thousands from across America, Canada, the British Isles, and other European countries converged in that city. So many English Saints migrated that the problem was acute among them. Joseph Fielding, a convert from England who gathered to Nauvoo, wrote a letter in which he addressed the problem of English women gathering to Nauvoo without their husbands. Fielding wrote to Apostle Parley P. Pratt, president of the English Mission. The letter revealed:

> There is one thing, in particular, I wish to caution the church against, namely this: some women, whose husbands persecute them for their religion, desire to come here; now, if such would lay their case before a council of the church and get a written statement from the presiding elder of their situation, so that the church here might know it, they might learn whether it would be lawful for them to be married again.

There has been a case or two of this sort here, which has been a source of trouble. I would advise no one to come in such a case without such certificate. (*Millennial Star* 3 [August 1842]: 78–79)

The *Millennial Star* soon published a letter from Hyrum and Joseph Smith, which gave an official ruling on this serious problem. The letter read:

ADDRESS FROM THE FIRST PRESIDENCY.
Nauvoo.
To our well beloved brother, Parley P. Pratt, and to the elders of the church of Jesus Christ of Latter-day Saints in England, and scattered abroad throughout all Europe, and to the Saints,—Greeting:

Whereas, in times past persons have been permitted to gather with the Saints at Nauvoo, in North America—such as husbands leaving their wives and children behind; also, such as wives leaving their husbands and children behind; and such as women leaving their husbands, and such as husbands leaving their wives who have no children, and some because their companions are unbelievers. All this kind of proceeding we consider to be erroneous and for want of proper information. And the same should be taught to all the Saints, and not suffer families to be broken up on any account whatever if it be possible to avoid it. Suffer no man to leave his wife because she is an unbeliever, nor any woman to leave her husband because he is an unbeliever. These things are an evil and must be forbidden by the authorities of the church, or they will come under condemnation; for the gathering is not in haste nor by flight, but to prepare all things before you, and you know not but the unbeliever may be converted and the Lord heal him; but let the believers exercise faith in God, and the unbelieving husband shall be sanctified by the believing wife; and the unbelieving wife by the believing husband, and families are preserved and saved from a great evil which we have seen verified before our eyes.

Behold this is a wicked generation, full of lyings, and deceit, and craftiness; and the children of the wicked are wiser than the children of light; that is, they are more crafty; and it seems that it has been the case in all ages of the world.

And the man who leaves his wife and travels to a foreign nation, has his mind overpowered with darkness, and Satan deceives him and flatters him with the graces of the harlot, and before he is aware he is disgraced forever: and greater is the danger for the woman that leaves her husband. The evils resulting from such proceedings are of such a nature as to oblige us to cut them off from the church.

There is another evil which exists. There are poor men who come here and leave their families behind in a destitute situation, and beg for assistance to send back after their families. Every man should tarry with his family until providence provides for the whole, for there is no means here to be obtained to send back. Money is scarce and hard to be obtained. The people that gather to this place are generally poor, the gathering being attended with a great sacrifice; and money cannot be obtained by labour, but all kinds of produce is plentiful and can be obtained by labour; therefore the poor man that leaves his family in England, cannot get means, which must be silver and gold, to send for his family; but must remain under the painful sensation, that his family must be cast upon the mercy of the people, and separated and put into the poorhouse. Therefore, to remedy the evil, we forbid a man to leave his family behind because he has no means to bring them. If the church is not able to bring them, and the parish will not send them, let the man tarry with his family— live with them—and die with them, and not leave them until providence shall open a way for them to come all together. And we also forbid that a woman leave her husband because he is an unbeliever. We also forbid that a man shall leave his wife because she is an unbeliever. If he be a bad man (*i. e.* the unbeliever) there is a law to remedy that evil. And if she be a bad woman, there is law to remedy that evil. And if the law divorce them, then they are at liberty; otherwise they are bound as long as they two shall live, and it is not our prerogative to go beyond this; if we do it, it will be at the expense of our reputation.

These things we have written in plainness, and we desire that they should be publicly known, and request this to be published in the [Millennial] STAR.

May the Lord bestow his blessing upon all the Saints richly, and hasten the gathering, and bring about the fulness of the everlasting covenant are the prayers of your brethren.

Written by Hyrum Smith, patriarch, by the order of Joseph Smith, president over the whole church of Jesus Christ of Latter-day Saints. HYRUM SMITH. (*Millennial Star* 3 [November 1842]: 115; RLDS *History of the Church* 2:640–641)

Brigham Young, Parley P. Pratt, and other members of the Quorum of Twelve Apostles did not heed the direction given by Joseph and Hyrum in the above letter. They not only separated wives from husbands, but they took some of the women for their own plural wives. In fact, at the time Hyrum penned his letter, Brigham Young had already plurally married two other men's wives. They were Lucy Ann Decker Seely, who was still married to William Seely; and Augusta Cobb, as previously noted. Soon other apostles who had served in England and Europe, along with their relatives and close friends, joined Brigham in secretly practicing polygamy. Apostle Parley P. Pratt was among them. After returning to Nauvoo, he secretly married his first plural wife, Elizabeth Brotherton, on July 24, 1843. She was a twenty-six-year-old convert from Manchester, England. All together Apostle Pratt married a total of twelve plural wives—four were from England and one from Scotland (Pratt, *Autobiography*, 462–464).

Whitehead Testified about Joseph's Conflict with Pratt

Joseph Smith's private secretary at the time of the martyrdom (June 1844) was High Priest James Whitehead, a convert from England. He testified that Joseph made a public statement against Apostle Pratt while preaching from the "Stand." Elder Whitehead had Joseph's private papers in his possession at the time of Joseph's death, and he delivered the records to the Twelve at Winter Quarters in December 1847, as instructed by the administrator of Joseph's estate (*Complainant's Abstract of Pleading and Evidence* [Temple Lot Case], 31). While at Winter Quarters near Omaha, Brother Whitehead saw the depravity which the polygamous apostles had brought upon the Saints. Therefore, he took his family to Alton, Illinois, and held himself aloof from all groups until he joined with the RLDS Church under Joseph III's administration. In a sermon he declared:

> Did Joseph [Smith] say anything about the church being led away into this terrible condition [polygamy and other evils]? He did, and I heard him. One Sunday afternoon after partaking of the sacrament, Joseph got up and spoke and said, "Brothers and sisters, I am going to warn you today of things to come. Do not let these things overthrow you, but be faithful and cleanse yourselves from filthiness and everything corrupt. Beware of all kinds of iniquity, for it is in high places."
>
> He then turned around to Parley Pratt, and pointing to him, said, "Brothers and sisters, if that brother knew what I know, he would turn around and want my life." ("Supplement," *Lamoni Gazette* [January 1888], 7; *Autumn Leaves* 1 [May 1888]: 203)

What secret had Joseph discovered—a deed so dark that Parley would want to take Joseph's life? The dark secret could have been that Joseph had learned that Parley had taken Elizabeth Brotherton as his plural wife.

Joseph Called upon Marks to Help Expel the Polygamists

Joseph was determined that polygamy was not going to continue in the Church. He was standing firmly between the polygamous conspirators and the Church. Standing with the Prophet were Emma, Hyrum, William Marks, and a few others. Most of the Saints were unaware of the deadly struggle going on behind the scenes. Both sides were growing more determined. When Joseph warned the Saints of iniquity in high places, and turned and spoke against Parley, he was aware that a conspiracy existed—that several apostles and others were planning to make polygamy a practice of the Saints and a doctrine of the Church. However, Joseph was determined to eradicate polygamy, even though he realized that his lack of cooperation with the polygamists could cost him his life.

The struggle between the pro-polygamists and Joseph became

more and more severe. A few weeks before Joseph's death it became apparent to him that polygamy could not be eradicated without bringing the struggle into the open. Therefore, Joseph went to High Priest William Marks, the president of the Nauvoo Stake and president of the High Council, as previously noted. He told Brother Marks that he would bring the polygamists to trial before the High Council, and that President Marks must expel them from the Church. Elder Marks later testified:

> I met with Brother Joseph. He said that he wanted to converse with me on the affairs of the church, and we retired by ourselves. I will give his words *verbatim*, for they are indelibly stamped upon my mind. He said he had desired for a long time to have a talk with me on the subject of polygamy. He said it eventually would prove the overthrow of the church, and we should soon be obliged to leave the United States, unless it could be speedily put down. He was satisfied that it was a cursed doctrine, and that there must be every exertion made to put it down. He said that he would go before the congregation and proclaim against it, and I must go into the High Council, and he would prefer charges against those in transgression, and I must sever them from the church, unless they made ample satisfaction. There was much more said, but this was the substance. The mob commenced to gather about Carthage in a few days after, therefore there was nothing done concerning it.
>
> After the Prophet's death, I made mention of this conversation to several, hoping and believing that it would have a good effect; but to my great disappointment, it was soon rumored about that Brother Marks was about to apostatize, and that all that he said about the conversation with the Prophet was a tissue of lies. (RLDS *History of the Church* 2:733)

A few weeks after this consultation with Elder Marks, Joseph was killed and the pro-polygamist apostles gained control of the Church. They continued their polygamous practices in Nauvoo, and later in Utah, where in 1852 they publicly proclaimed that Joseph had left a polygamous revelation commanding the Church to practice polygamy. They produced a document, now Section 132 in the LDS Doctrine and Covenants, and declared it to be Joseph's revelation—but it will be seen in later chapters that Joseph had no part in producing it.

If the apostles who went on missions to Europe had stood with Joseph against polygamy, that doctrine would have been kept out of the Church. Instead, they were the vehicle through which it entered—which caused the "mystery which is had in secret chambers" to almost destroy the Church in the "process of time."

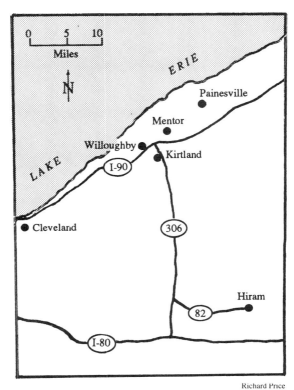

The Kirtland area, showing the close proximity of Willoughby (where Dr. John Bennett resided) to Kirtland, where the Church leaders lived.

Chapter 7

Dr. Bennett Laid the Foundation of Polygamy at Nauvoo

Though the Church was exposed to polygamy by the Cochranites, the practice of that evil doctrine at Nauvoo had its beginning through the instrumentality of a young medical doctor named John Cook Bennett.

Doctor Bennett taught that Joseph had received revelations from God on the subject of polygamy, and that "it was one of the mysteries of God, which was to be revealed when the people was strong enough in the faith to bear such mysteries" (see *Times and Seasons* 3 [August 1, 1842]: 870). This is the same doctrine that the Mormon Church uses as its basis for the practice of polygamy. It is also the doctrine which Jacob Cochran used twenty-five years earlier when he founded the Cochranite sect at Saco, Maine—which is proof that Utah Mormon polygamy originated with Jacob Cochran and not with Joseph Smith. Jacob Cochran provided material for Bennett to use in laying his polygamous foundation, and Brigham Young built upon it.

A Chronology of Events Which Led to Bennett's Coming to Nauvoo

Many have supposed that when Dr. Bennett arrived at Nauvoo in August 1840 he was an unknown stranger, but this was not true. Bennett and the Church leaders were acquainted. At the time the Church headquarters was in Kirtland in the early 1830s, Bennett was a young medical doctor living at Willoughby, Ohio, only three miles away. He was also a minister in Alexander Campbell's Christian Disciples Church, along with

Sidney Rigdon.
One biographer has written:

> At Willoughby he [Bennett] became acquainted with the Mormon leaders and knew Sidney Rigdon very well as he was for a time a licensed preacher in the Christian sect along with Rigdon. (Ralph V. Chamberlin, *The University of Utah: A History of Its First Hundred Years, 1850–1950*, Appendix Q, Biographical Notes, 577)

Other Saints at Kirtland knew Bennett, for they also had been members of the Christian Church prior to being converted to the Restored Gospel. The baptizing of one hundred and twenty-seven individuals in the fall of 1830, many of them Rigdon's followers, caused great excitement and resulted in Sidney and Campbell becoming bitter enemies. They proclaimed their differences publicly in the pulpits and the press. In the years which followed, Bennett kept a watchful eye upon the Saints and their problems, and joined the Church at Nauvoo in 1840 with a knowledge of its history and persecutions.

The following chronology traces the geographic movements of both the Church leaders and Bennett—the movements which helped bring them together at Nauvoo:

January 11, 1832: Elder William McLellin recorded in his journal that January 11 was "mostly spent" in talking with "Bennett a Campbellite Priest." McLellin had been baptized and ordained an elder the previous August, and was busily engaged in missionary work. The "Campbellite Priest" with whom he conversed was Dr. John C. Bennett. As McLellin and Bennett talked they agreed that on the following day McLellin would take Dr. Bennett to meet with Joseph and Sidney Rigdon, who were then living at Hiram, Ohio, about thirty miles southeast of Kirtland (see Jan Shipps and John W. Welch, editors, *The Journals of William E. McLellin, 1831–1836*, 69). At the time, Joseph and Sidney were engaged in correcting the Holy Scriptures to produce the Inspired Version. They had found it impossible to work without interruption in busy Kirtland, so they had moved to Hiram, hoping to find a quiet retreat. John and Elsa

Johnson, a Church couple who had a large, comfortable, colonial-style home at Hiram, provided Joseph and Emma and their adopted twin babies, Joseph and Julia, with a private bedroom in their home. They provided Sidney and his family with a log cabin on the farm (see Richard S. Van Wagoner, *Sidney Rigdon: A Portrait of Religious Excess*, 109). The Johnsons also made available a large, comfortable room for Joseph and Sidney to use while they worked on the Inspired Version.

January 12, 1832: McLellin recorded in his journal that he took Bennett in his sleigh to the Johnson home on that day. The meeting between Joseph and Bennett took place only one year and nine months after the Church was organized. Bennett stayed at Hiram long enough to hear Joseph, Sidney, and others expound the gospel. According to McLellin's journal, on the evening of January 13 Joseph and Bennett "talked considerable" (see Shipps and Welch, *Journals of William E. McLellin*, 69). Bennett was not baptized at that time, which must have been disappointing to McLellin, Joseph, and Sidney. However, Bennett kept a watchful eye on the Saints from January 1832 until 1840, when he was baptized at Nauvoo. He later wrote:

> My attention had been long turned towards the movements and designs of the Mormons, with whom I had become pretty well acquainted, years before, in the state of Ohio; and after the formation of their establishment at Nauvoo, in 1839. (John C. Bennett, *The History of the Saints; or, An Exposé of Joe Smith and Mormonism,* 5)

Don Carlos Smith, editor of the *Times and Seasons* and brother of the Prophet, substantiated Bennett's statement by publishing, "He [Bennett] has, likewise, been favorably known for upwards of eight years by some of the authorities of the church" (*Times and Seasons* 2 [June 1, 1841]: 432).

February 21, 1835: Dr. Bennett was serving as "President of our Medical Faculty, and Professor of the Principles and Practice of Midwifery, and the Diseases of Women and Children" at the Willoughby University of Lake Erie at Willoughby, Ohio

(Bennett, *History of the Saints*, 13). His presence there as a medical doctor and a minister in the church headed by Alexander Campbell brought him into contact with many Saints in Kirtland and vicinity.

March 14, 1838: Joseph Smith moved his family from Kirtland to Missouri, leaving behind many acquaintances, including Dr. John Bennett. Joseph and Emma made their home at Far West, Missouri, the headquarters for the Church (RLDS *History of the Church* 2:137; LDS *History of the Church* 3:8–9).

June 1838: Dr. Bennett moved from Ohio to Fairfield, Wayne County, Illinois (Bennett, *History of the Saints,* 14, 17). Fairfield is east of St. Louis in the southern part of Illinois. He had settled in a state adjacent to Missouri, where he had access to the Springfield *Sangamo Journal* and other newspapers which gave frequent reports concerning the Saints.

October 31, 1838: Joseph, Hyrum, Sidney, and other Church officials were arrested by the Missouri State Militia and imprisoned at Richmond, Missouri, which quickly became national news.

November 4, 1838: General Clark of the state of Missouri arrived at Far West, and informed the Saints:

> "The orders of the Governor to me were, that you should be exterminated, and not allowed to remain in the State. . . . [Y]ou must not think of staying here another season . . . . If I am called here again . . . you need not expect any mercy, but extermination, for I am determined the Governor's order shall be executed." (RLDS *History of the Church* 2:265–266; LDS *History of the Church* 3:203)

December 1, 1838: Joseph, Hyrum, Sidney, and three others were moved from the Richmond Jail to Liberty, Missouri. Dr. Bennett soon learned where they were imprisoned.

December 16, 1838: Joseph struggled to survive in the cold,

dark dungeon of the jail. He learned rumors were circulating that he was guilty of adultery and that the Saints believed in polygamy. He assured the Saints that he had not committed adultery and that polygamy was an abomination in the sight of God. Joseph wrote:

> *Liberty Jail, Missouri, Dec. 16, 1838.*
> To the church of Jesus Christ of Latter Day Saints in Caldwell county . . . who are persecuted and made desolate, and who are afflicted in divers manners, for Christ's sake . . . . [T]he world hated us. . . . And why? . . .Was it for commiting adultery? We are aware that false and slanderous reports have gone abroad, which have reached our ears, respecting this thing, which have been started by renagadoes, and spread by dissenters. . . . Some have reported that we not only dedicated our property, but likewise our families to the Lord, and Satan taking advantage of this has transfigured it into lasciviousness, a *community of wives [polygamy], which things are an abomination in the sight of God.*
> When we consecrate our property to the Lord, it is to administer to the wants of the poor and needy according to the laws of God, and when a man consecrates or dedecates his wife and children to the Lord, he does not give them to his brother or to his neighbor; *which is contrary to the law of God*, which says, "Thou shalt not commit adultery, Thou shalt not covet thy neighbors wife" "He that looketh upon a woman to lust after her has committed adultery already in his heart."—Now for a man to consecrate his property, his wife and children to the Lord is nothing more nor less than to feed the hungry, cloth the naked, visit the widows and fatherless, the sick and afflicted; and do all he can to administer to their relief in their afflictions, and for himself and his house to serve the Lord. . . . Now if any person, has represented any thing otherwise than what we now write they have willfully misrepresented us. . . . JOSEPH SMITH, Jr. (*Times and Seasons* 1 [April 1840]: 82–85; italics added)

February 20, 1839: Governor Thomas Carlin of Illinois issued a statement that J. C. Bennett had been "duly elected to the office of Brigadier-General of the Invincible Dragoons of the 2d Division of the Militia of the State of Illinois" (Bennett,

History of the Saints, 14). While holding this position Bennett offered assistance to free Joseph and the others from prison. He wrote letters to Joseph and Sidney which were encouraging, for he stated, "at that time I . . . proffered you my entire energies for your deliverance" (LDS *History of the Church* 4:168). Even though he was not specific concerning what kind of assistance, it was an important offer coming from a brigadier general of a division of the Illinois Militia.

April 1839: Sidney was discharged from prison because of ill health. Joseph, Hyrum, and other prisoners were taken to Gallatin, Missouri, for trial. Their attorney, General Alexander Doniphan, became convinced that the prisoners could not get a fair trial in Gallatin and secured a change of venue to Boone County. On the way there the sheriff, in collusion with unknown authorities, allowed the prisoners to escape. Joseph and Hyrum made their way to Quincy, Illinois, where they found their families. Thousands of Saints had also gathered to Quincy and the surrounding area.

Shortly thereafter the Church leaders purchased the deserted village of Commerce, Illinois, as a gathering place for the Saints. It was located at a beautiful bend on the east bank of the Mississippi River, about forty-six miles north of Quincy. The deserted land had a hidden menace—its swampy lowlands were malaria-ridden, which would cause the death of many of the Saints.

May 1839: Joseph moved his family to Commerce and the Saints began to gather. The name Commerce was soon changed to Nauvoo. Dr. Bennett was closely following the news and these movements of the Saints.

July 25, 1840: Bennett wrote to Joseph and Sidney with the news that he had resigned his office of brigadier general of the Invincible Dragoons, and had accepted an appointment by the governor to the office of quartermaster general of Illinois (ibid., 168–169). He had moved to a higher military rank.

July 27, 1840: Bennett wrote still another letter to Joseph and Sidney explaining that he had attended a meeting of the Saints at Springfield, Illinois, and he expressed hope that the time "will soon come when your people will become my people, and your God my God" (ibid., 169).

August 15, 1840: Bennett sent Joseph and Sidney another letter informing them that in about two weeks he would be with them at Nauvoo (ibid., 179). Joseph wrote, "Dr. J. C. Bennett . . . located himself in the city of Nauvoo, about the month of August 1840, and soon after joined the church" (*Times and Seasons* 3 [July 1, 1842]: 839). The history of the Church was changed forever!

Bennett Arrived When the Saints Were in Need of Leadership

Dr. Bennett's arrival at Nauvoo was very timely for his own climb up the social, political, economic, and religious ladders. The Saints at Nauvoo were in a weakened and critical condition, being physically and economically drained. Joseph and Hyrum and other Church leaders were shackled by threats from Missouri and Illinois law officials, who were seeking to seize and return them to Missouri to be tried on charges of treason. Several thousand destitute Saints were without homes and employment, and many were seriously ill because of malnutrition, exposure, and disease.

Even the Prophet was not exempt from losing members of his family and strong men upon whom he was depending. Some closest to him who died were: James Mulholland, Joseph's clerk, November 3, 1839 (*Times and Seasons* 1 [December 1839]: 32); Bishop Edward Partridge, May 27, 1840 (ibid. 1 [June 1840]: 127–128); Joseph Smith, Sr., the Prophet's father, September 14, 1840 (ibid. 1 [September 1840]: 170); Mary Smith, wife of Samuel, the Prophet's brother, January 25, 1841 (ibid. 2 [February 15, 1841]: 324); Don Carlos Smith, Joseph's brother and editor of the *Times and Seasons*, August 7, 1841 (ibid. 2 [August 16, 1841]: 503); Don Carlos, the Prophet's fourteen-month-old son, August 15, 1841 (ibid. 2 [September 1, 1841]: 533); Robert B. Thompson, Church clerk and another editor of the *Times and Seasons*, August 27, 1841 (ibid. 2 [September 1, 1841]: 519); and six-year-old Hyrum Smith, son of Joseph's brother, Hyrum, September 25, 1841 (ibid. 3 [November 1, 1841]: 592).

No doubt Joseph's personal losses and the suffering of other Saints weighed heavily upon him. A number of the members of the Twelve were in England as missionaries and therefore could not provide leadership. So Joseph welcomed the assistance of Dr. Bennett, who came prescribing a miracle medicine, quinine, for the malaria which was killing the Saints; and also bringing great visions and expertise in city planning, schools, a university, commerce, a militia, a Masonic Lodge, and political stability.

On January 15, 1841, Joseph, Hyrum, and Sidney, presidents of the Church, issued "A Proclamation to the Saints Scattered Abroad," in which they revealed that Dr. Bennett had been instrumental "in effecting our . . . deliverance from the . . . authorities of Missouri." They wrote:

> several of the principal men of Illinois . . . have become obedient to the faith . . . among whom is John C. Bennett, M.D., Quarter Master General of Illinois. . . . [D]uring our persecutions in Missouri, he became acquainted with the violence we were suffering, while in that State, on account of our religion—his sympathies for us were aroused, and his indignation kindled against our persecutors for the cruelties practised upon us. . . . [H]e addressed us a letter, tendering to us his assistance in delivering us out of the hands of our enemies, and restoring us again to our privileges, and only required at our hands to point out the way, and he would be forthcoming, with all the [military] forces he could raise for that purpose—He has been one of the principal instruments, in effecting our safety and deliverance from the unjust persecutions and demands of the authorities of Missouri, and also in procuring the [Nauvoo] city charter—He is a man of enterprize, extensive acquirements, and of independant mind, and is calculated to be a great blessing to our community. (*Times and Seasons* 2 [January 15, 1841]: 275)

Lucy Smith Asserted That Bennett Devised a Plan to Help Nauvoo

Lucy Smith, mother of the Prophet, referred to a "scheme" devised by Bennett which was to bring safety and peace to Joseph and other men who were being sought for prosecution by Missouri and Illinois law officers. She recalled:

> About this time [1840], John C. Bennett came into the city, and undertook to devise a scheme whereby Joseph and Hyrum, besides other brethren who were persecuted in like manner, might remain at home in peace. I do not know what he did, I only know that he seemed to be engaged in the law, as well as the gospel. My heart was then too full of anxiety about my husband [who died the month Bennett arrived], for me to inquire much into matters which I did not understand; however, the result was, that Joseph returned from Iowa [where he had been hiding from law officials]. . . . Joseph came in and told his father that he should not be troubled any more for the present with the Missourians. (Lucy Smith, *Biographical Sketches of Joseph Smith the Prophet and His Progenitors for Many Generations*, 336)

Mother Smith did not know what comprised Bennett's scheme. However, it can be pieced together by observing the things which Bennett the politician and statesman negotiated in his early months in Nauvoo. His plan would bring security to the city and the Saints by obtaining:

1. A city charter that made Nauvoo virtually independent of the state and county governments;
2. The Nauvoo city charter made provisions for a municipal court, which provided that the Saints could be tried by Church men in Nauvoo, rather than being judged by nonmembers at Carthage, the county seat;
3. Establishing of the Nauvoo Legion, with Joseph being its leader and the highest-ranking militia officer in the state;
4. Establishing the Masonic Lodge in Nauvoo, and making it large and strong by having the majority of men in the city join

it. In this way, the Nauvoo Lodge would be the largest in Illinois.

Dr. Bennett, as the quartermaster general of the state militia, with training in military leadership and with his shrewdness in political matters, was able to put the program into place. However, the plan was plagued with pitfalls, for it made the nonmember citizens throughout the state jealous. Soon they began to express fear that the Saints were beyond the law with their extraordinary charter and court, and with a militia that was so large and well trained that it was dangerous. Even the Masons feared being overwhelmed. But the greatest danger of all—and one which Joseph became aware of only after it had taken root—was that the unscrupulous doctor was building himself an empire, and that his actions would bring destruction upon the Saints.

Bennett Began His Spiritual Wifery Soon after Arriving in Nauvoo

The young doctor came to Nauvoo posing as a single man and was soon engaged in secret illicit sexual activity. Quickly he gathered a group around him (the majority were young men and women) and secretly taught them that "promiscuous intercourse between the sexes was a doctrine believed in by the Latter Day Saints." When they asked how such could be possible when they had heard Joseph preach much against polygamy, Bennett had a ready answer. He claimed that he was in a position to know exactly what was going on because he was boarding at Joseph's home—and was acting as a temporary member of the First Presidency in place of Sidney Rigdon, who was ill. He explained to them that Joseph was preaching so much against polygamy because of the prejudice of the public and Emma's strong opposition to that doctrine. (Emma's opposition to polygamy was well-known by the Saints.) Bennett's assurances were so convincing that his secret circle of friends accepted his lies as truth, and they began practicing spiritual wifery. Among those ensnared in his web were Sarah Pratt, wife of Apostle

Orson Pratt; Nancy Rigdon, daughter of Sidney; Chauncey and Francis Higbee, sons of Church Historian Elias Higbee; and others.

After Joseph, Emma, and Hyrum discovered this underground clique, they worked feverishly to eradicate Bennett's falsehood that Joseph had received a polygamous revelation and was practicing polygamy. But its roots had already gone too deep. When Apostle Brigham Young and others, who favored polygamy, returned to Nauvoo from their missions to the British Isles in the summer of 1841, they found Bennett's foundation in place. After Bennett left Nauvoo, his foundation served as a base for Brigham and others of the Twelve to secretly continue that false doctrine and practice. Between then and the time they left Nauvoo in 1846, Brigham and his many relatives and friends created their own secret inner circle wherein polygamy was practiced. They used Bennett's same wicked claim that Joseph had received polygamous revelations and was practicing polygamy, but was publicly denouncing it because of the prejudice of the public and Emma's opposition. Without Bennett's groundwork, Brigham could not have introduced polygamy into the Church as an official doctrine.

After August 1852, when Brigham made public his polygamous document (now Section 132 of the LDS Doctrine and Covenants) and claimed it had originally been received by Joseph, Brigham faced the enormous task of giving proof that Joseph was its author. Therefore, Bennett's claim of polygamous "revelations" to Joseph (see "Affidavit of Hyrum Smith" in *Times and Seasons* 3 [August 1, 1842]: 870) and charges that Joseph had plural wives, became the main defense for Brigham and his followers.

Joseph's Sons Declared the Secrecy Theory Absurd

The belief that Joseph taught and practiced polygamy, but did it secretly because he feared opposition, is a ridiculous, weak belief according to Joseph's sons, Joseph III, Alexander, and David.

Joseph Smith III was eleven and a half years old at the time of his father's death. The young lad had a deep respect for, and a close relationship with, his father. He was intelligent and studious, and knew more about the polygamy conspiracy against his father than most Saints, because he often witnessed his mother and father's joint work to counteract the false polygamous charges which Bennett had made. He had the opportunity to observe his father's behavior, language, and mindset in public and private, both in the Prophet's office and home. As an example, the father required that Joseph III sometimes accompany him upon the rostrum during worship services; and the boy stayed at least once with his father while the Prophet was in hiding. Joseph III had this to say in answer to Brigham Young and others' claims that his father kept a polygamous revelation and polygamous marriages secret because of fear of the public:

> To assert that Joseph Smith was afraid to promulgate that doctrine [polygamy], if the command to do so had come from God, is to charge him with a moral cowardice to which his whole life gives the lie. Nor does it charge him alone with cowardice, but brands his compeers with the same undeserved approbrium. The very fact that men are now found who dare to present and defend it, is proof positive that Joseph and Hyrum Smith would have dared to do the same thing had they been commanded so to do.
>
> The danger to the lives of those men would have been no more imminent, nor any greater in the preaching of "Celestial Marriage," than it was in preaching the "Golden Bible" and the doctrine that Joseph Smith was a prophet blessed with divine revelation. For the preaching of these tenets many lost their lives; Joseph and Hyrum Smith were repeatedly mobbed, were imprisoned and finally died, in the faith originally promulgated, but—if we may judge from their public records,—not believers in polygamy. (Joseph Smith III, *Reply to Orson Pratt* [tract], 4)

Alexander Hale Smith, a son of the Prophet, was six years old when his father was slain. After studying the polygamous charges against his father he wrote:

> We also learn another fact: . . . That in the brain of J. C. Bennett was conceived the idea, and in his practice was

the principle first introduced into the church; and from this hellish egg was hatched the present degrading, debasing, and destructive polygamic system, known as "spiritual wifery," or the "celestial marriage," so called.

It is said that Joseph Smith, the martyr, received a revelation revealing the "celestial marriage" and instituting "plurality of wives." I have already examined the testimony of Joseph Smith, concerning the marriage ceremony; and he declares that he knew of no other system of marriage than the one quoted from the Book of Doctrine and Covenants [1835 Kirtland Edition, 101; 1844 Nauvoo Edition, 109; 1866 Liverpool Edition, 109; RLDS DC, 111]. . . .

But says one, "that was only a sham to blind the eyes of our enemies." Shame on the man, or set of men, who will thus wilfully charge the two best men of the nineteenth century, the two Prophets of the most high God, with publishing to the church and the public at large a lie, and signing their names to it.

"Oh! but it was done to save their lives." A very likely story, when those two men had faced death and the world for fourteen long years, preaching the word of God to a sin-cursed generation. No, no, it will not do, you must meet the truth with better weapons than that, if you expect to make much of a battle. Besides all that, Is it not written, that "He who seeketh to save his life shall lose it, and he who loseth his life for my sake shall find it," and did not they know this. Yes, a thousand times yes; it was their hope, their consolation in times of danger. (Alexander H. Smith, *Polygamy: Was It an Original Tenet of the Church of Jesus Christ of Latter Day Saints?* [tract], 6)

Joseph's Fight against Polygamy Is Being Ignored by the LDS Church

In spite of all that Joseph did to proclaim that he was not lying when he said he had not had a polygamous revelation, and that he was honest in his condemning of polygamy, members of the LDS Church proclaim even to this day that Joseph did receive Section 132 and was a polygamist. Joseph's side of the story has been, and is being, purposefully ignored by the LDS

Church. They never give Joseph credit for having spoken the truth on this subject. In fact, they consider it was necessary and acceptable for the Prophet to lie, even though the Scriptures teach that lying is a major sin. It is ridiculous to believe that Joseph lied about polygamy because he feared a prejudiced public—for even the Mormons publish that Joseph bravely faced death at Carthage, saying, "I am calm as a summer's morning" (*Times and Seasons* 5 [July 15, 1844]: 585; RLDS DC 113:4b; LDS DC 135:4). When Joseph's statements against polygamy are taken at face value and are read with the realization that he was not a cowardly liar—an astounding fact becomes obvious—that it was Brigham and his pro-polygamist party that palmed a fraudulent polygamy conspiracy upon the Saints, which has blighted the Latter Day Saint Movement for over a century and a half.

Chapter 8

Dr. Bennett and Eliza R. Snow

It has been shown that polygamy did not enter the Church through the Prophet Joseph Smith's teachings, but through other avenues. One of the most devastating roads was the one paved by Doctor Bennett. There is evidence that Bennett seduced Eliza R. Snow and caused her to conceive a child during the Nauvoo period. There is also evidence that because Joseph and Emma Smith both felt that Eliza was a victim of Bennett's deceit, they shielded her from disgrace.

However, after becoming one of Brigham Young's many wives, Eliza allowed the rumor to spread in Utah that she had been a plural wife of Joseph the Prophet and had become pregnant with his child. Brigham sorely needed this type of rumor to be circulated in order to attach Joseph's name to the doctrine, and justify his own plural marriages and those of other church leaders. Therefore, the church officials, which included members of the Snow family (in both the presidency and the historical department), promoted this new rumor with such vigor in Utah that one hardly dared mention that President Brigham Young's wife, Eliza, had apparently been romantically linked with Doctor Bennett.

In order to piece together the account of what really happened at Nauvoo, it is necessary to give more of Dr. Bennett's background:

> John Cook Bennett was born in Fairhaven, Bristol County, Massachusetts, August 4, 1804.... In 1808 he moved with his parents to Ohio. There ... he acquired a knowledge of the classical languages and excelled especially in mathematics. Thereafter he was trained for the practice of medicine under

> Dr. Samuel Hildreth, a prominent physician of Marietta, Ohio. . . . He had a marked interest in founding colleges and universities and promoted the formation of such institutions in West Virginia, Indiana and Ohio. The last institution he was successful in organizing in Ohio was the medical school of Willoughby University, located only four miles from Kirtland. He was first dean of that college and at the same time professor of Gynecology and the diseases of children. At Willoughby he became acquainted with the Mormon leaders and knew Sidney Rigdon very well as he was for a time a licensed preacher in the Christian sect along with Rigdon. He moved to Illinois in 1838. . . . He soon won appointment as brigadier general of the Illinois Invincible Dragoons. In 1840 he was made Quartermaster General [of the state militia] of Illinois by Governor Carlin. That same year he joined the Mormon church at Nauvoo in which he had a meteoric career, within eighteen months attaining popularity and power second only to that of Joseph Smith. In addition to his positions of mayor of Nauvoo and "acting counselor" in the First Presidency of the church, he was made Chancellor of the University of Nauvoo, [and] did an excellent job of organizing and training the Nauvoo Legion. (Ralph V. Chamberlin, *The University of Utah: A History of Its First Hundred Years*, 577–578)

The Church headquarters was at Kirtland from 1831 to 1837, which was only four miles from where the doctor lived while in his twenties. Being a medical doctor and a fellow preacher with Sidney Rigdon in the Disciples of Christ Church (Campbellite), he had ample opportunity to hear and accept the gospel. But he chose not to join at that time.

Since he was Sidney Rigdon's close friend and fellow churchman, he was well-known in the five congregations over which Rigdon presided at the time Sidney heard and obeyed the gospel. No doubt Bennett was also well acquainted with many of Rigdon's followers who were baptized into the Church led by Joseph Smith, including Parley P. Pratt, Orson Hyde, Lyman Wight, Newell K. Whitney, and Isaac Morley. All of these last-named later became polygamists.

Bennett also knew the family of Oliver Snow, which included his poetic and scholarly daughter, Eliza—who was already noted for her writing ability. Bennett and Eliza Snow had many things in common at Kirtland—they were the same age, both teachers, intellectual, widely read, writers, liked poetry, and both were interested in the war between Greece and Turkey which occurred while the Church headquarters was at Kirtland. Eliza, using the pen name *Narcissa*, wrote a poem about the war, which was published in the Ravenna *Courier.* Dr. Bennett, who "acquired a knowledge of the classical languages," studied the Turkish practice of polygamy, for he mentioned it in his book, along with the polygamy practiced by Oriental and African rulers (see Bennett, *History of the Saints*, 218-219). His discussion of polygamous rulers and harems in his book demonstrates that he had more than an ordinary interest in the subject, and an extensive knowledge of it being practiced in various places.

When Doctor Bennett arrived in Nauvoo, he claimed to accept the gospel and was baptized by Joseph. Housing was scarce when he arrived, so he roomed for thirty-nine weeks (nine months) with Joseph and Emma and their children in the tiny log cabin with only three rooms, known as the Homestead. The account book for Joseph Smith's store shows that John C. Bennett owed Joseph $117 for thirty-nine weeks of board at a charge of three dollars a week (see Joseph Smith's *Red Brick Store Daybook* [December 8, 1843], account number 59).

Joseph Smith III had some vivid memories of Dr. Bennett. He recalled:

> While Doctor Bennett was boarding at our house every effort was made for his comfort, however. Mother would set a loaf of bread down in front of the wood fire until its end would be toasted a pleasing brown. Then she would slice that part off, thinly, and replace the loaf before the fire. In this manner she would get a goodly supply ready for his supper of browned bread and milk, prepared just as he liked it. (*Saints' Herald* 82 [January 8, 1935]: 49)

At the time Bennett came to Nauvoo, he had a wife and children in the East, but he posed as a single man. Immediately after arriving in August of 1840, he was dating a young woman in Nauvoo, whom he seduced. Joseph published on June 24, 1842, that "more than twenty months ago [September or October 1840] Bennett went to a lady in the city and began to teach her that promiscuous intercourse between the sexes was lawful and no harm in it" (LDS *History of the Church* 5:42–43). This act, along with other incidents of immorality, made it necessary to expel him from the Church in May 1842.

Joseph Described Bennett's Adulterous Activities

Joseph published:

> It becomes my duty to lay before the Church of Jesus Christ of Latter Day Saints, and the public generally, some important facts relative to the conduct and character of DR. JOHN C. BENNETT, who has lately been expelled from the aforesaid church; that the honorable part of [the] community may be aware of his proceedings, and be ready to treat him and regard him as he ought to be regarded, viz: as an imposter and base adulterer.
>
> It is a matter of notoriety that said Dr. J. C. Bennett, became favorable to the doctrines taught by the elders of the church of Jesus Christ of Latter Day Saints, and located himself in the city of Nauvoo, about the month of August 1840, and soon after joined the church. . . . He had not been long in Nauvoo before he began to keep company with a young lady, one of our citizens; and she being ignorant of his having a wife living, gave way to his addresses, and became confident, from his behavior towards her, that he intended to marry her; and this he gave her to understand he would do. I, seeing the folly of such an acquaintance, persuaded him to desist; and, on account of his continuing his course, finally threatened to expose him if he did not desist. This, to outward appearance, had the desired effect, and the acquaintance between them was broken off.
>
> But, like one of the most abominable and depraved beings which could possibly exist, he only broke off his publicly wicked actions, to sink deeper into iniquity and hypocrisy [by continuing to date her secretly]. When he saw that I would not submit to any such conduct, he went to some

of the females in the city, who knew nothing of him but as an honorable man, & *began to teach them that promiscuous intercourse between the sexes, was a doctrine believed in by the Latter-Day Saints, and that there was no harm in it*; but this failing, he had recourse to a more influential and desperately wicked course; and that was, to persuade them that myself and others of the authorities of the church not only sanctioned, but practiced the same wicked acts; and when asked why I publicly preached so much against it, said that it was because of the prejudice of the public, and that it would cause trouble in my own house [with Joseph's wife, Emma]. He was well aware of the consequence of such wilful and base falsehoods, if they should come to my knowledge; and consequently endeavored to persuade his dupes to keep it a matter of secrecy, persuading them there would be no harm if they should not make it known. *This proceeding on his part, answered the desired end; he accomplished his wicked purposes; he seduced an innocent female by his lying, and subjected her character to public disgrace, should it ever be known.*

But his depraved heart would not suffer him to stop here. Not being contented with having disgraced one female, he made an attempt upon others; and, by the same plausible tale, overcame them also; evidently not caring whose character was ruined, so that his wicked, lustful appetites might be gratified.

Sometime about the early part of July 1841, I received a letter from Elder H. [Hyrum] Smith and Wm. Law [a member of the First Presidency], who were then at Pittsburgh, Penn. This letter was dated June 15th, and contained the particulars of a conversation betwixt them and a respectable gentleman from the neighborhood where Bennett's wife and children resided. He stated to them that it was a fact that Bennett had a wife and children living, and that she had left him because of his ill-treatment towards her. This letter was read to Bennett, which he did not attempt to deny; but candidly acknowledged the fact.

Soon after this information reached our ears, Dr. Bennett made an attempt at suicide, by taking poison; but he being discovered before it had taken effect, and the proper antidotes being administered, he again recovered; but he very much resisted when an attempt was made to save him. The public impression was, that he was so much ashamed of his base and wicked conduct, that he had recourse to the above deed to escape the censures of an indignant community.

It might have been supposed that these circumstances transpiring in the manner they did, would have produced a thorough reformation in his conduct; but, alas! like a being totally destitute of common decency, and without any government over his passions, he was soon busily engaged in the same wicked career, and continued until a knowledge of the same reached my ears. I immediately charged him with it, and he admitted that it was true; but in order to put a stop to all such proceedings for the future, I publicly proclaimed against it, and *had those females notified to appear before the proper [Church] officers* that the whole subject might be investigated and thoroughly exposed.

During the course of investigation [by Church officials], the foregoing facts were proved by credible witnesses, and were sworn and subscribed to before an alderman of the city, on the 15th ult. The documents containing the evidence are now in my possession. (*Times and Seasons* 3 [July 1, 1842]: 839–840; RLDS *History of the Church* 2:585–587; italics added)

From the above it is seen that Dr. Bennett "seduced an innocent female by his lying, and subjected her character to public disgrace, should it ever be known." She was "a young lady, one of our citizens." He also "went to some of the [other] females in the city" and "accomplished his wicked purposes."

Lorenzo Wasson Testified of Bennett's Guilt and Joseph's Innocence

One of Joseph's primary witnesses to his fidelity and Bennett's immorality was Emma's nephew, Lorenzo D. Wasson, a son of Emma's sister, Elizabeth Wasson. Lorenzo joined the Church and lived with his Aunt Emma and Uncle Joseph, where Bennett also boarded. During the summer of 1841, Lorenzo was upstairs in Joseph and Emma's bedroom at the Homestead, and heard Joseph berating Bennett in the room below. The next summer, on July 30, 1842, while on a missionary journey, Lorenzo wrote Joseph these words:

> Uncle, . . . If I can be of any service in this Bennett affair I am ready. I was reading in your chamber last summer—yourself and Bennett came into the lower room, and I heard you give J. C. Bennett a tremendous flagellation for practicing iniquity under the base pretence of authority from the heads of the church—if you recollect I came down just before you were through talking. There are many things I can inform you of, if necessary, in relation to Bennett and his prostitutes. I am satisfied of your virtue and integrity. I have been with you to visit the sick, and time and again to houses where you had business of importance, you requested me to do so—many times I knew not why, but I am satisfied it was that you might not be censured by those that were watching you with a jealous eye, and I now solemnly protest before God and man, I never saw a thing unvirtuous in your conduct. . . . I am your most obedient nephew, L. D. WASSON. (*Times and Seasons* 3 [August 15, 1842]: 892)

Lorenzo was Joseph's faithful attendant in life and in death. In 1843 Joseph was taken prisoner by Sheriff Reynolds of Missouri at the Wasson home in Dixon, Illinois. Lorenzo and his father's quick action provided Joseph with attorneys and prevented Joseph from being taken to Missouri (see *Saints' Herald* 82 [January 22, 1935]: 112). It was Lorenzo who hastened to Nauvoo with a message from Emma, bearing the news to the Saints of Joseph's arrest. And alas, it was Lorenzo that Joseph III remembers seeing "covered with dust, bringing the news" that Joseph and Hyrum had been murdered at Carthage (ibid. [January 29, 1935]: 143).

After a mock funeral and entombment for Joseph and Hyrum in June of 1844, Lorenzo and others, carefully chosen by Emma, secretly buried the bodies of the Martyrs in the basement of the Nauvoo House (see George Q. Cannon, *The Life of Joseph Smith the Prophet*, 529–530). Lorenzo refused to follow the leadership of Brigham Young.

Who Was the "Young Lady" Whom Bennett "Disgraced"?

One of the best-kept secrets in the Church is the identity of the "innocent female" whom Bennett seduced. Joseph revealed the names of other women who were involved with Bennett, but never hers. The young lady's name was known, of course, to Church officials who tried Bennett's case, such as members of the Presidency and the High Council. Their official investigation of Bennett's immorality was reported in the *Times and Seasons* and the Nauvoo *Wasp;* yet her identity was kept secret. Why? Because as Joseph explained, she was "innocent"—she was looked upon as a victim. This was not the case with President Sidney Rigdon's daughter, Nancy; Apostle Orson Pratt's wife, Sarah; and several other women whose names were published (see *Affidavits and Certificates Disproving the Statements and Affidavits Contained in John C. Bennett's Letters*, published at Nauvoo, Illinois, August 31, 1842). The reason that their names were made public will be explained in later chapters.

The Snow Family Left Nauvoo Abruptly

Eliza Snow and John Bennett had known each other in Ohio; they were the same age; and both had good educations and were intellectual, as previously noted. Now they were in Nauvoo and were close friends of Joseph and Emma Smith and Sidney and Phebe Rigdon. These facts show a natural relationship between them. During this time an incident occurred which angered Eliza's father, Oliver Snow. Historian and author, Maureen Ursenbach Beecher, has written:

> Spring 1842 was a time of great turmoil for the Snow family. Apostate John C. Bennett was spreading falsehoods, dissension was breaking out among the Saints, and persecution from nearby settlers was mounting. For Oliver Snow, it was more trial than he had faith to match. Purchasing property at Walnut Grove, a settlement some seventy-five miles east of Nauvoo, he moved his family there, those who would go. He

wrote to his brother Franklin that "Eliza cannot leave our Prophet. Mother [Rosetta] did not like to. For my part I am very glad, at present, to be away. Turmoil and confusion, these stalk abroad at noon day." (*Ensign* 9 [June 1980]: 67)

Oliver Snow had endured all kinds of hardships with the Saints in Ohio, Missouri, and Illinois. Why was the spring of 1842 so much worse that Oliver decided to leave Nauvoo and the Church? The spring of 1842 was the time that Joseph brought Dr. Bennett to trial and exposed those who were involved in his seductive activities by publishing the information. Did those trials reveal to Oliver that Dr. Bennett, one of the heads of the Church, had seduced his daughter, Eliza? Mormon Church authorities insist that Eliza did become pregnant during the Nauvoo period. This may have been between the spring of 1841 when the family moved back to Nauvoo from La Harpe, and the spring of 1842 when Oliver departed so abruptly. This was the same time that Bennett was most involved in his promiscuous activities. If Eliza were that "innocent female," it would explain Oliver Snow's abrupt change of allegiance and departure from Nauvoo.

Dr. Wyl Implied Bennett Seduced Eliza

The German author and newspaper correspondent, Dr. W. Wyl, spent nearly five months in Salt Lake City in 1885 collecting material for a book on Mormonism. When the book was published, it contained information which he had acquired from his interviews with approximately eighty individuals, including a number of old-time Saints from the Nauvoo and Kirtland days.

Dr. Wyl implied that Dr. John C. Bennett had seduced Eliza Snow. He did this by quoting from an article by Eliza, published in the *Times and Seasons* of February 1, 1844 (5:430–431), entitled "Missouri," which spoke of polluting "female virtue." Wyl then suggested that it was "Joab," not Missouri, of whom Eliza had written. "Joab" was the pseudonym used by Bennett for some of his articles which were published in the Church paper (see *Times and Seasons* 2 [November 15, 1840]:

222; 2 [December 1, 1840]: 238; 2 [January 1, 1841): 267).

Wyl, who called Eliza's article a psalm, wrote of Eliza and Bennett:

> Sister Snow, in her great psalm . . . says of Missouri: "Thou art a stink in the nostrils of the Goddess of Liberty . . . . Thou art already associated with Herod, Nero and the bloody Inquisition—thy name has become synonymous with oppression, cruelty, treachery and blood." Oh, Sappho-Eliza-Roxanna-Snow-Smith-Young! But I think I sniff General Joab in this transcendent psalm. "Thou didst pollute the holy sanctuary of female virtue, and barbarously trample upon the most sacred *gems* of domestic felicity," is Pistol-Bennett, sure. (Dr. W. Wyl, *Mormon Portraits or the Truth About the Mormon Leaders from 1830 to 1886*, 186–187)

Why did Dr. Wyl write, "I sniff" Bennett in Eliza's psalm? Apparently because one or more old-time Saints, who had lived in Nauvoo, had confided to him the closely guarded secret that Eliza had been the "young lady" who was seduced by "Pistol-Bennett, [for] sure."

By applying the name *Sappho* to Eliza, Dr. Wyl was comparing her to the Greek poetess by that name (see *Encyclopedia Americana* 24 [1954]: 291–292). Dr. Wyl was acquainted with the play by Austria's most talented dramatist, Franz Grillparzer, which told the story of Sappho, the sixth century B.C. Greek lyric poet. The drama had received wide acclaim throughout Germany.

Eliza and Sappho had two things in common: each was the greatest poetess in her respective society, and each was rejected by her lover. Sappho was rejected by Phaon, a man who chose a younger woman (ibid.; see also Frank N. Magill, *Critical Survey of Drama—Foreign Language Series*, 2371). Eliza was rejected by Dr. Bennett after he promised to marry her, for he went to other women in Nauvoo and "overcame them also" (*Times and Seasons* 3 [July 1, 1842]: 840). He rejected her even further when he divorced his wife, Mary (see Springfield, Illinois, *Sangamo Journal* [July 22, 1842], 2), and did not marry Eliza.

The LDS Church authorities continually claim that the story

of Eliza being pregnant at Nauvoo is true, and there is no reason to doubt that she did conceive a child, but if she did, the child was not born at Nauvoo. However, there is absolutely no foundation for their claim that Joseph Smith was the father.

One month before he died, Joseph the Prophet proclaimed to thousands of Saints gathered for worship on Sunday May 26, 1844, that he was not a polygamist. He declared, "What a thing it is for a man to be accused of committing adultery, and having seven wives, when I can only find one" (LDS *History of the Church* 6:411). Also, the fact that Emma did not push Eliza down the Mansion House stairs (see chapter 9) is proof that the LDS Church's "tradition" that Joseph was the father, is false. Who then was the father? Dr. Wyl's book, from which LDS writers have often quoted in their efforts to prove that Joseph was a polygamist, implies that Bennett seduced Eliza—he could have been the father.

Joseph Smith said of Dr. John C. Bennett's case, "What I have stated I am prepared to prove, having all the documents concerning the matter in my possession" (*Times and Seasons* 3 [July 1, 1842]: 841–842).

At Joseph's death, those documents pertaining to John C. Bennett's case, referred to by the Prophet, fell into the possession of Brigham Young and his associates and were taken to Utah. If those records still exist and could be examined and made public, they would no doubt reveal that Dr. John C. Bennett was the father of the child, which the Mormon Church claims Eliza Snow gave birth to prematurely.

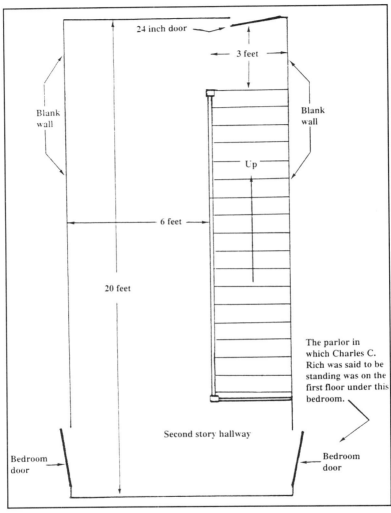

A diagram of the Mansion House stairs, showing that Charles C. Rich could not have seen Emma and Joseph coming from one bedroom and Eliza Snow coming from another (see also the photograph on page 126).

Chapter 9

Eliza Snow Was Not Pushed down the Mansion House Stairs

In an effort to prove that Joseph Smith was the author of polygamy in the Church, members of the LDS Church have proclaimed for over one hundred and fifty years that Eliza R. Snow was one of Joseph's plural wives in Nauvoo—and that Emma Smith in a jealous rage beat Eliza and shoved her down the Mansion House stairs, causing her to give birth prematurely to Joseph's child, who died. This story is false because the Mansion House stairs and hallway are constructed in such a way that the supposed altercation between Emma and Eliza could not have happened the way the story was reported. And even though Eliza lived with the Smiths for a short time at the Homestead, she never lived with them at the Mansion House, and her diary proves that she did not have an altercation with Emma.

In spite of these evidences, Fawn Brodie gave credence to this rumor by including it in her book, *No Man Knows My History*. She wrote:

> There is a persistent tradition that Eliza conceived a child by Joseph in Nauvoo, and that Emma one day discovered her husband embracing Eliza in the hall outside their bedrooms and in a rage flung her downstairs and drove her out into the street. The fall is said to have resulted in a miscarriage. (This tradition was stated to me as fact by Eliza's nephew, LeRoi C. Snow, in the Church Historian's Office, Salt Lake City.) Solon Foster, coachman for the prophet, was present in the Mansion House when the incident occurred. Years later he met Emma's sons, who were then publicly denouncing polygamy in Utah, and reproached them for their attitude: "Joseph, the night your mother turned Eliza R. Snow into the

> street in her night clothes you and all the family stood crying. I led you back into the house and took you to bed with me. You said, 'I wish mother wouldn't be so cruel to Aunt Eliza.' You called her aunt, because you knew she was your father's wife. He did not deny it."

C. G. Webb further corroborated the story in an interview with W. Wyl:

> There is scarcely a Mormon unacquainted with the fact, that Sister Emma, on the other side, soon found out the little compromise arranged between Joseph and Eliza. Feeling outraged as a wife and betrayed as a friend, Emma is currently reported as having had recourse to a vulgar broomstick as an instrument of revenge; and the harsh treatment received at Emma's hand is said to have destroyed Eliza's hopes of becoming the mother of a prophet's son. (Fawn Brodie, *No Man Knows My History*, 470–471)

Dr. Wilhelm Wyl had published Webb's account in his *Mormon Portraits*, page 58. In 1885 C. G. Webb made the above statement (as quoted by Fawn Brodie) to Dr. Wyl, an author and correspondent from Germany, who spent six months in Salt Lake City interviewing Mormons, including Webb, for a book which he was writing. His account demonstrates that by 1885 the story of Emma throwing Eliza down the stairs at the Mansion House was widespread among the Mormons—and they have been spreading that falsehood ever since. Even in March 1996 Mormon missionaries in the Independence, Missouri, area were trying to convert Saints in the Restoration branches by testifying that the Eliza Snow story was true.

Note that Fawn Brodie states that LeRoi C. Snow told her, "in the Church Historian's Office, Salt Lake City," the story that Solon Foster witnessed Emma Smith fling Eliza down the Mansion House stairs. Many heard and believed LeRoi Snow's testimony, not only because he worked at the Church Historian's Office, but because LeRoi was Eliza's nephew, and was the son of the Mormon Church President Lorenzo Snow, who was Eliza's brother.

Apostle Rich's Account Proven False

LeRoi Snow states that Apostle Charles C. Rich of the LDS Church saw Emma and Eliza at the head of the stairs, heard a commotion, then saw Eliza come tumbling down the Mansion House stairs. LeRoi's notes state:

> Charles C. Rich called at the Mansion House, Nauvoo, to go with the Prophet on some appointment they had together. As he waited in the main lobby or parlor, he saw the Prophet and Emma come out of a room upstairs and walk together toward the stairway which apparently came down center. Almost at the same time, a door opposite opened and dainty, little, dark-haired Eliza R. Snow (she was "heavy with child") came out and walked toward the center stairway. When Joseph saw her, he turned and kissed Emma goodbye, and she remained standing at the bannister. Joseph then walked on to the stairway, where he tenderly kissed Eliza, and then came on down stairs toward Brother Rich. Just as he reached the bottom step, there was a commotion on the stairway, and both Joseph and Brother Rich turned quickly to see Eliza come tumbling down the stairs. Emma had pushed her, in a fit of rage and jealousy; she stood at the top of the stairs, glowering, her countenance a picture of hell. Joseph quickly picked up the little lady, and with her in his arms, he turned and looked up at Emma, who then burst into tears and ran to her room. Joseph carried the hurt and bruised Eliza up the stairs and to her room. "Her hip was injured and that is why she always afterward favored that leg," said Charles C. Rich. "She lost the unborn babe." (Linda King Newell and Valeen Tippetts Avery, *Mormon Enigma: Emma Hale Smith*, 135)

When the stairways at both the Homestead and the Mansion House are examined, it is obvious that the event could not have happened at either place. The stairs in the Homestead are very narrow and they turn sharply near the bottom, so the top of the stairs cannot be seen while standing in the room below.

Neither can the hallway at the top of the stairs in the Mansion House be seen as Charles Rich described it. The stairway is narrow (only three feet wide) and at the top there is only a small landing three feet square—with a blank wall on the right, a small door straight ahead, and small hallway on the left. When standing at the foot of the stairs, one can only see the small door (see pages 88 and 126). It is straight ahead and it is the door to a small split-level room where the Smith children slept. The door to Joseph and Emma's room cannot be seen from the bottom of the stairs. No other door is visible, though Rich testified he "saw the Prophet and Emma come out of a room upstairs" and "a door opposite opened and dainty, little, dark-haired Eliza" came out of it. There was no "door opposite."

The shape of the stairways in both the Homestead and Mansion House makes Charles Rich's account false.

Foster's Story about Eliza Was Proven False by Joseph Smith III

The LDS Church's strongest witness to support their claim that Eliza was Joseph's plural wife was Solon Foster. In 1885, the year Dr. Wyl was gathering information from Salt Lake City Mormons for his book, Joseph Smith III (a son of the Martyr) was also in Salt Lake City obtaining evidence concerning polygamy to prove that his father, Joseph Smith, Jr., was not a polygamist. Joseph III had an interview with Solon Foster, and Solon tried to convince Joseph that he (Solon) had been present at the Mansion House and had seen Emma push Eliza down the stairs. John R. Young, Brigham Young's son, is said to have stated that he heard Solon Foster give a talk in which Foster told of the meeting between himself and Joseph III. According to John Young, Foster declared that he had told Joseph III that he (Solon) was present when Emma "turned Eliza R. Snow outdoors in her night clothes" (ibid., 134–135).

Joseph III gave an entirely different account of what was said during his interview with Foster. Joseph declared:

> Another person who called on me that summer at Brother Warnock's was a man whom I had known when I was a boy and whom I used to like very well as a young man—a genial, pleasant young fellow. His name was Solon Foster. When he heard that I was in the city, he came as he said from a

distance of one hundred and thirty miles to have a talk with me and *tell me what he knew*. Our conversation was pleasant until he proposed to tell me a good many things about my father's family, speaking as if he, personally, knew all about them. In the earlier part of our conversation I had learned that he was not at Nauvoo for about two years before Father's death. Therefore he could not possibly have known of things happening in 1843 and early in 1844 up to the time of the tragedy.

After he had "borne his testimony," I proceeded to interrogate him. It was but a little while until he was forced to admit that he was repeating *only what he had heard*. For instance, he had stated that my father was a polygamist and had other wives than my mother. I questioned him: "Brother Solon, were you ever present at a marriage ceremony of any kind which occurred between my father and any other woman than my mother, Emma Hale?"

"No; I was not even present at their marriage."

"When you were an inmate of my father's house at occasional stated periods as you have said, did you ever see any woman there whom you knew to be a wife to my father, other than my mother?"

"No, sir."

"Did you ever meet, in social gatherings anywhere in the city of Nauvoo at any time a woman in company with my father, introduced by him or others as his wife, other than my mother Emma?"

"No, sir."

"Did you ever see my father in his own home or elsewhere where people were assembled in a social meeting of any kind, conduct himself in a familiar, intimate, or endearing manner toward any woman other than my mother?"

"What do you mean by that?" he asked.

"I mean this, Solon. You know that husbands and wives sometimes express their affection for each other in the presence of other people, often using endearing terms or putting an arm around one another or offering some caress. Did you ever see a gesture of this kind offered by my father towards any woman whom you understood at the time to be in a position as his wife, to accept such caresses or endearments, other than my mother?"

With flushed face and a suspicion of confusion he said, "Brother Joseph, you have no business to ask me such pointed questions."

At this I said, "Yes, Brother Solon, I have, and a legitimate business, too. I was baptized by my father and confirmed a member of the church he organized. The faith into which I was baptized and confirmed was the faith which was held and taught by the church at that time, and *it included no provision concerning polygamy.* There were no polygamic marriages known to me to exist therein at that time. Now you say you have come down from the mountain to tell me what you know, and if I am to believe what you stated when you first came (before I began to question you), I would be compelled to believe that my father was a scoundrel, unfaithful and untrue to the commands he had received from God, and guilty of dealing treacherously with my mother; that he broke not only the laws of God given to the church through him as Prophet and Revelator but also the vows he had pledged with my mother at the altar in 1827. So I repeat, it is my business to find out the truth even if it should involve the necessity on my part of losing faith in my father's purity of life and conduct and believing him to be a libertine and an evil-minded man!

"However, now that I have questioned you closely, I discover that, like others, you know nothing at all, personally, that would so convict and condemn him, for you say he never taught you the doctrine; you say you never saw him married to any woman other than my mother; you say you never saw him act toward any other woman as though she were his wife, in any form; and that you were never introduced to any other woman who posed or was recognized, either in his house or at the house of anyone else, as his wife.

"I say I have indeed, the right to ask you any question which would either confirm your original statements or refute them. I have the right to bring out the truth from you as to what you really do know and what you have only just heard from others."

He seemed quite abashed at the vigor and earnestness with which I spoke. I told him I did not hold him responsible for that which he had heard, but that he had no business to repeat or to testify to things that had not come within his own personal knowledge and to the truthfulness of which he could not swear.

I do not know that he ever forgave me for the cross-examination to which I subjected him, but I do know that I had gone to Salt Lake City with the firm intention of examining closely every statement presented to me by anyone which bore upon the differences existing between my church and the one dominant in that western valley and intended to use every means in my power to ascertain and establish either their truth or falsity. Solon Foster was just another specimen of the kind of witness, and his statements the kind of testimony which those people out there were asking me to accept. (*Saints'Herald* 83 [March 24, 1936]: 368)

Joseph Smith III was a primary witness, for he was almost eleven years old when he moved with his mother and father into the Mansion House, and would have known if Joseph were practicing polygamy. His testimony is much more convincing than Fawn Brodie's "persistent tradition" and Solon Foster's claims—for, as previously noted, Eliza *never* lived with Joseph and Emma in the Mansion House.

There is a great difference in the accounts given by Charles C. Rich and Solon Foster. Rich asserts that he saw Joseph carrying Eliza "up the stairs and to her room," while Foster declares that Emma "turned Eliza R. Snow into the street in her night clothes." Both men claim that they saw Eliza tumble down the stairs at the Mansion House—while history shows Emma and Joseph did not move to the Mansion House until *after* Eliza moved away from their home.

Joseph Smith III Declared Eliza Did Not Bear a Child in Nauvoo

As early as the 1850s, the Mormons were spreading their false story about Eliza (see *Saints' Herald* 59 [May 15, 1912]: 465–467). In 1862 Elder Charles Derry and Joseph Smith III discussed the Mormon Church's claim that Eliza Snow had conceived a child by Joseph Smith. Elder Derry had gathered from England to Salt Lake City in 1854 and because of the apostasy he witnessed there, he left Utah in 1859 (*Journal of History* 1 [July 1908]: 273; ibid. [October 1908]: 437). Brother Derry soon joined the Reorganized Church and became one of its most distinguished missionaries. In December 1862 he visited Joseph III at Nauvoo before leaving on a missionary assignment to Salt Lake City. While Joseph was taking Derry the first thirty miles of his journey, the two men discussed the subject of polygamy, including the Mormon claim that Eliza Snow had been pregnant with the Prophet's child. Derry recorded:

> Bro. Joseph [III] is taking me out to Colchester [Illinois] in his wagon, the distance of thirty miles. We have some interesting conversation. He does not believe his father ever practiced polygamy, and he gives good reasons for it. He says there were several young women lived at his father's house, but they were destitute of homes. They were not his father's wives. If they had been it is probable some evidence would have been visible, especially as we are told that polygamy was instituted to bring forth a holy seed, and surely no means [of birth control] would have been taken to have prevented this result. But he [Joseph III] knows that none of these females [who lived with Emma and Joseph] had children until 1846, which was nearly two years after Joseph's death.
>
> As for Eliza Snow, it is reported that she had a child by Joseph; but he [Joseph III] knows that she never bore children while she was in Nauvoo, which also was about two years after Joseph's death. (*Journal of History* 2 [April 1909]: 168–169)

Eliza's Journal Proves That the "Altercation" Story Is False

Eliza was born in 1804 to Oliver and Rosetta Snow and had lived with her parents, brothers, and sisters in northern Ohio at the time the Church headquarters was in Kirtland in the early 1830s. The Snows were friends of Sidney Rigdon and belonged to the Disciples of Christ Church (Campbellite) which had recently been formed, with Sidney as one of its founders, along with Alexander Campbell. After Sidney left the Disciples of Christ and joined the Church, the Snow family joined also. The Snows moved to Missouri with the Saints and suffered the persecutions there. Later they moved to Nauvoo.

Eliza Snow's Nauvoo journal has now been published, which shows the entire altercation story was fabricated. A study of her life and writings reveal the following:

Spring 1838: In the spring of 1838 when Eliza was thirty-four, she moved with her father, mother, brothers, and sister from Kirtland to Adam-ondi-Ahman in Daviess County, Missouri, not far from the Church's headquarters at Far West (see Maureen Ursenbach Beecher, *The Personal Writings of Eliza Roxcy Snow*, 12).

December 1838: Eliza was still living with her parents, brothers, and sister in the Far West area (ibid., 12–13).

March 5, 1839: Eliza and her family left Missouri, where they had lived for nine months, and traveled together to Quincy, Illinois. Eliza's parents and her two teenage brothers settled temporarily in Quincy, while Eliza and her sister, Leonora, went to live in nearby Lima, Illinois, and worked as seamstresses (Maureen Ursenbach Beecher, *Ensign* 9 [June 1980]: 66–67; see also Beecher, *Personal Writings*, 15).

July 16, 1839: On this day Eliza Snow moved from Lima to Commerce (Nauvoo) at the invitation of Sidney Rigdon, her former Church of Christ minister. She lived at the Rigdon home and taught the Rigdon family school (ibid.). At that time the Rigdons were living in the James White stone house at the foot of what later became Parley Street. (When that area was flooded by water from the Keokuk Dam, the house was inundated.)

October 6, 1839: Eliza was still living with the Rigdons (ibid., 18).

Winter 1839–1840: Oliver Snow came for his daughter,

Eliza, and she moved away from Nauvoo to the home of her parents (ibid.).

Spring 1840: Eliza moved with her parents to La Harpe, Illinois, where they lived for one year—until the spring of 1841 (ibid.).

Spring 1841: Eliza and her parents moved to Nauvoo, and she lived there in her parents' home until June 20, 1842 (ibid., 52).

June 20, 1842: Eliza's father, Oliver Snow, became so distraught about events connected with Dr. John C. Bennett that he left Nauvoo and the Church, and moved seventy-five miles away to Walnut Grove, Illinois (Beecher, *Ensign* 9 [June 1980]: 67). Eliza's mother and brothers went also, but Eliza chose to stay at Nauvoo even though no other member of her family was living there. Her sister, Leonora, whom Eliza had left in Lima, had become a polygamous wife of Patriarch Isaac Morley and was living in the Morley Settlement at Lima (ibid.). (It must be remembered that Brigham Young and others were practicing polygamy in 1842.) Housing was so scarce in Nauvoo that Eliza was desperate to find a place to live.

August 13, 1842: On this date Emma Smith sent for Eliza. Emma was aware of Eliza's sad plight—a thirty-eight-year-old unmarried woman now bereft of family and home. Emma's heart and home were always open to the oppressed and lonely, especially needy women and children. No doubt Emma knew the full story behind Oliver Snow's quick exit from the city, and Emma's heart went out to Eliza—so she invited Eliza to share her home (Beecher, *Personal Writings*, 54).

August 18, 1842: Eliza moved into Emma and Joseph's home (the Homestead) on this date (ibid.). Eliza's diary shows that she was treated kindly by Joseph and Emma and there is no evidence of plural marriage or contention. During this time Eliza taught school at the Red Brick Store, and the Smith children were some of her pupils.

February 11, 1843: Eliza moved out of the Homestead on this date, after having lived with Emma and Joseph almost six months (ibid., 64). The day after she moved, Eliza taught school as usual, with no evidence of having received a beating or having suffered a fall or a miscarriage. If Eliza had been injured so severely that she suffered a life-threatening miscarriage, she would have had to close her school for the rest of the term—but the records show that she did not miss a single day of teaching (Newell and Avery, *Mormon Enigma*, 136).

March 17, 1843: This was the last day of school, and Eliza was happy to record in her diary that at her closing school program she had "the pleasure of the presence of Prest. J. Smith, [and] his lady" (Beecher, *Personal Writings*, 66). Her "pleasure" at their presence shows a friendly regard for both the Prophet and Emma, and is another proof that the entire story about Eliza being a plural wife, who had been battered by Emma, is totally false.

Shortly after her school term ended, Eliza moved from Nauvoo to Lima to live with her sister, Leonora (Maureen Ursenbach Beecher, *Eliza and Her Sisters*, 58). Leonora was still a plural wife of Isaac Morley. Eliza's journal shows that she never again lived with Emma and Joseph. According to Mormon Church history, Joseph and Emma moved into the Mansion House August 31, 1843, six months after Eliza moved from their home at the Homestead (LDS *History of the Church* 5:556).

Eliza's diary verifies that she was not married to Joseph, for in it she never alludes to any intimacy toward him. Though she showed respect for him as the Prophet and President, she did not use any term which a wife would naturally use in referring to her husband. Her writings in relation to him were always formal. If she had been his wife, there would have been some reference to the fact in her personal record. Also, the diary proves the charges against Emma to be false, because Eliza's journal shows that she respected Emma. There is no hint of any ill will between them, which would have appeared in her journal if Emma had beaten her and pushed her down the stairs. Eliza's journal portrays only a high regard for the beautiful, capable, and kindhearted Emma, who had given the sad, middle-aged, homeless woman a place to live. Eliza's diary is in itself sufficient proof that Joseph and Eliza were not married.

The question must be asked, Why did Eliza allow the rumor to circulate throughout Utah Mormondom and the world, that Emma had beaten her in the Mansion House? The answer is, because Eliza was a devoted and favored wife of Brigham Young while in Utah and a woman of great influence, and therefore she chose to uphold Brigham's doctrine of polygamy. She was called a " 'priestess' and 'prophetess,' " and "queen among Mormon women" (Beecher, *Personal Writings*, 2, xvii). Her testimony was of tremendous importance in the struggle between polygamy and antipolygamy which raged during the last thirty years of her life. She could have stopped the malicious lies about her being a plural wife of Joseph Smith. Instead, she chose to feed the fires of untruth for over a quarter of a century by not publishing that those stories were false. She supported Brigham Young's false dogma that polygamy was introduced by Joseph the Prophet in order to keep Brigham's Rocky Mountain empire from crumbling.

Chapter 10

More Evidence Concerning Eliza Snow

Years after Joseph Smith's death, many of the women who were married to prominent church leaders in Utah, claimed to have been married to Joseph while in Nauvoo. This was because Joseph's three sons, Joseph III, Alexander, and David, went to Utah and challenged the polygamous system there by claiming their father was not a polygamist. Under this attack, the LDS leaders had to find women who would swear that they had been Joseph's wives in order to keep the empire from collapsing. Eliza R. Snow was Brigham Young's most prominent wife, so of course she would have desired to uphold the system. And the best way to do it was to issue public statements that she had been Joseph's wife. One of Eliza Snow's declarations that she was married to Joseph is found in Edward W. Tullidge's *The Women of Mormondom*, 294–295.

The publication of Emma Smith's last testimony by Joseph Smith III brought a strong contradictory statement from Eliza Snow. Emma's testimony, given in February 1879 (two and a half months before her death) stated that her husband, Joseph, had not given a revelation on polygamy nor practiced that doctrine (see RLDS *History of the Church* 3:352–358). Eliza's rebuttle to Emma's testimony was published in the *Deseret News* (weekly) of October 22, 1879. It was then republished by Assistant LDS Historian Andrew Jenson in an article entitled "Plural Marriage" in the *Historical Record* 6 [May 1887]: 224.

Eliza claimed to have married Joseph on June 29, 1842, which is interesting in view of this being the approximate date that Dr. Bennett departed from Nauvoo—the time when Joseph was making a tremendous fight against polygamy.

Eliza Abstained from Writing about Polygamy in Nauvoo

More than thirty-two years later, after being Brigham's wife for over a quarter of a century, Eliza wrote in the book, *The Women of Mormondom*:

> Polygamy was undoubtedly introduced by Joseph himself, at Nauvoo, between 1840 and 1844. Years afterwards, however, a monogamic rival church [the RLDS Church], under the leadership of young Joseph Smith, the first born of the prophet, arose, denying that the founder of Mormondom was the author of polygamy, and affirming that its origin was in Brigham Young, subsequent to the martyrdom of the prophet and his brother Hyrum. This, with the fact that nearly the whole historic weight of polygamy rests with Utah, renders it expedient that we should barely touch the subject at Nauvoo, and wait for its stupendous sensation after its publication to the world by Brigham Young. (Edward W. Tullidge, *The Women of Mormondom*, 293)

Why did Eliza find it "expedient that we should barely touch the subject at Nauvoo," when that which happened there determined the whole matter of the polygamy question? Why did she say that "Polygamy was undoubtedly introduced by Joseph himself" when she knew Joseph did not introduce it? Eliza Snow knew exactly what happened in Nauvoo, for as an officer in the Ladies' Relief Society she gave her support to Emma and Joseph, and stood with them in Nauvoo as they fought a losing battle against polygamy.

Eliza knew that Joseph was innocent in 1842, and she knew it in 1876–1877 as she assisted Edward Tullidge in writing *The Women of Mormondom*. Since she was one of the central figures in the polygamy controversy at Nauvoo and had become a co-conspirator with her husband, Brigham Young, in placing the blame for the introduction of that doctrine upon Joseph, any in-depth attempt by her in 1877 to write historically of polygamy would have been risky. With only a minority of the Saints in Utah practicing polygamy, and many of the former old Nauvoo Saints still alive, Eliza no doubt touched lightly on the subject of polygamy to keep her past from being unveiled.

Eliza Signed a Certificate Which Said There Was No Polygamy in the Church at Nauvoo

One of the reasons Eliza wanted to barely touch on the subject of polygamy at Nauvoo was because she had helped lead a thousand women in signing a petition, stating that Joseph was not guilty of polygamy as Bennett had charged (see *Times and Seasons* 3 [August 1, 1842]: 869). After Dr. Bennett left Nauvoo in late June 1842 and published many statements declaring that Joseph was a polygamist, Joseph made a great effort to fight against that false doctrine. Joseph himself published that he "preached ... much against it" (*Times and Seasons* 3 [July 1, 1842]: 840). Also, the Ladies' Relief Society, with Emma as the president and Eliza Snow as the secretary, made a strong public stand against polygamy. The Relief Society prepared and published a certificate which declared:

> We the undersigned members of the ladies' relief society, and married females do certify and declare that we know of no system of marriage being practised in the church of Jesus Christ of Latter Day Saints save the one contained in the Book of Doctrine and Covenants. . . .
> Emma Smith, President . . .
> Eliza R. Snow, Secretary. (*Times and Seasons* 3 [October 1, 1842]: 940)

No wonder Eliza said that it was "expedient that we should barely touch the subject at Nauvoo"! Her stories conflicted—she had signed a statement printed on October 1, 1842, that no system of polygamy existed in the Church. But years later (when she was trying to support Brigham's polygamy) she claimed to have married Joseph on June 29, 1842, which was *only three months* prior to her signing the statement by the Relief Society. Signing the certificate made her 1879 claim of marriage to Joseph an obvious falsehood.

The statement in the certificate, signed by Eliza and other leading women of the Church, stated that they knew of no system of marriage but the one in the Doctrine and Covenants—

the official law of the Church entitled "On Marriage." It was Section 101 in the 1835 Edition which Joseph used in Nauvoo, and Section 109 in LDS editions from 1844 to 1876, but was removed when the 1876 Edition was printed (see *The Doctrine and Covenants Student Manual* [1981], 2). The polygamous Section 132 was inserted in the LDS Doctrine and Covenants for the first time in the 1876 Edition (ibid., 327). The article on marriage is Section 111 in the editions published by the Reorganized Church.

Joseph, who was the editor of the *Times and Seasons* in 1842, published the Church's official law "On Marriage" in conjunction with the Relief Society's certificate to prove that polygamy was a crime and not a doctrine of the Church. Joseph published that,

> Inasmuch as this church of Christ has been reproached with the crime of fornication, and polygamy: we declare that we believe, that one man should have one wife; and one woman, but one husband, except in case of death, when either is at liberty to marry again. . . . *We have given the above rule of marriage as the only one practiced in this church.* (*Times and Seasons* 3 [October 1, 1842]: 939; italics added)

It should be emphasized that Joseph declared here that polygamy was a crime.

Eliza and the Book Entitled
The Women of Mormondom

Eliza's keen intellect and superior writing and executive abilities, along with being married to the master of Utah, made her the most prominent woman in the LDS Church. She needed Brigham, and he needed her. She needed him so she could be elevated to supreme prominence, and he needed her to convince the women of Utah, and the world, that polygamy was a divine doctrine and that Joseph was its author.

After Joseph and Emma Smith's three sons went to Utah to convert the Saints back to the true faith, Eliza responded by preparing the book, as previously mentioned, to prove that Joseph was the author of polygamy.

Leonard J. Arrington, former LDS historian, wrote that the idea for the book to be written was Eliza's. Arrington stated:

> In 1876–77 Eliza directed the preparation of a manuscript which, with the assistance of Edward W. Tullidge, was published under the title *The Women of Mormondom* (New York, 1877). This book containing the personal histories and important talks of twenty-six LDS women and shorter sketches of fifty-six additional women was remarkable. . . . The idea of the 552-page book was Eliza's; she induced the women to write the personal histories that form the basis of the book, and she raised the funds for its publication. (*The John Whitmer Historical Association Journal* 10 [1990]: 11)

Eliza's self-glorification is seen in many places in the book, which bears Tullidge's name as the author. Eliza's portrait appears in the front of the book. On page 63 she refers to herself as "Eliza R. Snow, the high priestess." On page 66 she writes of the "interesting relationship between the prophet [Joseph] and the inspired heroine [Eliza] who became his celestial bride, and whose beautiful ideals have so much glorified celestial marriage." She refers to herself as "the prophetess, Eliza R. Snow," on page 69; and on page 194 she calls herself "prophetess and high priestess." The book gives interesting accounts of the lives of many of the LDS Church's leading women (some were plural wives of leading men). Interwoven in the accounts were their testimonies that Joseph Smith brought polygamy into the Church.

Until Brigham's death, he and Eliza worked very closely together. She always sat on his immediate right at dinner and during evening family worship, and held a place in his life that no other wife, not even his wives who bore him children, could challenge.

Brigham's daughter, Clarissa Young Spencer, wrote:

> Aunt Eliza R. Snow . . . held a most honored place in our household. . . . She always sat on Father's right at the dinner table and also in the prayer room. He valued her opinion greatly and gave her many important commissions. (Clarissa Young Spencer, *Brigham Young at Home*, 82–83)

Another of Brigham's daughters wrote that Eliza was the last one with whom Brigham counseled prior to his death. Susa Young Gates stated:

> After prayers that evening [August 19, 1877] he sat in council with Aunt Eliza R. Snow in the prayer-room. . . . At 11 o'clock that night he was seized with an attack of what was supposed to be "cholera morbus". . . . On . . . August 29, 1877, he passed away. (Susa Young Gates, *The Life Story of Brigham Young*, 360-361)

Together, Eliza and Brigham convinced millions that Joseph was the author of polygamy. But the truth is finally coming forth—that Eliza lied and that Joseph actually fought against polygamy.

"Joseph forbids it [polygamy] and the practice thereof"

The LDS Church history quotes a statement which purports to be an exact entry from Joseph's journal for October 5, 1843, to prove that Joseph had commanded that polygamy be practiced. The statement is monogamous in the original journal, but was changed by Mormon historians to have a polygamous meaning. Joseph's October 5, 1843, entry as it now appears incorrectly in the Mormon history is:

> "Gave instructions to try those persons who were preaching, teaching, or practicing the doctrine of plurality of wives; for, according to the law, I hold the keys of this power in the last days; for there is never but one on earth at a time on whom the power and its keys are conferred; *and I have constantly said no man shall have but one wife at a time, unless the Lord directs otherwise.*" (LDS *History of the Church* 6:46)

Modern Mormon scholars, who have had access to records in the Mormon Church's archives, have found that this statement has been changed. Originally it condemned polygamy. The original quotation is in "an untitled journal of 278 manuscript pages," which is thought to be in the handwriting of Willard Richards, one of Joseph's scribes. Richards made the following entry:

> Walked up and down St[reet] with Scribe and gave instructions to try those who were preaching, teaching, or ~~practicing~~ the doctrine of plurality of wives on this Law. Joseph forbids it and the practice thereof. No man shall have but one wife. [*rest of page blank*] {page 116} (Scott H. Faulring, ed., *An American Prophet's Record: The Diaries and Journals of Joseph Smith*, 417)

Richard S. Van Wagoner, author and historian, agreed that this is true, saying,

> The prophet's most pointed denial of plural marriage occurred on 5 October 1843 in instructions pronounced publicly in the streets of Nauvoo. Willard Richards wrote in Smith's diary that Joseph "gave instructions to try those who were preaching, teaching, or practicing the doctrine of plurality of wives. . . . Joseph forbids it and the practice thereof. No man shall have but one wife." (Van Wagoner, *Sidney Rigdon*, 292)

Van Wagoner continued by explaining:

> When incorporating Smith's journal into the *History of the Church*, church leaders, under Brigham Young's direction, deleted ten key words from this significant passage and added forty-nine others. (ibid., 303, note 17)

What a tremendous difference between the way Joseph gave this instruction against polygamy and the way the LDS polygamists published it in their doctored history! They changed the history as part of the conspiracy to legalize their own polygamous crimes by making the dead Prophet the author of it. The original version of the October 5 entry agreed with all of Joseph's writings which were published during his lifetime—including those found in the Three Scriptures and his sermon of May 26, 1844, against the dissenters.

Joseph Was Either a Monogamist or a Hypocrite and Fraud

Presiding Patriarch Elbert A. Smith of the RLDS Church was the son of David Hyrum Smith, who was the youngest son of Joseph the Martyr and Emma Smith. Elbert spent a lifetime studying the polygamy conspiracy. He commented on his grandfather's May 25, 1844, sermon by stating:

> On page 411 of the sixth volume of the church history published by the Utah Mormon church appears a remarkable statement, purporting to come from the lips of Joseph Smith the Martyr. It is found in a synopsis of a sermon delivered by the prophet from the stand in Nauvoo, Sunday, May 26, 1844 (only a month before his death). He is replying to the charges made in the Nauvoo *Expositor*. He says: "What a thing it is for a man to be accused of committing adultery, and having seven wives, when I can find only one." Our Gentile friend may twist the statement as made here in a ridiculous way. But our Mormon friends claim to present Joseph Smith as a prophet whose testimony may be relied upon. Clearly his intention was to say plainly that at that time he had but the one wife. We are indebted to our Utah friends for having preserved and published this statement unwittingly.
>
> In the same volume, on page 474, is a report of a sermon by the prophet from the stand in Nauvoo, June 6 [16], 1844. In one passage they report him as saying: "I have taught *all* the *strong* doctrines *publicly*, and always taught *stronger* doctrines in public than in private." This was about ten days before his death and effectually disposes of the Utah claim that he taught the strong (and rank) doctrine of polygamy in private, not daring to teach it in public. Salt Lake can hardly repudiate its own version of these sermons. . . .
>
> There is no halfway ground. Either Joseph Smith was true and clean, open and above board, as the Reorganized Church claims; or else he was a hypocrite and a fraud through and through, as his enemies claim. The Utah Mormons cannot long continue seriously to contend that he was a real prophet of God, and a good man, yet blowing hot in private and cold in public, a monogamist in the pulpit and press and a polygamist in his home, a pure milk of the word man by

daylight and a strong meat man after dark. (*Saints' Herald* 65 [February 27, 1918]: 204)

Joseph's grandson, Elbert, was correct when he said that Joseph was either monogamous, or he was a hypocrite and a fraud. Joseph's writings, and the fact that he had no polygamous children, are proofs that he was not a polygamist. The LDS Church's position is based upon the theory that Joseph was a hypocrite—that he denounced polygamy in public and practiced it in private. This is indeed a fragile foundation for the Mormon Church, considering that Joseph was a bold man who never hesitated to proclaim all the doctrines of the gospel, regardless of the opposition.

Chapter 11

Bennett and Francis Higbee's Polygamous Activities Discovered in 1841

Doctor John C. Bennett arrived at Nauvoo in September of 1840 and did much to help the Saints in their time of desperate need. It was through his efforts that a city charter was obtained and the Nauvoo Legion and the Nauvoo Municipal Court were organized and functioned so quickly and so well. He took such an active part in Church affairs that he soon became a temporary member of the First Presidency in the place of Sidney Rigdon who was ill. He was also the prime organizer of a Masonic Lodge in Nauvoo (Andrew F. Smith, *The Saintly Scoundrel*, 75–77). The Nauvoo lodge soon mushroomed into the largest one in the state, which caused members of other lodges to be jealous—bringing more persecution upon the Saints.

With all of his successes and talents, it seemed to many that the doctor would become one of the most valuable members of the Church's leadership—but alas, there was a dark side to his personality—his polygamous nature and philosophy—which he kept carefully hidden until it unexpectedly came to light in the summer of 1841, less than a year after he arrived at Nauvoo.

News of Bennett's Baptism Brought a Warning

The *Times and Seasons* for January 15, 1841 (3:275), announced Bennett's baptism into the Church—the news spread quickly. Bennett was widely known, for he had lived in several states and not less than twenty towns. He had been a prominent person in and about colleges and universities (*Times and Seasons* 3 [July 1, 1842]: 842; RLDS *History of the Church* 2:591).

Some individuals, especially those in Ohio, had a special interest in him because he had married Mary Barker, the daughter of Colonel Joseph Barker of Marietta, Ohio—one of the foremost citizens of the area (see Smith, *Saintly Scoundrel*, 1, 5).

Some newspapers responded to the news of Bennett's baptism by questioning his motives for being baptized. However, Bennett's apparent religious sincerity, visible accomplishments, and tremendous popularity made it necessary for Joseph to proceed with caution in discovering the truth about him before attempting to remove him from the Church, if that should be necessary.

Shortly after Bennett's baptism, Joseph received a letter from an individual warning that Bennett had a living wife, and was "a very mean man." Joseph reported:

> Soon after it was known that he had become a member of said church, a communication was received at Nauvoo, from a person of respectable character, and residing in the vicinity where Bennett had lived. This letter cautioned us against him, setting forth that he was a very mean man, and had a wife, and two or three children in McConnelsville, Morgan county, Ohio; but knowing that it is no uncommon thing for good men to be evil spoken against, the above letter was kept quiet, but held in reserve. (*Times and Seasons* 3 [July 1, 1842]: 839)

As soon as Bennett began dating "a young lady, one of our citizens" (undoubtedly Eliza Snow), Joseph and Emma became alarmed. In order to protect the young woman and the Church, and to be sure of the facts, Joseph sent Bishop George Miller to Ohio to discover the truth about Bennett's marital status. On March 2, 1841, Bishop Miller wrote a letter to Joseph, which must have almost devastated the Prophet. The letter revealed:

> By your request I have made inquiries into the history of John Cook Bennett. . . . It was soon manifest that he was a superficial character, always uneasy, and moved from place to place . . . it is not presumed that less than twenty towns has been his place of residence at different times; he has the vanity to believe he is the smartest man in the nation; and if

he cannot at once be placed at the head of the heap, he soon seeks a situation; he is always ready to fall in with whatever is popular; by the use of his recommendations he has been able to push himself into places and situations entirely beyond his abilities; he has been a prominent personage in and about colleges and universities, but had soon vanished; and the next thing his friends hear of him he is off in some other direction; at one time he was a promine[n]t Campbellite preacher.

During many years his poor, but confiding wife, followed him from place to place, with no suspicion of his unfaithfulness to her; at length however, he became so bold in his departures, that it was evident to all around that he was a sore offender, and his wife left him under satisfactory evidence of his adulterous connections. . . . Mrs. Bennett now lives with her father; has two children living, and has buried one or two . . . . [I]t has been Dr. Bennett's wish that his wife should get a bill of divorcement, but as yet she has not; nor does my informant know that she contemplates doing so;—in fine, he is an imposter, and unworthy of the confidence of all good men. . . . [W]e withhold the names of our informants, and other correspondents; but hold ourselves in readiness, at all times, to substantiate by abundant testimony, all that has been asserted, if required, as the documents are all on hand. George Miller. (ibid., 842; RLDS *History of the Church* 2:591–592)

Armed with Bishop Miller's letter and the "abundant testimony" which the bishop had brought to him, Joseph confronted Bennett with the facts. Joseph reported:

He had not been long in Nauvoo before he began to keep company with a young lady, one of our citizens; and she being ignorant of his having a wife living, gave way to his addresses, and became confident, from his behavior towards her, that he intended to marry her; and this he gave her to understand he would do. I, seeing the folly of such an acquaintance, persuaded him to desist; and, on account of his continuing his course, finally threatened to expose him if he did not desist. This, to outward appearance, had the desired effect, and the acquaintance between them was broken off. (*Times and Seasons* 3 [July 1, 1842]: 839)

Joseph Continued the Investigation

From all outward appearances, Bennett seemed to have severed his relationship with the young woman, but Joseph was determined to investigate the doctor's background even further. Meanwhile, the industrious doctor as mayor of Nauvoo was diligently at work organizing and planning—making various improvements in the city, such as draining the unhealthy swamps, stressing more healthful eating, promoting schools, the university, the strong municipal government, and the state-approved Nauvoo Legion. At the same time he was writing articles for the Church paper, the *Times and Seasons*, and debating publicly (which was popular at the time). The fluent doctor was amiable, entertaining, friendly, and a popular figure among the Saints. Many must have sought his presence as a guest at dinner parties and other social gatherings in their homes. Did they vie for his presence, and the presence of the young lady he had courted until Joseph stopped their courtship? Joseph and Emma were heavily burdened with the knowledge that Bennett was a wolf in sheep's clothing among the Saints, while the weeks of investigation of his character continued.

Next, Joseph sent William Law, his second counselor in the First Presidency, and Hyrum Smith, the presiding patriarch, to gather additional information. The Prophet reported:

> Sometime about the early part of July 1841, I received a letter from Elder H. Smith and Wm. Law, who were then at Pittsburgh, Penn. This letter was dated June 15th, and contained the particulars of a conversation betwixt them and a respectable gentleman from the neighborhood where Bennett's wife and children resided. He stated to them that it was a fact that Bennett had a wife and children living, and that she had left him because of his ill-treatment towards her. This letter was read to Bennett, which he did not attempt to deny; but candidly acknowledged the fact.
>
> Soon after this information reached our ears, Dr. Bennett made an attempt at suicide, by taking poison; but he being discovered before it had taken effect, and the proper antidotes being administered, he again recovered; but he very much resisted when an attempt was made to save him. The public

impression was, that he was so much ashamed of his base and wicked conduct, that he had recourse to the above deed to escape the censures of an indignant community. (ibid., 840; *The Wasp* 1 [June 25, 1842]; RLDS *History of the Church* 2:586–587)

Francis Higbee Became Bennett's Protégé in Sin

About July 1, 1841, the Prophet received a request to administer to Francis M. Higbee, a young man in his early twenties whom Joseph greatly respected. Higbee was the son of Judge Elias Higbee, a long-time personal friend of the Prophet and a member of the Church's High Council at Nauvoo. Francis was one of the most promising young men in the Church. He had shown strength at Far West and during the exodus of the Church from Missouri, and had aided Joseph's younger brother, Don Carlos, in preparing the paper for the printing of the first issue of the *Times and Seasons* at Nauvoo. At the time he became ill, he was courting Miss Nancy Rigdon, daughter of President Sidney Rigdon.

Francis called upon Dr. Bennett to act as his physician, but Bennett's medicine failed to cure him—so in desperation Francis sent for the Prophet to administer to him. Joseph was horrified at what he found. Joseph later testified under oath in civil court that when he went to administer, he discovered that Francis was suffering from a venereal disease. Joseph stated:

> I must tell the story in its true light, under oath; then I can be forever set free. . . . The peace of myself, my family, my happiness, and the happiness of this city depend upon it. . . . I want to testify . . . of what occurred a long time before John C. Bennet left this city. I was called on to visit Francis M. Higbee; I went and found him on a bed on the floor. (*Times and Seasons* 5 [May 15, 1844]: 538)

Joseph continued to testify about the immorality of Higbee, Bennett, and their associates. Joseph's testimony was so graphic that Apostle John Taylor, the editor of the *Times and Seasons,* felt it unwise to print it. The editor explained:

> [Here follows testimony which is too indelicate for the public eye or ear; and we would here remark, that so revolting, corrupt, and disgusting has been the conduct of most of this clique, that we feel to dread having any thing to do with the publication of their trials; we will not however offend the public eye or ear with a repetition of the foulness of their crimes any more.] (ibid., 538-539)

Others testified concerning Francis Higbee's immoral activities. H. J. Sherwood stated:

> I recollect a French woman coming up from Warsaw, and that Francis M. Higbee had medical assistance * * * * * * Dr. Bennet attended him, Joseph Smith administered unto him but it was irksome; Higbee assented that it was so, he did not contradict it, he promised to reform—he would do better, he would do so no more. (ibid., 540)

Joel S. Miles testified:

> I have seen Francis M. Higbee go into rooms with females, but what their intentions were I did not know, I might have seen him two or three times; I think he has done that which is not right, I should judge from conversations with him, that was the case: I presume he has a good many times; I might recollect twenty times, he has frequently told me things of that kind, it is a private case to be sure . . . I recollect the time that he was sick, when Dr. Bennet attended him, I went to see him nearly every day." (ibid.)

Upon further investigation, Joseph discovered that Francis had seduced "six or seven" women. But worst of all, the Prophet found that Francis was only one of a group of young men and women whom Dr. Bennett had gathered around himself and taught them that "spiritual wifery" was a *doctrine believed in by Latter Day Saints and that Joseph Smith had received a revelation commanding the practice of it!* The prophet declared that Bennett taught that "we believed in and practiced polygamy" (ibid. 3 [August 1, 1842]: 869).

Joseph continued:

> Bennet said Higbee pointed out the spot where he had

seduced a girl, and that he had seduced another. I did not believe it, I felt hurt, and labored with Higbee about it; he swore with uplifted hands, that he had lied about the matter. I went and told the girl's parents [Elder and Mrs. Rigdon], when Higbee and Bennet made affidavits and both perjured themselves, they swore false about me so as to blind the family [by saying that Francis was innocent and Joseph was lying]. I brought Francis M. Higbee before Brigham Young, Hyrum Smith and others; Bennet was present, when they both acknowledged that they had done these things, and asked us to forgive them. I got vexed, my feelings had been hurt; Higbee has been guilty of adulterous communication, perjury, &c.; which I am able to prove by men who heard them confess it. (ibid. 5 [May 15, 1844]: 539)

Bennett, in his eagerness to distance himself from Higbee's illness, told Joseph in detail about Higbee's seduction of several young ladies, including Nancy Rigdon. The involvement of the two young people from the Rigdon and Higbee families was a severe blow to the Prophet. To have a devoted young man like Francis, who had a wonderful future in the Church and prospects of marrying a daughter of a member of the Presidency, toss it away in the manner Bennett described, seemed out of character to Joseph.

The Prophet reported Higbee's case at once to the proper Church authorities and called for a Church court to handle the matter—and ordered an undercover investigation of Bennett, for he suspected far more was involved than what Bennett had told him about Francis. He suspected Bennett was behind the terrible turn of events. Joseph also reported the seduction of Nancy Rigdon to her parents.

Joseph explained that Bennett

professed to be virtuous and chaste, yet did he pierce the heart of the innocent, introduce misery and infamy into families, reveled in voluptuousness and crime, *and led the youth that he had influence over to tread in his unhallowed steps.* (ibid. 3 [August 1, 1842]: 868–869; italics added)

Joseph also testified:

But, like one of the most abominable and depraved beings which could possibly exist, he only broke off his publicly wicked actions, to sink deeper into iniquity and hypocrisy. When he saw that I would not submit to any such conduct, he went to some of the females in the city, who knew nothing of him but as an honorable man, & *began to teach them that promiscuous intercourse between the sexes, was a doctrine believed in by the Latter-Day Saints, and that there was no harm in it; but this failing, he had recourse to a more influential and desperately wicked course; and that was, to persuade them that myself and others of the authorities of the church not only sanctioned, but practiced the same wicked acts;* and when asked why I publicly preached so much against it, said that it was because of the prejudice of the public, and that it would cause trouble in my own house. He was well aware of the consequence of such wilful and base falsehoods, if they should come to my knowledge; and consequently endeavored to persuade his dupes to keep it a matter of secrecy, persuading them there would be no harm if they should not make it known. This proceeding on his part, answered the desired end; he accomplished his wicked purposes; he seduced an innocent female by his lying, and subjected her character to public disgrace, should it ever be known. (ibid. [July 1, 1842]: 839–840; italics added)

Because Dr. Bennett was teaching that Joseph had received a polygamous revelation, Joseph realized that the situation was extremely serious and that he must do all within his power to eradicate it. Therefore, Joseph fought polygamy by doing everything he could to stop it, including (1) preaching much against it, and (2) taking Bennett and Higbee into an elders' court. They were both brought before the court which included President William Law, Presiding Patriarch Hyrum Smith, and Apostle Brigham Young.

Brigham Young, president of the Twelve Apostles, testified:

With regard to Francis M. Higbee, at the time that is spoken of, I stopped opposite Mr. Laws' store, we had been conversing with Dr. Bennet[;] when I came into the room, Francis Higbee rather recoiled and wished to withdraw; he went out and sat upon a pile of wood. He said it is all true, I am sorry for it, I wish it had never happened. I understood

Joseph and Emma Smith*

"I had not been married scarcely five minutes, and made one proclamation of the Gospel, before it was reported that I had seven wives. . . . This spiritual wifeism! Why, a man dares not speak or wink, for fear of being accused of this . . . . I am innocent of all these charges. . . . *What a thing it is for a man to be accused of committing adultery, and having seven wives, when I can only find one.* I am the same man, and as innocent as I was fourteen years ago [when the Church was organized]; and I can prove them all perjurers"—Joseph Smith (*History of the Church of Jesus Christ of Latter-day Saints, Period 1,* 6 [Salt Lake City, Utah: Deseret Book Company, 1962]: 410–411; italics added).

*This picture was created by combining the well-known pictures of Joseph and Emma which were painted in 1843 at Nauvoo. ©PPC-CBI

122

Beautiful Nauvoo as seen from Montrose, Iowa, across the Mississippi River.

Nauvoo as painted by David H. Smith, son of Joseph and Emma.

Joseph Smith's General Store (Red Brick Store) after reconstruction. It also served as Church headquarters and a meeting place for various groups.

The upper room in the Red Brick Store (as reconstructed), where important meetings were held.

The Homestead at sunset—the first home of Joseph and Emma Smith in Nauvoo. The Mississippi River may be seen in the background.

The Mansion House—Joseph and Emma's second home in Nauvoo. The Mansion House was operated as a hotel, with Joseph and his family occupying six rooms.

Home of Nauvoo Stake President William Marks, northwest of the Red Brick Store. William assisted Joseph in the fight against polygamy.

Home of Apostle Brigham Young in Nauvoo. Brigham secretly led the movement toward introducing polygamy into the Church.

The narrow Mansion House stairs—showing the falseness of Charles C. Rich's story that while standing in the lobby or parlor behind the wall on the right, he saw Joseph and Emma coming from their bedroom and Eliza Snow coming from another, and that Emma pushed Eliza down the stairs (see page 88).

Bennet who related some of the circumstances, he cried and begged of us to forgive him, and said if he could be permitted to stay in the city as a private individual he should be happy ... he said; it is true, I am sorry for it I wish it had never been so; as we came up, Dr. Bennet, Mr. Higbee, and Mr. [Joseph] Smith, had been talking about it ... I knew of the whole affair, it was on the 4th of July [1841], or a few days after—it was shortly after I came from England.... I have heard Dr. Bennet say all these things were facts; he acknowledged that Higbee had the _____ and that he had doctored him, he acknowledged that, and a great deal more.

I will make one statement in our conversation with Dr. Bennet. I told Dr. Bennet that one charge was seducing young women, and leading young men into difficulty—he admitted it—if he had let young men and women alone it would have been better for him. (ibid. 5 [May 15, 1844]: 539)

Hyrum Smith testified concerning Higbee's case:

Francis M. Higbee acknowledged that it was the truth, that he was sorry, and had been a thousand times; he acknowledged his connection with the woman on the hill; I did think he was with Dr. Bennet at the time, the statement of Bennet was, that he was guilty, he was sorry and asked forgiveness, he said he had seduced six or seven [women], he acknowledged it, and said if he was forgiven, he would not be guilty any more. Francis said he knew it was true, he was sorry and had been a hundred times.... Francis did not say any thing about his sickness, but Dr. Bennet made those observations to him [Joseph] that he had doctored him in the time of his sickness .... [H]e [Francis] said he should not have been seduced, if it had not been by Dr. Bennet, when charged with them, Francis said they were true; that they were alledged a hundred times; he said "I will alter, I will save my character." (ibid., 539–540)

The Results of the 1841 Trial of Bennett and Higbee

John Bennett and Francis Higbee were tried before the elders' court and were found guilty. They confessed and both begged for forgiveness. Joseph described Bennett's seeming repentance in these words:

> he would acknowledge his iniquity, ask and pray for forgiveness, beg that he might not be exposed, on account of his mother, and other reasons, saying, he should be ruined and undone. He frequently wept like a child, and begged like a culprit for forgiveness, at the same time promising before God and angels to amend his life, if he could be forgiven. (ibid. 3 [August 1, 1842]: 869)

The brethren who heard their cases forgave them, which meant their confessed sins were not made public. Dr. Bennett was permitted to keep all of his official positions, including the office of mayor. Joseph and the other leaders carefully refrained from saying anything derogatory about either man. From all outward appearances, Bennett, Francis, and those involved with them ceased their promiscuity. However, the polygamous spirit was not dead as Joseph soon realized.

OTHER EVIDENCES THAT JOSEPH AND THE CHURCH FOUGHT POLYGAMY IN 1841

Bennett's House of Ill Fame

Since Dr. Bennett was a medical doctor who specialized in the diseases of women, it was legitimate for him to go alone into the homes of those who were ill. This gave him opportunity to continue his promiscuity without Joseph being able to know whether or not he was remaining chaste. But Joseph and Hyrum suspected that Bennett had not repented, and asked certain men holding the office of teacher in the priesthood to investigate Bennett's conduct. Teacher John Taylor (not the apostle by that name) was one of those who did the investigating. He testified under oath:

> I held the position of teacher in the original church from September, 1832, until Joseph Smith's death in 1844. . . . It was our duty in case we found anybody *with more wives than one to report them to the President of the Teachers' Quorum* . . . . [O]ur instructions were if we found *any case of that kind*

> *to report it to the President of the Teachers' Quorum*, and the president [of the Teachers' Quorum] would report them to Hyrum Smith. . . . [I]t was about that time that John C. Bennett's secret wife system came to be heard of. . . . [We] were told to search it out and find what there was to it if we could. That was the way it was, and so I got after him [Bennett], and followed him, and saw him go into a house that did not have a very good reputation. I followed him to the house there in Nauvoo where this secret wife business was practiced,—saw him go into it.
>
> He was said to be a doctor and was going about treating people. . . . He would go into these houses, and the women there were suspicious women,—did not bear good characters. I heard about his doing this, and I went around to watch him and see if I could not catch him going there. And one evening I traced him and saw him go right into the house. During the time that I was a teacher from 1832 up to 1844, *there was no rule or law of the original church that permitted the practice or principle of polygamy*. (*Abstract of Evidence*, 190–191; italics added)

It is important to remember that Hyrum Smith directed the teachers to investigate and report any man who might be found to have "more wives than one"; and also that Teacher Taylor testified that there was no "rule or law" that permitted the practice of polygamy up to 1844—while Joseph and Hyrum were alive.

Teacher John Taylor testified further:

> John C. Bennett *and a lot of them* built an ill-fame house near the Temple in Nauvoo. . . . After they had built it, John C. Bennett and the Fosters,—I knew all their names at the time, they were the head men of it,—after they got it built, they wrote on it in large letters what it was,—a sign declaring what it was, and what it was there for. . . .
>
> The City Council held a council over it, and they considered it was a nuisance to the city. . . . [The police] took the building, and put it on rollers; and there was a deep gully there, and they pitched the house into it. (ibid.,192; italics added)

One may wonder if this was the house "on the hill" where Francis Higbee visited the French woman who had come to Nauvoo from Warsaw. Dr. Robert Foster, a resident of Nauvoo at the time, declared that Bennett "plead the cause of the house of ill fame in Nauvoo when he was Mayor and the City Council unanimously declared it a public nuisance" (*Wasp* 1 [October 2, 1842]: 2). The *Times and Seasons* for November 15, 1841, published a notice of the destruction of the house with the statement, "The city authorities manifest a determination to carry out strictly the temperance ordinances of the city, and in this we wish them 'God speed' " (*Times and Seasons* 3:599–600).

Sidney Roberts and the "Holy Kiss"

Another incident which demonstrated that the Church was fighting polygamous activities in 1841, was the cutting "off from the church" of Elder Sidney Roberts. He advocated a practice which was similar to, or patterned after, the teachings of Jacob Cochran, head of the polygamous Cochranite sect in Maine. Joseph's brother, Don Carlos Smith, editor of the *Times and Seasons*, reported that the New York City Branch expelled Roberts for claiming to have had a revelation that he should salute "the sisters with what he calls a holy kiss, taking them on his lap, and putting his arms around them, &c." (ibid. 2 [February 1, 1841]: 307). Jacob Cochran had practiced the so-called "holy kiss" in his church services. "Females in the craze of their fanaticism would embrace him in public meeting and unblushingly kiss him, and he found apology for it in 'the holy kiss' of Scripture" (see "Cochran Fanaticism," 8; Maine Historical Society).

Joseph Told the Conference He Had but One Wife

Joseph made it a point to tell the Saints gathered for the fall Conference of 1841, that he had only one wife. Joseph's statement was published by the Twelve, with Brigham Young's name appearing first on the list of apostles who signed the document. When it is realized that Joseph was at the time being charged with polygamy, the Prophet's statement takes on new meaning. Brigham and the other apostles reported:

> When Br. Joseph stated to the general conference the amount and situation of the property of the church, of which he is trustee in trust by the united voice of the church, he also stated the amount of his own possessions on earth; and what do you think it was? we will tell you; his old Charley horse, given him in Kirtland; two pet deer; two old turkeys, and four young ones; the old cow given him by a brother in Missouri, his old Major, dog; his wife [singular], children, and a little household furniture, and this is the amount of the great possessions of that man whom God has called to lead his people in these last days; this the sum total... (*Times and Seasons* 2 [October 15, 1841]: 569)

Polygamy Was Not Practiced by the Church in 1841

In order to stress that the Church was not in favor of polygamy, an article from the St. Louis, Missouri, *Atlas* was republished in the *Times and Seasons*. It read:

> An intelligent friend, who called upon us this morning, has just returned from a visit to Nauvoo and the Mormons .... He believes—just as we do—that they have been grossly misunderstood and shamefully libeled.... [I]t is a faith which they say encourages no vice, nor immorality, nor departure from established laws and usages; neither polygamy, nor promiscuous intercourse, nor community of property. (ibid., 580)

Joseph Preached against Polygamy

The records show that throughout the year 1841 Joseph made a valiant fight against the encroachment of polygamy into the Church. Let it be remembered that Bennett even stated that Joseph preached "much against it" (ibid. 3 [July 1, 1842]: 840).

Where are the records of the many sermons which the Prophet preached against polygamy in 1841 and 1842? Were his sermons recorded by Church clerks? Do they exist in the LDS Church Archives in Salt Lake City, Utah? If the missing sermons do exist and are published in the future, they will denounce polygamy and further vindicate the Prophet. His missing sermons would give still more evidence that the Prophet was, and still is, a victim of an insidious conspiracy to attach his name to a doctrine which he abhorred and vigorously opposed.

Chapter 12

Chauncey L. Higbee Expelled for Polygamous Activities

Although Dr. John C. Bennett claimed that he had repented when he was brought to trial in July 1841, he and his group of young followers continued their practice of spiritual wifery in secret. Bennett "led the youth that he had influence over to tread in his unhallowed steps . . . even to the seduction of the virtuous" (*Times and Seasons* 3 [August 1, 1842]: 869). Even though Joseph felt that those in Bennett's "clique" were continuing their activities, the Prophet had to wait until definite proof could be obtained before charges could be filed. In the meantime, Joseph was ever watchful and continued to preach against it.

An example of Joseph's constant fight against polygamy is found in an account of a sermon which he preached on April 10, 1842. According to the LDS *History of the Church*, Joseph preached in the Grove near the Temple on this date, and condemned "all adulterers, and fornicators, and unvirtuous persons, *and those who have made use of my name to carry on their iniquitous designs"* (LDS *History of the Church* 4:587; italics added). He was speaking, of course, of Bennett and his friends, who were using Joseph's name to teach polygamy, or spiritual wifery as it was popularly called.

During the fall of 1841 and the first five months of 1842, at least three polygamy-related cases were in varying stages of development, with which Joseph had to labor:

1. Dr. Bennett's promiscuity with Sarah Pratt, the wife of Apostle Orson Pratt;
2. The claim by Martha Brotherton, a young English

immigrant, that Brigham Young had tried to force her to become his plural wife, and that Joseph assisted him;

3. An escalation of the Francis Higbee-Nancy Rigdon case.

These three cases will be discussed in a later volume.

In the spring of 1842 another case erupted which involved Chauncey L. Higbee—who was a brother of Francis, a Church member, a prominent lawyer, and also a colonel in the Nauvoo Legion. An investigation of Chauncey's activities was begun after Joseph delivered a sermon before the Nauvoo Choir, in which he denounced polygamy.

Information about the choir is found in an article in the *Times and Seasons*—a news item relating how the choir brought a petition to the Board of Regents of the Nauvoo University. The article, which was entitled "Choir of the Stake of Zion in the City of Nauvoo," stated:

> The Choir of Singers presented a petition to the Board of Regents of the University, at their last sitting, for the appointment of a "Professor and Wardens in the Department of Music in the University of the City of Nauvoo," to constitute a board for the regulation of Music in this city, which was adopted. (*Times and Seasons* 3 [January 1, 1842]: 653)

Dr. Bennett was Chancellor of the University, and Joseph Smith was a member of the Board of Regents (see ibid. [December 15, 1841]: 630–631).

In his speech to the choir Joseph condemned polygamy, which caused Sarah Miller, a choir member, to become alarmed (see Sarah Miller's testimony which follows). She was one of Bennett's clique and one of Chauncey L. Higbee's spiritual wives. After hearing Joseph, she confessed to Church authorities, and it was quickly learned that Chauncey had also seduced at least three other women—two sisters, Margaret and Matilda Nyman, and a widow named Catharine Fuller. When questioned, these women readily admitted that Chauncey had seduced them by using Bennett's "plausible tale" that (1) promiscuous intercourse was acceptable if kept secret, (2) that Joseph had received a polygamous revelation, (3) that Joseph and other heads of the

Church were practicing polygamy, and (4) that Joseph preached much against polygamy as a cover-up, because of the public's prejudice against it and Emma's hatred of that doctrine.

The Women Gave Their Testimonies before the High Council

During May 1842, the Church's High Council met day after day to investigate this situation. The women testified before the Council about circumstances surrounding their seductions, after which Joseph took their written affidavits before the city's Municipal Court in an attempt to also convict Chauncey in civil court. The testimonies of the four women were published in the *Nauvoo Neighbor* under the title "Chauncey L. Higbee" and are given below.

[Affidavit of Margaret J. Nyman]
Testimony of Margaret J. Nyman, vs Chauncey L. Higbee, before the High Council of the Church of Jesus Christ of Latter-Day Saints, in the City of Nauvoo, May 21, 1842.

Some time during the month of March last, Chauncey L. Higbee, came to my mother's house, early one evening, and proposed a walk to a spelling school. My sister Matilda, and myself accompanied him; but, changing our design on the way, we stopped at Mrs. [Catharine] Fullers: During the evening's interview, he, (as I have since learned,) with wicked lies proposed that I should yield to his desires, and indulge in sexual intercourse with him, stating that such intercourse might be freely indulged in, and was no sin: That any respectable female might indulge in sexual intercourse, and there was no sin in it, providing the person so indulging, keep the same to herself; for there could be no sin, where there was no accussor;—and most clendestinely, with wicked lies, persuaded me to yield by using the name of Joseph Smith: and, as I have since learned, totally false and unauthorised; and in consequence of those arguments, I was influenced to yield to my Seducer, Chauncey L. Higbee.

I further state that I have no personal acquaintance with Joseph Smith, and never heard him teach such doctrines, as stated by Chauncey L. Higbee, either directly or indirectly.

I heartily repent before God, asking the forgiveness of my brethren.
Margaret J. Nyman.
State of Illinois, ss
County of Hancock,
City of Nauvoo.

May 24th, 1842.

Personally appeared before me, George W. Harris, alderman, of the city aforesaid, Margaret J. Nyman, the signer of the above instrument, and testified, under oath, that the above declaration is true.
Geo. W. Harris, alderman.

[Affidavit of Matilda J. Nyman]
Nauvoo, May 21*st*, 1842.

During this spring Chauncy L. Higbee, kept company with me from time to time, and, as I have since learned, wickedly deceitfully, and with lies in his mouth, urged me vehemently to yield to his desires; that there could be no wrong in having sexual intercourse with any female that could keep the same to herself;—most villianously and lyingly stating that he had been so instructed by Joseph Smith, and that there was no sin where there was no accuser:—Also vowing he would marry me. Not succeeding, he, on one occasion, brought one, who affirmed that such intercourse was tolerated by the heads of the Church. I have since found him also to be a lying conspirator against female virtue and chastity, having never received such teachings from the heads of the church; but I was at the time partially influenced to believe in consequence of the source from whom I received it.

I yielded and become subject to the will of my seducer, Chauncey L. Higbee: and having since found out to my satisfaction, that a number of wicked men have conspired to use the name of Joseph Smith, or the heads of the Church, falsely and wickedly to enable them to gratify their lusts, thereby destroying female innocence and virtue, I repent before God and my brethren and ask forgiveness.

I further testify that I never had any personal acquaintance with Joseph Smith and never heard him teach such doctrines as Higbee, stated either directly or indirectly.

Matilda J. Nyman.
State of Illinois, ss
City of Nauvoo.

May 24*th*, 1842.

Personally appeared before me, George W. Harris, alderman, of said city, Matilda J. Nyman, the signer of the above instrument, and testified, under oath, that the above declaration was true.

Geo. W. Harris, alderman.

[Affidavit of Sarah Miller]

Nauvoo, May 24*th*, 1842.

Some two or three weeks since, in consequence of brother Joseph Smith's teachings to the singers, I began to be alarmed concerning myself, and certain teachings which I had received from Chauncey L. Higbee, and questioned him (Higbee) about his teaching, for I was pretty well persuaded from Joseph's public teachings that Chauncey had been telling falsehoods; but Chauncey said that Joseph now taught as he did through necessity, on account of the prejudice of the people, and his own family particularly [Emma], as they had not become believers in the doctrine.

I then become satisfied that all of Chauncey's teaching had been false, and that he had never been authorized by any one in authority to make any such communication to me. Chauncey L. Higbee's teaching and conduct were as follows. When he first came to my house soon after the special conference this spring, Chauncey commenced joking me about my getting married, and wanted to know how long it had been since my husband died, and soon removed his seat near me; and began his seducing insinuations by saying it was no harm to have sexual intercourse with women if they would keep it to themselves, and continued to urge me to yield to his desires, and urged me vehemently, and said he and Joseph were good friends, and he [Joseph] teaches me this doctrine, and allows me such privileges, and there is no harm in it and Joseph Smith says so.

I told him I did not believe it, and had heard no such teaching from Joseph, nor from the stand [the place where preaching services were held at Nauvoo], but that it was wicked to commit adultery, &c. Chauncey said that did not mean single women, but married women; and continued to press his instructions and arguments until after dark, and until I was inclined to believe, for he called God to witness of the truth, and was so solemn and confident, I yielded to his temptations, having received the strongest assurance from him that Joseph approved it and would uphold me in it. He also told me that many others were following the same course of conduct. As I still had some doubts, near the close of our interview, I again suggested my fears that I had done wrong, and should loose the confidence of the brethren, when he assured me that it was right, and he would bring a witness to confirm what he had taught.

When he come again, I still had doubts, I told him I understood he (Higbee), had recently been baptized, and that Joseph, when he confirmed him, told him to quit all his iniquitous practices,—Chauncey said it was not for such things that he was baptized for, [he said] do you think I would be baptized for such a thing and then go into it so soon again? Chauncey Higbee, said it would never be known, I told him it might be told in bringing forth [a child]. Chauncey said there was no danger, and that Dr. Bennet understood it, and would come and take it away, if there was any thing.

Sarah Miller.
State of Illinois, ss
City of Nauvoo.

May 24th, 1842.

There appeared Sarah Miller, the signer of the above instruments, and made oath that the above declaration is true before me.
Geo. W. Harris, alderman.

[Affidavit of Catharine Fuller Warren]
Nauvoo, May 25th, 1842.

Extract from the testimony of Catharine [Fuller] Warren, vs. Chauncey L. Higbee, *before the High Council of the Church, &c.*

I have had unlawful connexion with Chauncey L. Higbee. Chauncey Higbee, taught the same doctrine as was taught by J. C. Bennet, and that Joseph Smith, taught and practiced those things, but he [Chauncey] stated that he did not have it from Joseph, but he had his information from Dr. John C. Bennet. He, Chauncey L. Higbee, has gained his object about five or six times, Chauncey L. Higbee, also made propositions *to keep me with food if I would submit to his desires."* (*Nauvoo Neighbor*, May 29, 1844; *Millennial Star* 23:657–658)

The affidavits of the women involved in the trials of Chauncey Higbee and Bennett in 1842 were not published at the time the trials occurred, in hopes these men would repent of their evil ways and Nauvoo and the Church would be spared the notoriety of such gross practices. However, in 1844 these affidavits were published when the Higbee brothers joined a group of conspirators who eventually brought about the martyrdom of Joseph and Hyrum. When the affidavits were published in 1844, Editor (Apostle) John Taylor commented:

We have abundance of like testimony on hand, which may be forth coming if we are compelled, at present the foregoing may suffice.

Why have you not published this before?—We answer, on account of the humility and entreaties of [Chauncey] Higbee, at the time,—and on account of the feelings of his parents, who are highly respectable,—we have forborne until now. The character of C. L. Higbee, is so infamous, and his exertions such as to destroy every principle of righteousness, that fo[r]bearance is no longer a virtue.

After all that this Chauncey L. Higbee has done, in wickedly and maliciously using the name of Joseph Smith, to persuade innocent females to submit to gratify his hellish lusts: and then blast the characters of the most chaste, pure virtuous, and philanthropic man on earth [Joseph Smith], he, to screen himself from the law of the land, and the just indignation of insulted people, and save himself from the Penitentiary, or whatever punishment his unparralled crimes merit; has entered into a conspiracy with the Laws [William and Wilson], and others against the like of those, who are knowing to his abandoned conduct; thus hoping to save himself from the disgrace which must follow an exposure, and wreak his vengeance and gratify his revenge for his awful disappointments. (ibid.)

The above testimonies show that "a number of wicked men" were indeed involved in Bennett's polygamous scheme, and that they used seven basic steps to seduce undiscerning young Church women. Their seven steps were:

1. To convince women that Joseph Smith had received a revelation which allowed men to have plural wives;
2. They brought witnesses (some of their own clique) to testify that this was true;
3. They taught their victims that which Joseph called Bennett's "plausible tale"—which was the false claim that Joseph was preaching and teaching so vigorously against polygamy in order to fool Emma and the prejudiced public;
4. They "vehemently" requested intercourse with the women;
5. They pledged that if pregnancies occurred Dr. Bennett would perform abortions;
6. They offered to furnish the women with the necessities of life (to care for them as their wives);
7. They promised to marry the women (see *Times and Seasons* 3 [July 1, 1842]: 839; 3 [August 1, 1842]: 870; *Nauvoo Neighbor*, May 29, 1844).

To this day the Mormon Church still uses Bennett's item 1 and item 3 as a part of their theology—that Joseph had a revelation commanding that polygamy be practiced, and that Joseph denied polygamy openly while practicing it secretly to fool Emma and the prejudiced public. If Joseph did bear false witness to deceive Emma and the public, he was one of the greatest liars in the history of mankind, and a false prophet. But he was neither. He was a truthful prophet who gave his life fighting against plural marriage.

It should be noted that Margaret Nyman testified that Chauncey Higbee took her to the home of Mrs. Fuller, where he seduced her. The Nauvoo *Wasp* for April 30, 1842, announced that Catharine Fuller and William Warren were married on April 27, 1842. This confirms that Catharine Fuller is the same person as Catharine Fuller Warren. Mrs. Fuller not only was seduced by Chauncey, but she allowed her home to be used by him to seduce innocent young girls.

The "abundance of like testimony" mentioned previously was undoubtedly taken to Utah when Brigham Young took Joseph's official papers West. If they are still extant, the leaders of the LDS Church could do justice to the cause of truth by publishing those records. No doubt the records would give the names of others who were led into plural marriage at Nauvoo by Bennett's "plausible tale." Those documents would also give additional proof that Brigham Young used Bennett's platform as a springboard to officially introduce the doctrine of polygamy into the Church.

Lawyer Higbee Made an Affidavit of Joseph's Innocence

Joseph brought Chauncey before the Church's High Council for trial. According to the LDS *History of the Church*, Joseph's journal for May 21, 1842, states: "I spent the day with the High Council of Nauvoo, investigating the case of . . . Chauncey L. Higbee and others" (LDS *History of the Church* 5:14). Chauncey was found guilty of cohabitating with several spiritual wives. He made the following affidavit that Joseph had not taught him that illicit intercourse with women was justifiable under any circumstance:

> Affidavit of C. L. Higbee
> State of Illinois
> City of Nauvoo
>
> Personally appeared before me Daniel H. Wells, an alderman of said city, C. L. Higbee, who being duly sworn according to law, deposeth and saith, that he never was taught anything in the least contrary to the strictest principles of the gospel or of virtue, of the laws of God or of man, under any circumstances or upon any occasion, either directly or indirectly, in word or deed by Joseph Smith, and that he never

knew said Smith to countenance any improper conduct whatever, either in public or in private, and that he never did teach me in private or public that an illicit intercourse with females was under any circumstances justifiable and that he never knew him so to teach others.

Sworn to and subscribed before me this 17th day of May 1842. Daniel H. Wells, Alderman. (*Affidavits and Certificates*, August 31, 1842)

Chauncey Was Expelled from the Church

On May 24, 1842, the High Council voted to expel Chauncey L. Higbee from the Church because of his adulterous sins (see LDS *History of the Church* 5:18).

Joseph desperately desired to put an end to the polygamy in the Church by stopping the polygamists from using his name. Therefore, in addition to preferring charges against Chauncey in the High Council and Nauvoo Municipal Court, he also sued Chauncey in the Circuit Court at the county seat in Carthage, Illinois. This was a determined attempt by Joseph to stop polygamy and clear his name of polygamous allegations. The account of this court case in Carthage has never been discussed in writing by scholars, but will be discussed in the next chapter of this work.

Chapter 13

Joseph Sued Chauncey L. Higbee in Court at Carthage

Joseph Smith took immediate action when he discovered that Lawyer Chauncey L. Higbee had used his name to seduce women into practicing spiritual wifery. The Prophet was so disturbed by this news that he not only brought Chauncey before the Church's High Council and had him expelled from the Church, but he took the case two steps further: He sued Chauncey in Nauvoo before Justice of the Peace Ebenezer Robinson, and later in the Hancock County Circuit Court at the county seat at Carthage. In doing so Joseph provided one of the strongest evidences that (1) he was not a polygamist, (2) that he had not had a revelation commanding the practice of polygamy, and (3) that polygamy had its origin in some other source (which was in Dr. Bennett's brand of Cochranism).

How the Chauncey L. Higbee Court Case Was Found

The records of Joseph's court case against Chauncey were kept in the Hancock County Courthouse files at Carthage, Illinois, under the title, *The People vs. Chauncey L. Higbee*. They were deposited in the office of the County Clerk and Recorder of the Circuit Court. These documents have remained unknown to Saints and scholars because Brigham Young and the historians, who rewrote Church history after Joseph's death, excluded the details of this court case from their history. Therefore, the Carthage records have not been previously treated in writings on the subject of polygamy.

We (Richard and Pamela Price) began seriously studying the

polygamy question in the early 1950s. Our vacations were spent studying in libraries in Missouri, Kansas, Illinois, Iowa, Utah, and Washington, D.C. Notes were laboriously taken in longhand and typed later. Information on the subject of polygamy in the Church was also discovered by sending inquiries to libraries throughout the United States, and to Manchester and London, England (where thousands of Saints were converted in the 1840s). Information gathered from these sources made the story of Joseph's fight against polygamy more evident. In all of our studies, the Chauncey Higbee case was one of our most important discoveries.

Richard recorded in his journal for November 7, 1962:

> In our studies in preparation of the book, *Joseph Smith Fought Polygamy,* . . . Pamela and I felt directed that we should go to Carthage and study the court records firsthand. We sent a letter to which they replied that the records were open to the public. On the above date we . . . drove to Carthage, taking two cameras and two typewriters.

Pamela's notes state:

> We left Independence, November 7, 1962, after work. . . .
>
> We spent the next day in the Hancock County Courthouse, in the office of the County Clerk and Recorder of the Circuit Court. There we found that the archives contained the court records dating back to the beginning of the county. We searched all day long and found six indictments which were brought against Joseph in 1844 by some of the Nauvoo conspirators who brought about his death, but nothing pertaining to the question of polygamy in 1842.
>
> During the first day we had searched through everything to no avail. We called in Mr. P_____, the circuit court clerk, and asked him to help us find more information on Joseph Smith, but he was unable to do so. We were very disappointed as we left that evening and retired to the Hotel Carthage across the street south of the courthouse.
>
> The next day we searched the [Hancock] county public library and were amazed to find so little that would be helpful. We went back with prayer to the County Clerk's archives and began searching the 1842 files again. With great surprise

and delight, we found a court case in File Box 18, Case Number 40, with an innocent-looking title, *"People vs. Higbee* Oct. 1842 No 40."

To our amazement we found in File Box 18 a jacket of faded blue paper with the title of this case on the outside. This was Case Number 40. Inside the jacket were seven papers which were the actual court documents of the suit which the Prophet brought against Chauncey Higbee. This included an affidavit signed by the Prophet Joseph Smith. What a tremendous find! There was Joseph's signature on a sworn affidavit that his character, and also the character of his wife, Emma, had been defamed by Chauncey L. Higbee "in seducing certain females."

This affidavit has great significance when it is studied in connection with the testimonies of Margaret and Matilda Nyman, Sarah Miller, and Catharine Warren, as given in the previous chapter. The documents within the jacket were:

1. Joseph Smith's affidavit;
2. A warrant for the arrest of Lawyer Chauncey Higbee to have him appear before Justice Ebenezer Robinson in Nauvoo;
3. A subpoena for three of the women named above to appear as witnesses for Joseph, before Justice Robinson in Nauvoo;
4. Justice Ebenezer Robinson's "transcript" with which he remanded the case to the circuit court in Carthage;
5. Chauncey Higbee's bond that he would appear before the Carthage Circuit Court;
6. A subpoena for three of the women named above and one man to appear as Joseph's witnesses at Carthage;
7. Another subpoena to have five women appear as Chauncey's witnesses at Carthage.

**THE DOCUMENTS WITHIN THE JACKET OF
THE CASE OF *PEOPLE VS. HIGBEE***

The documents have been given numbers in this chapter to assist in their identification. Documents Number 1 through Number 4 reveal that on May 24, 1842, Chauncey had a hearing before Justice of the Peace Ebenezer Robinson in Nauvoo.

[Document Number 1—Joseph's Affidavit]

State of Illinois } ss
County of Hancock

Before me, Ebenezer Robinson, one of the Justices of the Peace for said county personally came Joseph Smith, who, being duly sworn according to law, deposeth and saith, that at sundry times, in the City of Nauvoo, county aforesaid, one Chancy L. Higbee has slandered and defamed the character of the said Joseph Smith, and also the character of Emma Smith, his wife, in using their names, the more readily to accomplish his purpose in seducing certain females, and further this deponont saith not.

Sworn to, and subscribed before me, in the county aforesaid, this 24th day of May A.D. 1842. E. Robinson J. P.

[Signed] Joseph Smith

On another sheet inside the jacket which contained the case was written:

J. Smith's Affidavit Filed September 14th, 1842. . . . Davis Clerke

We were familiar with photocopies of Joseph Smith's signature, and as we viewed the document we felt certain that it was indeed the Prophet's signature. We were honored to hold in our hands a document which had been signed by the Prophet—the document upon which this entire case was based.

[Document Number 2—State Warrant for the Arrest of Chauncey Higbee]

State of Illinois } ss
County of Hancock

The People of the State of Illinois, to all sheriffs, coronors

and constables of said State.
Greeting:

Whereas complaint has been made before me, one of the Justices of the Peace in and for the county aforesaid, upon the oath of Joseph Smith, that Chancy Higbee, late of the county aforesaid did, at sundry times, slander the character of the said Joseph Smith, and also the character of Emma, his wife.

These are therefore, to command you to take the said Chancy L. Higbee, if he be found in your county; or if he shall have fled, that you pursue after the said into any other county within this state, and take and safely keep the said ~~Higbee~~ Chancy L. Higbee so that you have his body forthwith before me, or some other Justice of the Peace to answer the said complaint, and be further dealt with according to law.

Given under my hand and seal this 24th day of May A.D. 1842.

      E. Robinson ss
      Justice Peace

On the back of the warrant were the words:

<u>State Warrant</u>
State of Illinois
 vs.
Chancy L. Higbee
costs 50
Filed September 14th, 1842
J. C. Davis Clerk

I have taken the within named Chauncey L Higbee and He is know preasent [now present].
May 24th 1842. fees 31 cts, Lewis Robison Constable.

[Document Number 3—Subpoena for Joseph's Witnesses at Nauvoo]

STATE OF ILLINOIS, } Sct.
HANCOCK COUNTY,

THE PEOPLE OF THE STATE OF ILLINOIS To Margaret J.

Nyman, Matilda Nyman, Sarah Miller,
 You are hereby commanded to appear before me at my office in Nauvoo, forthwith then and there to testify the truth, in a matter in suit, wherein The State of Illinois is plaintiff and Chancy L. Higbee defendant and this you are not to omit under the penalty of the law. Given under my hand and seal, this 24th day of May, 1842.
E. Robinson J. P. [Seal]

The following is written in longhand on this page:

 Names of Witnesses in case of State of Illinois vs.
Chancy L. Higbee
Margaret J. Nyman
Matilda Nyman
Sarah Miller &
Alexander McRae
Issued

The following information is written on the back of the subpoena:

Subpoena
State of Illinois
      vs
Chancy L. Higbee
costs .25 [cents]
    50
    31
 Served on the witnesses named May 24th 1842 Fees 50 [cents]
            Lewis Robison Constable

(Adding authenticity to this subpoena are these descriptive words, "E. Robinson, Printer, Nauvoo," which shows that Ebenezer had printed the subpoenas that were used in Nauvoo.)

State of Illinois) Slander and Defamation
  vs.   ) of Character.
Chauncy L. Higbee)
Justices fees $1.62½) May 24, 1842. Upon
Const ..   ) the affidavit of Joseph
Witness fees $2.00) Smith, a Warrant issued
                    against Chauncy L. Higbee
                    for Slander and defama-
tion committed against the said Joseph Smith
and Emma Smith his wife, at sundry times
in the city of Nauvoo, and county of Hancock.
May 24, 1842 Warrant executed
by Lewis Robison constable, by bringing
the defendant forward. At request of
complainant Subpoena issued for Margaret
J. Nyman, Matilda Nyman and Sarah Miller, and was served by Constable Robison.
And the witnesses attended.
    On hearing the Defendant is
required to give bail in the sum of
Two Hundred dollars, for his appearance at
the next term of the Circuit Court for
said county, to answer said complaint.
    Whereupon, the Defendant and
Francis M. Higbee entered into bond acc'd-
ingly.

State of Illinois)
County of Hancock) ss. I, Chauncey Robinson, justice
of the peace, do certify that the foregoing is
a true copy from my docket of the proceedings
in the above case.

Justice Robinson's transcript by which the case of **The People** vs. **Chauncey L. Higbee** *was remanded to the county circuit court in Carthage.*

[Document Number 4—Robinson's "Transcript" Remanding the Case to the Carthage Court]

Joseph pressed the case further and Justice Ebenezer Robinson prepared the necessary papers to be entered in the records at Carthage in preparation for the trial. The documents were entered by a clerk at Carthage on September 14, 1842, in the office of the circuit clerk. The trial date was set for October 3, 1842. Robinson's transcript stated:

Slander and Defamation of Character.

State of Illinois
    vs.
Chancy L. Higbee
Justice fees $1.62 1/2
Const.   "   4 Witnesses $2.00

May 24 1842. Upon the affidavit of Joseph Smith, a Warrant issued against Chancy L. Higbee for slander and defamation committed against the said Joseph Smith and Emma Smith his wife, at sundry times in the City of Nauvoo, and county of Hancock.

May 24, 1842. Warrant executed by Lewis Robison, Constable, by bringing the Defendant [Chauncey Higbee] forward. At request of complainant [Joseph Smith] subpoena issued for Margaret J. Nyman, Matilda Nyman and Sarah Miller, and was sworn by Constable Robison and the witnesses attended.

On hearing, the Defendant is required to give bail in the sum of Two Hundred Dollars, for his appearance at the next term of the Circuit Court for said county, to answer said complaint.

Whereupon, the Defendant, and Francis M. Higbee [his brother] entered into bond accordingly.

State of Illinois   } ss
County of Hancock

    I, Ebenezer Robinson, Justice of the peace, do certify that

151

the foregoing is a true copy from my Docket, of the proceedings in the above case. September 1, 1842. E. Robinson J. P.

On the cover of this important document these words are written:

Transcript
State of Illinois
   vs
Chauncey L. Higbee
   Filed in my office Septem 14th 1842 J. C. Davis Clerke

[Document Number 5—Chauncey's Bond, Agreement to Appear at the October 3 Trial]

State of Illinois   }
County of Hancock } ss.

Be it remembered, that on the Twenty-fourth day of May, in the year of our Lord one thousand Eight hundred and forty Two Chancy L. Higbee and Francis M. Higbee personally appeared before me, Ebenezer Robinson, one of the justices of the peace in and for the county aforesaid, and jointly and severally ackrowledged themselves to owe the people of the State of Illinois the sum of Two Hundred Dollars, to be levied of their goods and chattels, lands and tenements, if default be made in the condition following, to wit:

The condition of this recognizance is such, that if the above bound Chancy L. Higbee shall personally be and appear before the Circuit Court on the first day of the term thereof, next to be holden in and for the County aforesaid; then and there to answer the a charge of slander and defamation against the character of Joseph Smith, and abide the judgment of the Court, and not default without leave; then this recognizance shall be void: otherwise, it shall be and remain in full force and virtue in law.

C. L. Higbee
F. M. Higbee

The subpoena which was issued to summon Joseph's witnesses to testify in the Carthage court.

Taken and acknowledged before me, on the day and year first above written.

      E. Robinson
      Justice Peace

On the outside of the above document is written:

Chancy L. Higbee's Bond.
 Filed September 14, 1842, J. C. Davis Clerke C

[Document Number 6—A Subpoena for Joseph's Witnesses for the Carthage Trial]

Three women and one man were subpoenaed to appear at Carthage as witnesses for Joseph. The subpoena ordered:

STATE OF ILLINOIS, } Sct.
HANCOCK COUNTY.

 THE PEOPLE OF THE STATE OF Illinois. TO THE SHERIFF OF SAID COUNTY, GREETING: WE COMMAND YOU TO SUMMON Margaret J. Nyman, Matilda Nyman, Sarah Miller & Alexander McRae if to be found in your County, personally to be and appear before the Circuit Court of said Hancock County, at the Court House, in Carthage, on the 3d day of October in the year of our Lord one thousand eight hundred and forty two to testify, and the truth to speak, in relation to a certain matter in controversy, now depending in the said Court, between The People of of [sic] the State of Illinois Plaintiffs and Chauncey L. Higbee Defendant at the instance of the said Plaintiff [Joseph Smith] laying aside all pretences and excuses whatsoever, under penalty of what the law directs. And make due return of this writ, and of the manner in which you execute the same.

 WITNESS, J. C. DAVIS, Clerk of our said Circuit Court, at Carthage, this 14th day of September in the year of our Lord one thousand eight hundred and forty-two.

      J. C. Davis, Clerk.
      By [ ] Avise D. C.

This information was recorded on the back of this subpoena:

1st Day.   No.
Pltffs [Plaintiffs] SUBPOENA FOR Matilda J. Nyman et als
IN THE CASE OF
The People of the State Ills
    vs
Chauncey L. Higbee
HANCOCK COUNTY CIRCUIT COURT, ILL.
To October TERM, A. D. 1842
SHERIFF'S FEES:
4 Services of Subpoena $1.00
72 Miles travel   4.50
4 Returning Subpoena   50
                       $6.00

William Backinstos SHERIFF, H. C. ILL
by Henry Marks [ ]

"I have served the within writ by reading the same to the within named Margaret Neiman, Matilda Neiman, Sarah Miller, Alexander McRae Sept. 17th 1842
                William Backinstos
                SHERIFF, H. C. ILL
                by Henry Marks [ ]

[Document Number 7—A Subpoena for Chauncey's Witnesses to Appear at Carthage]

To defend himself, Chauncey had five women subpoenaed to testify against Joseph. That subpoena ordered:

STATE OF ILLINOIS, } Sct.
HANCOCK COUNTY.

THE PEOPLE OF THE STATE OF ILLINOIS,
TO THE SHERIFF OF SAID COUNTY, GREETING:
    WE COMMAND YOU TO SUMMON Nancy Ridgon, Sarah Pratt, Emeline White, Amanda Gee and Melissa Schindle if to be found in your county, personally to be and appear before

the Circuit Court of said Hancock County, at the Court House in Carthage, on the 3d day of October in the year of our Lord one thousand eight hundred and forty-two to testify, and the truth to speak, in relation to a certain matter in controversy, now depending in the said Court, between the People of the State of Illinois Plaintiffs and Chauncey L. Higbee Defendant at the instance of said Defendant, laying aside all pretences and excuses whatsoever, under penalty of what the law directs. And make due return of this writ, and of the manner in which you execute the same. WITNESS, J. C. DAVIS. Clerk of our said Circuit Court at Carthage this 19th day of September in the year of our Lord one thousand eight hundred and forty-two.

> J. C. Davis Clerk.
> By [ ] Avise D. C.

On the outside of this subpoena was written:

1st Day. No. 23. Defts [Defendant's] SUBPOENA FOR Nancy Rigdon, Sarah Pratt, Emeline White, Amanda Gee & Melissa Schindle IN THE CASE OF The People vs C. L. Higbee Hancock Circuit Court, Ill. TO October TERM, A. D. 1842 . . . SHERIFF, H. C. ILL.

The Case Was "Disposed of" Because Joseph Was Forced into Hiding

Unfortunately, this case never came to court because Dr. John C. Bennett caused charges to be brought against Joseph, which forced the Prophet into hiding until January 1, 1843—long after the court date had passed. The case was closed with this one-line entry:

> Circuit Court Record: P; page: 4, file no.: 18; plaintiff: People; Defendant: C. L. Higbee; kind of action: indictment; Term disposed of: Oct. 1842. (Index to Court Papers A, listed under index H)

It should be remembered that on May 6, 1842, Lilburn W. Boggs, the ex-governor of Missouri, was shot and severely wounded at his home in Independence, Missouri. Boggs had been the governor at the time the Saints were driven out of Missouri in 1838–39, and had given the cruel extermination order that the Saints must leave Missouri or die. Though Boggs had many political enemies (at the time of the shooting he was a candidate for the Missouri state senate), Joseph Smith was blamed for the attempted assassination.

Dr. John Bennett was expelled from the Church May 11, 1842 (see *Times and Seasons* 3 [June 15, 1842]: 830). He soon left Nauvoo and began publishing letters filled with accusations against Joseph and the Church in an attempt to bring about the downfall of both. The accusation which caused law officials to seek Joseph's arrest, and forced the Prophet into hiding was Bennett's claim that Joseph had told him that he had sent Orrin Porter Rockwell to Independence to assassinate ex-Governor Lilburn Boggs. A letter from Bennett was published in the *Sangamo Journal* of Springfield, Illinois, in which Bennett boasted, "I am now going over to Missouri to have Joe [Smith] taken to justice" (*Sangamo Journal*, July 15, 1842).

After causing much animosity against Joseph in Illinois, Bennett went to Jefferson City, the capital of Missouri, where he assured authorities that Joseph was the perpetrator behind the attempted murder of Boggs. As a result, Governor Reynolds of Missouri requested that Governor Carlin of Illinois extradite Joseph to Missouri for trial. On October 2, the day before the Higbee trial was to take place at Carthage, Joseph learned of a plot to capture him while he was attending the court. It is recorded that

> About ten o'clock in the forenoon, a messenger arrived [at Nauvoo] from Quincy, stating that the governor [Carlin of Illinois] had offered a reward of $200 for Joseph Smith, Jun., and also $200 for Orrin P. Rockwell. This report was fully established on receipt of the mail papers. The *Quincy Whig* also stated that Governor Reynolds [of Missouri] has offered a reward, and published the governor's proclamation offering a reward of $300 for Joseph Smith, Jun., and $300 for Orrin P. Rockwell. (LDS *History of the Church* 5:167)

Sidney Rigdon, who was visiting in Carthage,

> ascertained that [Governor] Carlin had intentionally issued an illegal writ, expecting thereby to draw President Joseph to Carthage to get acquitted by habeas corpus before [Judge Steven A.] Douglas, and having men there waiting with a legal writ to serve on Joseph as soon as he was released under the other one, and bear him away to Missouri, without further ceremony. (ibid., 168)

Judge Elias Higbee, father of Francis and Chauncey, reported to Joseph that he [Elias] had

> been informed that many of the Missourians are coming to unite with the militia of this state voluntarily, and at their own expense; so that after the court rises at Carthage, if they don't take me [Joseph] there, they will come and search the city [Nauvoo], &c. (ibid., 168–169)

In view of these reports Joseph had to make a choice—to go to Carthage and risk being captured, or go into hiding. He chose the latter. The words *after the court rises* in Judge Higbee's statement is in reference to Joseph's court case against Chauncey. If Joseph had appeared at Chauncey's trial at Carthage on October 3, the Prophet could have been captured by civil authorities and extradited to Missouri; or perhaps he would have been captured or killed by bounty hunters eager to collect the $500 reward, which was a large sum of money in that day. Joseph dared not go to Carthage under these circumstances, and therefore the case of *The People vs. Chauncey L. Higbee* was "disposed of."

The question has been asked: Why didn't Joseph renew the suit against Chauncey at a later time? The answer is, because Joseph only lived eighteen months longer, and had to remain in semi-hiding during that time because the Missouri officials considered him to be a fugitive from justice. He narrowly escaped being taken to Missouri in June 1843, when he was kidnapped by Jackson County Sheriff Joseph H. Reynolds and Constable Harmon T. Wilson of Carthage, Ilinois, after they disguised themselves and posed as "Mormon elders" (see RLDS *History of the Church* 2:657; LDS *History of the Church* 5:439–440).

The Fate of Joseph's Affidavit

In 1962 when we first examined the papers pertaining to this case, no copier was available in the circuit court office where the documents were deposited. We used slide film to photograph the documents, but when the film was processed, the text was not legible. We also made typed copies of the papers, including Joseph's affidavit, which we proofread again and again to be sure we had copied it correctly.

We realized that the papers were of great value; therefore, we took *The People vs. Chauncey L. Higbee* case (Case #40 in File Box 18) to a clerk in the office. After explaining their value to her, we suggested that they put the documents into a vault for protection, which she did immediately.

In 1968 we returned to the Carthage Courthouse to try to obtain photocopies of these official papers, since a copier was then available. We requested permission to examine this file again and it was brought to us, but Joseph Smith's affidavit (Document Number 1 above) was missing! We immediately reported the absence of that document to a clerk, who informed us that one of the county commissioners had taken it home for study. Richard requested her to give him the name of the commissioner, so we might contact him and ask the privilege of making a copy of the affidavit, but she refused. However, we still had our 1962 copy of Joseph's affidavit. We did make photocopies of all the other documents at that time (1968).

In 1979 we again returned to the same office and examined the files. Joseph's affidavit was still missing.

In June 1998 we went once more to Carthage to search for Joseph's affidavit, but it had not been returned. When Richard went to view the papers, on June 22, 1998, he found none of the documents of this case in File Box 18. This fact was reported to the clerks, who made an unsuccessful search for them. Richard then explained to them that the case involved Joseph Smith—whereupon they replied that many papers which had to do with Joseph had been recently taken to Salt Lake City, Utah, but had been returned. Further searching in a locked vault produced the packet of documents which the clerk said had been taken to Salt Lake City. The papers were fragments from several court cases, all mixed together and in great disorder. Among them Richard found the jacket for *The People vs. Chauncey L. Higbee* case. Only two other documents of the case were there—the subpoenas for Joseph's witnesses (Margaret, et al) and Chauncey's witnesses (Nancy, et al). The clerks did say that all of the Joseph Smith papers had been recently microfilmed, and that they *may be* available through the Mormon Church. The clerks did not disclose the name of the person or persons who took the documents to Utah for study. The remainder of the documents concerning this case were not found at that time.

Mormon Church Writers Purposefully Avoided Reporting Chauncey's Case

It is important to be aware that the Mormon Church did not address *The People vs. Chauncey L. Higbee* case in its official history. It mentioned Chauncey's promiscuity, but refrained from giving details of the case.

Of course Apostle Brigham Young, his first cousin Apostle Willard Richards, and the others who were involved in writing the LDS Church's history after Joseph's death, knew all of the facts of the Chauncey Higbee case. For example, Brigham and Ebenezer Robinson were brothers-in-law, for they had married sisters. (Brigham's first wife, Miriam Works, and Ebenezer's wife, Angeline Works, were sisters.) If the LDS historians had written that Joseph had sued Chauncey for falsely stating that Joseph had received a polygamous revelation and "the heads of the church" were practicing polygamy, the true facts would have destroyed their false claims that Joseph had plural wives. In other words, if the Saints had been told how emphatically Joseph had denied having a polygamous revelation, and that he had brought a charge of slander against a prominent member of the Church for saying that he had, the Saints would have discerned that Joseph was not a polygamist—and that the entire polygamy doctrine and practice was a fraud.

The Significance of the Chauncey Higbee Case

Even though the case against Chauncey L. Higbee did not come to trial at Carthage on October 3, 1842, it was a very significant factor in Joseph Smith's fight against polygamy. It showed that Joseph vigorously contended against that evil doctrine in private and in public. If Joseph had been guilty, he certainly would not have sued a competent lawyer and insisted that the case be tried at Carthage among his enemies. Would a man with plural wives sue a lawyer—in the state of Illinois, where polygamy was a crime at that time (see *Statutes of Illinois, Criminal Code*, Section 121–122)? If Joseph had been guilty, Chauncey could have easily proven it, and no doubt Joseph would have gone to jail for that crime.

One needs to be aware that the women Chauncey chose for his witnesses were a part of "Bennett's clique." As already stated, his witnesses (those who were members of the Church) had suffered the shame of an investigation before the Nauvoo High Council. Dr. John C. Bennett published their names in newspapers across the land, and in his book, claiming that Joseph had attempted to take them as his plural wives. No doubt Chauncey hoped that by using these women as witnesses, he could convince the world that he was innocent and that Joseph was a polygamist, so the blame would be on Joseph and not himself. The cases of these women are to be treated later.

Because Joseph was innocent, he did not hesitate to have Chauncey arrested and charged. The case of *The People vs. Chauncey L. Higbee* attests to the innocence of the Prophet, and to his courageous fight to clear his and Emma's names of the fraudulant charges that he had received a polygamous revelation and had plural wives.

Chapter 14

Dr. Bennett Expelled from the Church

It would seem that Dr. Bennett would have been afraid to have continued his promiscuity after coming so close to being expelled in July 1841, but he continued his crimes unabated. When Bennett heard that Chauncey L. Higbee was being tried before the High Council in May of 1842, he feared that his name would be mentioned—that some of the women would name him as also seducing them. Therefore, Bennett hurried to President William Law, Joseph's counselor in the First Presidency, and asked Law to intercede in his behalf if anyone tried to implicate him.

Law testified:

> he came to me and told me that a friend of his [Chauncey Higbee] was about to be tried by the High Council, for the crime of adultery, and that he feared his name would be brought into question.—He entreated me to go to the council and prevent his name from being brought forward, as, said he, "I am not on trial, and I do not want my mother to hear of these things, for she is a good woman." (*Times and Seasons* 3 [August 1, 1842]: 873)

Dr. Law went to the Church authorities to plead for Dr. Bennett, but in spite of Law's pleadings, Bennett's crimes were so horrible that he was ordered to appear before the High Council for another trial.

Women's Names Published

Bennett had reason to fear the investigation by the High Council into Chauncey's activities, because the hearings had barely begun when the doctor's name was linked to women both in and out of the Church, with whom he had practiced spiritual wifery. Those women who were members of the Church were immediately brought before the High Council to face interrogation. The names of five Church women were published in the *Wasp*, a Nauvoo newspaper edited at that time by Joseph's brother, Apostle William Smith. Church leaders close to Joseph advised him not to publish the women's names. However, William published a letter from Dr. Robert Foster, Surgeon General of the Nauvoo Legion, in which the names of six of the women were listed. The five who belonged to the Church were: Sarah Pratt, wife of Apostle Orson Pratt, who was accused of having an affair with Bennett while her husband was a missionary in England; Martha Brotherton, a teenage English immigrant; and two young sisters, Margaret and Matilda Nyman. A nonmember, Emmeline Hibbard White, ex-wife of Captain Hugh White from whom Joseph had purchased the Homestead and adjoining land, was also named.

Dr. Robert Foster wrote a letter to the editor of the New York *Herald*, in which he named some of the women who had been involved with Bennett. Foster gave William Smith a copy of that part of his letter for publication in the *Wasp*. The letter stated:

> I challenge Bennett or any other man or woman to show a more examplary man beneath the sun, or cite to any time or place when he [Joseph Smith] has violated the laws of his country, or when he has taught, either publicly or privately, by precept or example, any thing repugnant to the laws of the Holy Bible, or worthy of bonds or death. It can't be done; it is too well known that he stamps with indignation and contempt every species of vice—if it had not been so Bennett would have been with us yet. . . . Alas, none but the seduced join the seducer; those only who have been arraigned before a just tribunal [the Church's High Council] for the same unhallowed conduct can be found to give countenance to any of his black hearted lies, and they, too, detest him for his seduction, these are the ladies to whom he refers his hearers to substantiate his assertions. Mrs. [Emmeline] White, Mrs. [Orson] Pratt, Niemans [Margaret and Matilda Nyman], [Sarah] Miller,

[Martha] Brotherton, and others. Those that belong to the church have had to bear the shame of close investigation as to their adulteries, and have been dealt with according to church order, in such case made and provided, in the Book of Covenants, (Sec. 91 and Sec. 13, page 122 [of the 1835 Edition], and the Holy Bible, Book of Mormon &c.) Mrs. [Emmeline] White never was a member of the Mormon church, but really did Bennett try to seduce her from her father's home to wander with him, God knows where. . . . Why does he not . . . contribute to the wants of his wife and helpless family in Ohio? (*Wasp* 1 [October 15, 1842]: 2)

Section 13 of the Doctrine and Covenants is now Section 42 in both the RLDS and LDS Editions. In that section God commands: "Thou shalt love thy wife with all thy heart, and shall cleave unto her and none else; and he that looketh upon a woman to lust after her, shall deny the faith, and shall not have the Spirit; and if he repents not, he shall be cast out. Thou shalt not commit adultery; and he that committeth adultery and repenteth not, shall be cast out" (RLDS DC 42:7d–e; LDS DC 42:22–23).

One week after Foster's letter appeared in the *Wasp*, Apostle William Smith published:

> We have two presses in Nauvoo [the *Wasp* and the *Times and Seasons*], and it has yet to be shown that either of them has spread falsehood or held back the truth. (*Wasp* 1 [October 22, 1842]: 2)

Hyrum Smith's Affidavit Described Bennett's Crimes

Hyrum Smith, ever a foe of polygamy, gave the following affidavit concerning Bennett:

> On the seventeenth day of may, 1842, having been made acquainted with some of the conduct of John C. Bennett, which was given in testimony under oath before Alderman G. W. Harris, by several females, who testified that John C. Bennett endeavored to seduce them and accomplished his designs by saying it was right; that it was one of the mysteries

of God, which was to be revealed when the people was strong enough in the faith to bear such mysteries—that it was perfectly right to have illicit intercourse with females, providing no one knew it but themselves, vehemently trying them from day to day, to yield to his passions, bringing witnesses of his own clan to testify that their was such revelations and such commandments, and that it was of God; also stating that he would be responsible for their sins, if their was any; and that he would give them medicine to produce abortions, providing they should become pregnant.

One of these witnesses, a married woman [who was not named] that he attended upon in his professional capacity, whilst she was sick, stated that he made proposals to her of a similar nature; he told her that he wished her husband was dead, and that if he was dead he would marry her and clear out with her; he also begged her permission to give him [her husband] medicine to that effect; he did try to give him medicine, but he would not take it—on interogating her [of] what she thought of such teaching, she replied, she was sick at the time, and had to be lifted in and out of her bed like a child. Many other acts as criminal were reported to me at the time. On becoming acquainted with these facts, I was determined to prosecute him [Bennett], and bring him to justice.—Some person knowing my determination, having informed him of it, he sent to me Wm. Law and Brigham Young, to request an interview with me and to see if their could not be a reconciliation made. I told them I thought there could not be, his crimes were so henious; but told them I was willing to see him; he immediately came to see me; he begged on me to forgive him, this once, and not prosecute him and expose him, he said he was guilty, and did acknowledge the crimes that were alleged against him; he seemed to be sorry that he had committed such acts, and wept much, and desired that it might not be made public, for it would ruin him forever; he wished me to wait; but I was determined to bring him to justice, and declined listening to his entreaties; he then wished me to wait until he could have an interview with the masonic fraternity; he also wanted an interview with Br. Joseph; he wished to know of me, if I would forgive him, and desist from my intentions, if he could obtain their forgiveness; and requested the privilege of an interview immediately.

I granted him that privilege as I was acting as master *pro. tem.* at that time; he also wished an interview first with Br. Joseph; at that time Brother Joseph was crossing the yard from the house to the store, he immediately come to the store and met Dr. Bennett on the way; he reached out his hand to Br. Joseph and said, will you forgive me, weeping at the time; he said Br. Joseph, I am guilty, I acknowledge it, and I beg of you not to expose me, for it will ruin me; Joseph replied, Doctor! why are you using my name to carry on your hellish wickedness? Have I ever taught you that fornication and adultery was right, or poligamy or any such practices?

He said you never did.

Did I ever teach you any thing that was not virtuous—that was iniquitous, either in public or private?

He said you never did.

Did you ever know anything unvirtuous or unrighteous in my conduct or actions at any time, either in public or in private? he said, I did not; are you willing to make oath to this before an Alderman of the city? he said I am willing to do so.

Joseph said Dr. go into my office, and write what you can in conscience subscribe your name to, and I will be satisfied—I will, he said, and went into the office, and I went with him and he requested pen ink and paper of Mr. Clayton, who was acting clerk in that office, and was also secretary *pro. tem.* for the Nauvoo Lodge U. D.

Wm. Clayton gave him paper, pen and ink, and he stood at the desk and wrote the following article which was published in the 11th No. of the Wasp [newspaper]; sworn to and subscribed before Daniel H. Wells, Alderman, 17th day of May, A. D. 1842; he [Bennett] called in Br. Joseph, and read it to him and asked him if that would do, he [Joseph] said it would, he then swore to it as before mentioned; the article was as follows:

STATE OF ILLINOIS, }
City of Nauvoo.

Personally appeared before me, Daniel H. Wells, an Alderman of said city of Nauvoo, John C. Bennett, who being duly sworn according to law, deposeth and saith: that he never was taught any thing in the least cantrary to the strictest principles of the Gospel, or of virtue, or of the laws of God, or man, under any occasion either directly or indirectly, in word or deed, by Joseph Smith; and that he never knew the said Smith to countenance any improper conduct whatever, either in public or private; and that he never did teach me in private that an illegal illicit intercourse with females was, under any circumstances, justifiable, and that I never knew him so to teach others.

JOHN C. BENNETT.

Sworn to, and subscribed, before me, this 17th day of May, 1842.
DANIEL H. WELLS, Alderman. (*Times and Seasons* 3 [August 1, 1842]: 870–871)

Affidavit of [President] Wm. Law.

I believe it was on the evening of the 11th day of May ... I had some conversation with J. C. Bennett and intimated to him that such a thing [as his expulsion] was concluded upon, which intimation I presume led him to withdraw immediately. I told him we could not bear with his conduct any longer—that there were many witnesses against him, and that they stated that he gave Joseph Smith as authority for his illicit intercourse with females. J. C. Bennett declared to me before God that Joseph Smith had never taught him such doctrines, and that he never told any one that he (Joseph Smith) had taught any such things, and that any one who said so told base lies; nevertheless, he said he had done wrong, that he would not deny, but he would deny that he had used Joseph Smith's name to accomplish his designs on any one; stating that he had no need of that, for that he could succeed without telling them that Joseph approbated such conduct .... He plead with me to intercede for him, assuring me that he would turn from his iniquity, and never would be guilty of such crimes again.... I accordingly went to Joseph Smith and plead with him to spare Bennett from public exposure, on account of his mother. On many occasions I heard him acknowledge his guilt, and beg not to be destroyed in the eyes of the public, and that he would never act so again, "So help him God." From such promises, and oaths, I was induced to bear with him longer than I should have done.

On one occasion I heard him state before the city Council

that Joseph Smith had never taught him any unrighteous principles, of any kind, and that if any one says that he ever said that Joseph taught such things they are base liars, or words to that effect. This statement he made voluntarily; he came into the council room about an hour after the council opened, and made the statement, not under duress, but of his own free will, as many witnesses can testify.

On a former occasion he came to me and told me that a friend of his was about to be tried by the High Council, for the crime of adultery, and that he feared his name would be brought into question.—He entreated me to go to the council and prevent his name from being brought forward, as, said he, "I am not on trial, and I do not want my mother to hear of these things, for she is a good woman."

I would further state that I do know from the amount of evidence which stands against J. C. Bennett, and from his own acknowledgements, that he is a most corrupt, base, and vile man; and that he has published many base falsehoods since we withdrew the hand of fellowship from him.

About the time that John C. Bennett was brought before the Masonic Lodge he came to me and desired that I would go in company with B. Young, to Hyrum Smith, and entreat of him to spare him—that he wished not to be exposed. . . . WM. LAW. (ibid., 872–873)

Dr. Bennett Was Expelled from the Church

John C. Bennett was tried before the Church's High Council and was expelled from the Church on May 11, 1842 (ibid. [June 15, 1842]: 830). He was tried by the Masonic Lodge and Nauvoo Legion and expelled from both. He was also tried before the Nauvoo City Council, which removed him from the office of mayor.

Joseph reported part of the proceedings which took place in the City Council meeting:

> The following conversation took place in the City Council, and was elicited in consequence of its being reported that the Doctor had stated that I [Joseph] had acted in an indecorous manner, and given countenance to vices practised by the Doctor, and others:

Dr. John C. Bennett, ex-Mayor, was then called upon by the Mayor [Joseph Smith] to state if he knew aught against him; when Mr. Bennett replied:

"I know what I am about, and the heads of the Church know what they are about. I expect I have no difficulty with the heads of the church. I publicly avow that any one who has said that I have stated that General Joseph Smith has given me authority to hold illicit intercourse with women is a liar in the face of God, those who have said it are damned liars; they are infernal liars. He never, either in public or private, gave me any such authority or license, and any person who states it is a scoundrel and a liar. I have heard it said that I should become a second Avard by withdrawing from the church, and that I was at variance with the heads and should use an influence against them because I resigned the office of Mayor; this is false. I have no difficulty with the heads of the church, and I intend to continue with you, and hope the time may come when I may be restored to full confidence, and fellowship, and my former standing in the church; and that my conduct may be such as to warrant my restoration—and should the time ever come that I may have the opportunity to test my faith it will then be known whether I am a traitor or a true man."

Joseph Smith then asked: "Will you please state definitely whether you know any thing against my character either in public or private?"

Gen. Bennett answered: "I do not; in all my intercourse with Gen. Smith, in public and in private, he has been strictly virtuous.

Aldermen. GEO. A. SMITH,
N. K. WHITNEY, WILSON LAW,
HIRAM KIMBALL, B. YOUNG,
ORSON SPENCER, JOHN TAYLOR,
GUST. HILLS, H. C. KIMBALL,
G. W. HARRIS, W. WOODRUFF,
Counsellors. JOHN P. GREEN,
WILLARD RICHARDS,
JAMES SLOAN, City Recorder.
May 19th 1842. (ibid. [July 1, 1842]: 841)

Joseph's Official Statement Concerning Dr. Bennett

The Prophet Joseph made the following statement concerning the promiscuous doctor:

> After I had done all in my power to persuade him to amend his conduct, and these facts were fully established, (not only by testimony, but by his own concessions,) he having acknowledged that they were true, and seeing no prospects of any satisfaction from his future life, the hand of fellowship was withdrawn from him as a member of the church, by the officers; but on account of his earnestly requesting that we would not publish him to the world, we concluded not to do so at that time, but would let the matter rest until we saw the effect of what we had already done.
> It appears evident, that as soon as he perceived that he could no longer maintain his standing as a member of the church, nor his respectability as a citizen, he came to the conclusion to leave the place; which he has done; and that very abruptly; and had he done so quietly, and not attempted to deceive the people around him, his case would not have excited the indignation of the citizens, so much as his real conduct has done.
> In order to make his case look plausible, he has reported, "that he had withdrawn from the church because we were not worthy of his society;" thus instead of manifesting a spirit of repentance, he has to the last, proved himself to be unworthy the confidence or regard of any upright person, by lying, to deceive the innocent and committing adultery in the most abominable and degraded manner.
> We are credibly informed that he has colleagued with some of our former wicked persecutors, the Missourians, and has threatened destruction upon us; but we should naturally suppose, that he would be so much ashamed of himself at the injury he has already done to those who never injured, but befriended him in every possible manner, that he could never dare to lift up his head before an enlightened public, with the design either to misrepresent or persecute; but be that as it may, we neither dread him nor his influence; but this much we believe, that unless he is determined to fill up the measure of his iniquity, and bring sudden destruction upon himself from

the hand of the Almighty; he will be silent, and never more attempt to injure those concerning whom he has testified upon oath he knows nothing but that which is good and virtuous.

Thus I have laid before the Church of Latter Day Saints, and before the public, the character and conduct of a man who has stood high in the estimation of many; but from the foregoing facts it will be seen that he is not entitled to any credit, but rather to be stamped with indignity and disgrace so far as he may be known. What I have stated I am prepared to prove, having all the documents concerning the matter in my possession. . . . JOSEPH SMITH. Nauvoo, June 23, 1842. (ibid., 841–842)

Dr. John Bennett left Nauvoo soon after his expulsion from the Church, and immediately began a campaign to blacken the name of Joseph Smith by declaring many falsehoods, including the charge that Joseph was practicing polygamy. Bennett wrote letters to the editors of the *Sangamo Journal* at Springfield, Illinois, and other newspapers, which were reprinted far and wide. Bennett attempted to prove that Joseph was guilty in order to take the focus from himself. Dr. Robert D. Foster said of Bennett, "He tried to father all his own iniquity upon Joseph Smith" (*Wasp*, September 24, 1842). To this day the Mormon Church declares that some of Dr. Bennett's claims that Joseph was a polygamist are true.

Brigham Young Learned More of Polygamy from Bennett

Brigham Young learned from the High Council hearings how polygamy could be practiced secretly without Joseph's approval. He was one of the judges in the 1841 trial of Bennett and Francis Higbee, and in the 1842 trials of Bennett and Chauncey Higbee. In 1844 Brigham testified under oath, "I knew of the whole affair, it [Francis Higbee's trial] was on the 4th of July [1841], or a few days after—it was shortly after I came from England" (*Times and Seasons* 5 [May 15, 1844]: 539).

Joseph said, "I brought Francis M. Higbee before Brigham Young, Hyrum Smith and others; Bennet was present" (ibid.). Of course Brigham had learned about polygamy from the Cochranites, among whom he ministered in Maine in the 1830s—and he claimed that God had given him a vision favorable to polygamy while he was in England, as previously noted.

Bennett's "plausible tale" was just what Brigham needed to assist him in taking plural wives. On June 15, 1842, less than one month after the Chauncey Higbee-John Bennett Church trials ended, Brigham secretly took Lucy Decker Seely (Mrs. William Seely) as his first plural wife (Stewart, *Brigham Young and His Wives*, 85).

In spite of Joseph's constant battle against polygamy, Brigham led others into the practice of that doctrine.

The question is, Who was telling the truth? Was it Joseph and Hyrum and their supporters who declared Joseph was not a polygamist? Or was it Brigham Young and other polygamists who asserted that Joseph was practicing polygamy in secret? In the final analysis, one should remember that the supposed purpose of polygamy was to produce many children. However, Joseph and Hyrum fathered no children by plural wives, while Young fathered fifty-six! This is another strong proof that Joseph was truthful and Brigham was lying.

Chapter 15

Dr. Bennett Persecuted Joseph and the Church

After Dr. John C. Bennett was expelled from the Church in 1842 and it became obvious that he could no longer be a prominent and respected person in Nauvoo, he left the city and began a campaign of persecution against Joseph Smith and the Saints which has never been equaled in severity. So many significant events occurred during that spring and summer, which involved the doctor and had such important bearings upon the subject of polygamy, that they need to be kept in mind in the order of their dates. Some of these events were:

> May 6—Lilburn Boggs, ex-governor of Missouri who had issued the order to drive the Saints out of the state in 1838, was shot and wounded in his home in Independence.
> May 7—General Bennett supervised a sham battle of the Nauvoo Legion, in which it was believed that he intended to have Joseph assassinated (see Cannon, *Life of Joseph Smith*, 393-394).
> May 11—The Church authorities voted to withdraw the hand of fellowship from Dr. Bennett, and published the fact on June 15 (see *Times and Seasons* 3:830).
> May 17—Bennett resigned as mayor (see *Wasp* 1 [May 21, 1842]: 3). He also made affidavit that Joseph "never did teach to me in private that an illegal illicit intercourse with females was, under any circumstances, justifiable; and that I never knew him so to teach others" (*Times and Seasons* 3 [July 1, 1842]: 840-841).
> May 19—Joseph Smith was elected mayor of Nauvoo and Bennett made an official statement before the City Council in which he stated that Joseph was "strictly virtuous" (ibid. [July 1, 1842]: 841; [August 1, 1842]: 872).

May–June—The Church authorities discovered that Bennett was continuing his illicit activities (ibid., 872).

June 15—A notice that Bennett had been disfellowshipped appeared in the *Times and Seasons*, volume 3, page 830.

June 18—Joseph preached a public sermon against Bennett and his false teachings (see LDS *History of the Church* 5:34–35).

June 22—Bennett went to Springfield, the capital of Illinois, and made an agreement with Editor Simeon Francis to write letters exposing alleged crimes of Joseph Smith for Francis to publish in the *Sangamo Journal* (see *New York Herald* [July 26, 1842], 2).

June 25—Joseph published a lengthy article detailing Bennett's sins (see *Wasp* 1 [June 25, 1842]; *Times and Seasons* 3 [July 1,1842]: 839–843).

June 27—Bennett returned to Nauvoo from Springfield and stayed at the home of his devoted friend, George W. Robinson, where he had been boarding (see Bennett, *History of the Saints*, 290–291). Robinson, whom Bennett had made a brevet major general in the Nauvoo Legion, was Sidney Rigdon's son-in-law.

June 30—Bennett was cashiered out of the Nauvoo Legion (see LDS *History of the Church* 5:49).

July 1—Bennett went to Carthage (see Bennett, *History of the Saints*, 282). He remained there until July 10, writing some of his infamous six letters against Joseph to be printed in the *Sangamo Journal.*

July 13—Bennett arrived in St. Louis and met with Martha Brotherton—who in answer to Bennett's request, made an affidavit charging Joseph with polygamy and related crimes (see Bennett, *History of the Saints*, 236–240). Bennett also met with newspaper editors and sought their support in having Joseph extradited to Missouri for trial in the Boggs case.

August 8—Joseph went into hiding to avoid extradition to Missouri.

August 29—While conference was in session, Joseph suddenly appeared on the stand. He requested that elders volunteer "to declare the truth" in the case of Dr. John C. Bennett. Three hundred and eighty elders volunteered (Cannon, *Life of Joseph Smith,* 410).

August 31—Joseph defended himself by publishing a broadside entitled *Affidavits and Certificates Disproving Statements and Affidavits Contained in John C. Bennett's Letters* for the elders to distribute.

August 1842 through 1843—Bennett traveled to the East and gained widespread notoriety by lecturing in New York City, Boston, and elsewhere—charging those who attended his lectures a considerable fee.

October 1842—Bennett's book entitled *History of the Saints; or, an Exposé of Joe Smith and Mormonism,* was published (see *New York Herald* [October 21, 1842], 2).

Bennett Continued His Promiscuity

After the intense hearings before members of the High Council, the City Council, and the Masonic Lodge, Dr. Bennett pretended to repent on the one hand, but continued his spiritual wifery on the other. At the same time he was plotting revenge against Joseph. The Prophet and other officials had hoped that their charges and Bennett's admission of guilt would cause him to repent and leave Nauvoo without a public exposure. President William Law tried to persuade him to go to Texas. Law said under oath:

> On many occasions I heard him acknowledge his guilt, and beg not to be destroyed in the eyes of the public, and that he would never act so again, "So help him God." From such promises, and oaths, I was induced to bear with him longer than I should have done. . . .
>
> About the time that John C. Bennett was brought before the Masonic Lodge . . . I advised him to go to Texas, and when he returned, if he would behave well we would reinstate him. He said he had no means to take him to Texas, and still insisted on B. Young and myself to intercede for him. (*Times and Seasons* 3 [August 1, 1842]: 873)

Bennett hoped to be forgiven as in previous cases and to stay in Illinois, where he had made a name for himself. After all, he was a candidate for the Illinois House of Representatives, a position he greatly desired—and a break with Joseph and the Church would mean a loss of the election. But Joseph and Hyrum discovered that Bennett was continuing his illicit activities in spite of the severe reprimands and threats of public exposure. Hyrum testified:

> Still after all this we found him guilty of similar crimes again, and it was found to our satisfaction that he was conspiring against the peace and safety of the citizens of this state—after learning these facts we exposed him to the public; he then immediately left the place abruptly; threatening to drink the hearts blood of many citizens of this place. (ibid., 872)

Because of the doctor's continuing promiscuity, Joseph began publishing the truth about him, which made him even more determined to wreak revenge upon the Prophet, and to clear his own name by destroying Joseph's character. The Church officials published a notice in the *Times and Seasons* for June 15, 1842, stating they had withdrawn the hand of fellowship from John C. Bennett.

Bennett Conspired with Editor Francis

When Bennett left Nauvoo, he knew that he could never obtain his goals without a publisher to tell his story. The year of 1842 was an election year and the Whig Party was desperately trying to win over the Democrats. At an earlier date, Editor Simeon Francis of the *Sangamo Journal,* which was published in the state capital at Springfield, had printed an article against the Saints at Nauvoo in order to swing votes in favor of the Whigs. Bennett, who was still mayor when that issue of the *Sangamo Journal* arrived, answered him in a long, scathing letter in the *Wasp* for June 18. (Ironically, it was the same issue of the *Wasp* which announced Bennett's expulsion from the Church. Bennett's letter was probably written days earlier, before he knew he was going to be exposed.)

After the hand of fellowship was withdrawn, the shrewd

doctor devised a diabolical scheme—he traveled to Springfield on June 22 and entered into a pact with Editor Francis. Bennett agreed to write letters against Joseph and the Saints. In turn, Francis would publish the letters to swing votes to the Whig Party, and both the editor and Bennett would profit financially. Therefore, Bennett was able to publish six lengthy letters which still live in infamy.

The truth of this matter was published by the editor of the *Illinois State Register,* a political opponent and competitor of Editor Francis. That paper published:

> About two weeks ago Gen. Bennett, a master spirit among the Mormons, was in this city. He was seen in conversation with several of the leaders of the Junto [leaders of the Whig Party], who made arrangements with him to make sundry awful disclosures about the Mormons. (*Illinois State Register,* July 8, 1842)

Two weeks prior to July 8 places this meeting with the Whig politicians around June 22, six days after the notice of Bennett being disfellowshipped was published, and three days after Joseph had preached against him in the Grove near the Temple. The editor of the *Register* explained the purpose of the conspiracy between Bennett and Editor Francis:

> We have no confidence in this exposition [by Bennett], because it is designed to affect the approaching gubernatorial election. . . . The Mormon General Bennett is thrust from the temple at Nauvoo as to unclean to mingle with those who minister there and forthwith with the Springfield Junto, a herd of kindred spirits, send for him—they hug him to their bosoms with a grin of infernal joy. Promises, flattery and perhaps money are bestowed upon him. Finally a plan of horrible disclosures is proposed and agreed upon, and the [*Sangamo*] *Journal,* miserable harlot of Junto, is made to bring forth to the world, a litter of crippled and misshapen monsters, to frighten half-witted men, women and children, and divert the attention of the people from a sober consideration of the important interest involved in the election. By such foul means—by such base trickery the managers of the Whig party hope to elect the corrupt Prince of town-lot speculators,

Governor of the State of Illinois. (ibid.; republished in the *New York Herald* [July 26, 1842], 2)

The editor of the *Register* also announced in his paper for July 14 that

> Many thousands of copies of Bennett's letters have been struck off at the expense of Gov. Duncan [to sway the election in favor of the Whigs], as we have been credibly informed, and distributed gratuitously everywhere.

The use of Bennett's six letters may have pleased the Whig Party, but it greatly increased the persecution of the Saints. In spite of this, the Democrats won the election.

The Writing of Bennett's Six Letters

When the doctor left Nauvoo, he did not have far to travel to find sympathetic friends. He went sixteen miles southeast to Carthage, where he found enemies of the Saints. Politicians in that village feared that the ever-increasing number of Saints in Nauvoo would vote as a block and control elections. Bennett's first letter, which appeared in the *Sangamo Journal* for July 8, was written on June 27 while he was still in Nauvoo; the second was written in Carthage July 2; and the third one was dated July 4, 1842. His fourth letter was dated July 15 in St. Louis, where he met with Martha Brotherton, who made affidavit that Joseph had tried to get her to become Brigham Young's plural wife. The fifth letter was written on the river steamer *Importer* and was dated July 23. This letter was first published in the *Louisville Journal*. The sixth letter (the most famous of all) was dated August 2, 1842, and written aboard a boat on the Erie Canal, as Bennett was traveling to the East. These letters were published in the *Sangamo Journal* and were couched in the most vehement language, charging Joseph with polygamy, seduction, murder, treason, and other crimes.

Before leaving Carthage, Bennett filed for a divorce from his wife, Mary Barker Bennett, of Ohio. The divorce was granted October 15, 1842. The record of this divorce, at the Hancock County Courthouse at Carthage, verifies the findings which Bishop George Miller, William Law, and Hyrum Smith reported when they investigated Bennett's background in Ohio—that he was a married man at the time he became engaged to a young Church woman at Nauvoo, "one of our citizens," and taught and practiced spiritual wifery.

Only a few of the charges which Bennett made against Joseph in his six letters can be treated here.

Bennett's Charge about the Danites

John Bennett returned to Nauvoo on June 27 and as previously mentioned, stayed at the home of his supporter, George W. Robinson. Bennett later wrote in his book that Joseph sent the "Danites" to Robinson's home to kill him. (While the Church headquarters was at Far West, a Dr. Sampson Avard had formed a secret organization, named after Dan in the Old Testament, called Danites. Bennett claimed that Joseph now maintained this group to kill his opponents.) Bennett declared:

> We shall have full disclosures [of alleged crimes against Joseph] if the *Danites* don't catch me—they are after me like prowling wolves, by Joseph's special orders. (*Sangamo Journal,* July 15, 1842)

Bennett claimed that the Danites tried to kill him during his last night in Nauvoo. He wrote:

> on the evening of the 29th of June, the DESTROYING ANGEL approached my boarding-house, (General Robinson's,) in Nauvoo, with their carriage wheels wrapped with blankets, and their horses' feet muffled with cloths, to prevent noise, about ten o'clock, for the purpose of conveying me off for "*sudden destruction,*" or assassination, so as to make me "*silent,*" and thus prevent disclosures. Dead men tell no tales! But, as I had an intimation of the matter in the afternoon, I borrowed two pistols of General Robinson, and one of Mr. Hunter, a merchant, and loaded them with slugs. Besides these, I had two good Bowie-knives, and some of my friends were, likewise, well armed,—well prepared to give

the ANGEL a warm reception. So, after prowling around the house (the lights in which were extinguished) for some time, the "*hand of the Almighty*" withdrew! (Bennett, *History of the Saints,* 290-291)

Joseph and other Church leaders denied the existence of Danites in Nauvoo or that Joseph had used any manner of threat or force against Bennett (see *The Wasp Extra* [July 27, 1842], 2). On July 20, members of the Nauvoo City Council made an affidavit denying Bennett's accusation by stating, "there is no such thing as a Danite Society in this city" (*Times and Seasons* 3 [August 1, 1842]: 870).

The Charge of Duress

Another charge which the devious doctor made was that Joseph had forced him to make his affidavit on May 17, in which he declared that

> he never knew the said Smith to countenance any improper conduct whatever, either in public or private; and that he never did teach to me in private that an illegal illicit intercourse with females was, under any circumstances, justifiable; and that I never knew him so to teach others. (ibid. [July 1, 1842]: 841)

Bennett also claimed that he was under duress when he made a similar statement before the City Council on May 19. In his six letters Bennett published that Joseph had taken him into a room on May 17, locked the door, drew a pistol, and said:

> The peace of my family requires that you should sign an affidavit, and [also] make a statement before the next City Council, on the 19th, exonerating me from all participation whatever, either directly or indirectly, in word or deed, in the SPIRITUAL WIFE DOCTRINE, or *private intercourse with females in general*; and if you do not do it *with apparent cheerfulness*, I will make CAT FISH-BAIT of you, or deliver you over to the Danites for execution to-night. (Bennett, *History of the Saints,* 287; *Warsaw Signal* [July 23, 1842], 2)

Upon reading Bennett's charge of duress in the newspapers, Nauvoo Church and civil authorities made affidavits to prove that Bennett was not under duress when he made his affidavit of May 17 and his statement on May 19, in which he stated that Joseph was virtuous. Justice Daniel Wells, who witnessed Bennett's affidavit on May 17, declared that Bennett showed no signs of being under duress. Wells asserted:

> The door of the room was open and free for all or any person to pass or repass. . . . During all this time if he was under duress, or fear, he must have had a good faculty for concealing it, for he was at liberty to go and come when and where he pleased. . . . I know that I saw him in different parts of the city, even after he had made these statements, transacting business as usual. (*Times and Seasons* 3 [August 1, 1842]: 873-874)

Wells was a resident of Nauvoo before the Saints located there, and was not a member of the Church at the time he witnessed Bennett sign the affidavit.

Members of the City Council also signed an affidavit in which they declared that Bennett was not under duress at the time he made a statement at their May 19 meeting, stating that Joseph was virtuous (see ibid., 869-870).

The editor of the Nauvoo *Wasp* published:

> In fact, until the whole City Council of Nauvoo are *impeached*, the Doctor must stand before the public as a perjured man.—There let him stand. (*Wasp Extra* [July 27, 1842], 2)

One factor that lends evidence toward Bennett not being under duress was that he remained in Nauvoo for over five weeks after he made the affidavit, and went about the city as usual. Being a medical doctor he had patients to see. And Justice Daniel Wells said under oath that Bennett completed some work in the mayor's office, and performed work connected with the streets of Nauvoo (see *Times and Seasons* 3 [August 1, 1842]: 874). If Joseph had threatened to murder Bennett, as he claimed, the doctor surely would have left Nauvoo immediately. The duress charge was a falsehood fabricated by Bennett.

Of course he found it necessary to make the charge of duress in order to convince the public that he was the victim and not the criminal. If he had not made the claim that he was under duress, the public would not have believed any of his charges against Joseph.

Bennett Claimed That Joseph Ordered the Assassination of Boggs

During the same time that Bennett was being tried and disfellowshipped, word came from Missouri that Lilburn Boggs, the former governor of Missouri, had been shot and wounded. Bennett lost no time in proclaiming that he had previously heard Joseph declare that he was sending Orrin Porter Rockwell to Independence to kill Boggs. From Carthage Bennett wrote:

> I am now going over to Missouri to have Joe taken to justice; and then I am going to New York to publish a book called "The History of the Saints," in which I shall tell most of the actings and doings at Nauvoo for the last two years, of most of their great men, and some of their great women too; so look out for the breakers. We shall have full disclosures if the Danites don't catch me—they are after me like prowling wolves, by Joe's special orders. (*Sangamo Journal,* July 15, 1842)

In order to assist the Missourians in arresting Joseph Smith, Dr. Bennett corresponded with Dr. Joseph O. Boggs of Independence, Missouri, a brother of Lilburn Boggs (see Bennett, *History of the Saints*, 151–152). In July Bennett went to Missouri to promote the prosecution of Joseph. On August 27, 1842, he wrote:

> I . . . stand in readiness to obey the mandate of Missouri, to testify in the premises. The Mormon Pontiff [Joseph] shall tremble at the sight of gathering hosts, in the days of his captivity, like an aspen leaf in the wilderness. . . . I will tear the ermine of sanctity from the shoulders of His Pontifical Holiness, and dim the glory of his mitred head. . . . Nothing short of an excision of the cancer of Mormonism will effect a cure of that absorbing delusion, and the strong arm of military

power must perform the operation at the edge of the sword, point of the bayonet, and mouth of the cannon. (ibid., 151)

These statements reveal that Dr. Bennett was so intent on destroying Joseph that he would even call for a military invasion of Nauvoo!

As a result of Bennett's efforts, Missouri authorities sent a requisition to Illinois to have Joseph extradited to Missouri, which made it necessary for the Prophet to avoid capture by going into hiding from August 1842 to January 1843. Orrin Porter Rockwell was captured and imprisoned in Independence. Alexander Doniphan, the attorney who had often aided the Saints, defended him and he was acquitted. In later years RLDS Historian Heman C. Smith wrote:

> We were surprised to find that Rockwell was not even indicted for this crime, but the most serious indictment found against him by the grand jury of Jackson County, Missouri, was for "breaking jail." On this indictment he was found guilty as charged, and sentenced to five minutes' imprisonment. That is all there is to the story that has so long been circulated about O. P. Rockwell shooting Ex-Governor Boggs, and Joseph Smith being accessory before the fact. (*Saints' Herald* 66 [July 2, 1919]: 647)

Bennett Charged Joseph with Treason

The Saints were loyal to the United States Government during the lifetime of Joseph Smith. They were mainly law-abiding and peace-loving, and desired that all men might enjoy freedom. In spite of this, John Bennett convinced multitudes that Joseph was guilty of treason. For two years after he left Nauvoo, the doctor proclaimed the treason charge. It was this same charge which held Joseph and Hyrum in Carthage Jail on June 27, 1844—long enough to be murdered.

Bennett taught that the Saints believed in Zion, the Kingdom of God on earth, and purposefully projected it to mean a civil and military kingdom with Joseph Smith as dictator and tyrant-king. The idea of Zion (a spiritual government of the Saints, religiously speaking) was construed by him to mean that Joseph intended to raise an army and overthrow the American Government by force and establish "a great Mormon empire." Bennett's charges struck terror in the hearts of many. He published:

> Joe Smith designs to abolish all human laws, and establish a *Theocracy*, in which the word of God, *as spoken by his (Joe's) mouth,* shall be the only law. (Bennett, *History of the Saints*, 149)

> The States of Missouri, and Illinois, and the Territory of Iowa, are the regions to which the Prophet has hitherto chiefly directed his schemes of aggrandizement, and which were to form the NUCLEUS of the great MORMON EMPIRE. The remaining states were to be licked up like salt, and fall into the immense labyrinth of glorious prophetic dominion, like the defenceless lamb before the mighty king of the forest! (ibid., 293)

Bennett Claimed That Joseph Was Practicing Polyamy

In his infamous six letters and his book, Dr. Bennett charged Joseph with other crimes, including polygamy. General Bennett declared that Joseph had introduced "a new degree of masonry [in the Nauvoo Masonic Lodge] called, 'Order Lodge,' " in which leading men of Nauvoo promoted their polygamous activities (*Quincy Whig,* July 16, 1842).

Bennett also went into great detail in describing an alleged women's lodge, which he said was connected with the Order Lodge. He called it a "seraglio" (harem) and claimed that the women who were in it were classified in three degrees (see Bennett, *History of the Saints*, 220-225). He asserted that the Female Relief Society, of which Emma Smith was president, used devious means to recruit women to become a part of this harem (ibid., 220). Bennett linked Emma with polygamy and used derogatory names to describe her. In referring to her as part of the alleged seraglio, Bennett described her as:

> Emma, the *Electa Syria* of the Church, and wife of the Holy

Joe, the male Cassandra of the Mormon Hierarchy. . . the delectable Emma, the Lady Abbess of the Seraglio, or "Mother of the Maids." (ibid., 227)

Emma and other members of the Ladies Relief Society were furious when they learned that Bennett was telling the world that the members of the Relief Society were engaged in polygamy and recruiting young women for polygamous relationships with the heads of the Church. They took the following action:

> The "Ladies Relief Society," also drew up a petition signed by about one thousand Ladies speaking in the highest terms of the virtue, philanthrophy, and benevolence of Joseph Smith. (*Times and Seasons* 3 [August 1, 1842]: 869)

The one thousand women also published a declaration that no system of polygamy existed in the Church. They declared:

> We the undersigned members of the ladies' relief society . . . certify and declare that we know of no system of marriage being practised in the church of Jesus Christ of Latter Day Saints save the one contained in the Book of Doctrine and Covenants, and we give this certificate to the public to show that J. C. Bennett's "secret wife system" is a disclosure of his own make.
> Emma Smith, President . . .
> Eliza R. Snow, Secretary. (ibid. [October 1, 1842]: 940; RLDS *History of the Church* 2:598)

The law in the Doctrine and Covenants, which the women referred to, contained these words:

> Inasmuch as this church of Christ has been reproached with the crime of fornication, and polygamy: we declare that we believe, that one man should have one wife; and one woman, but one husband, except in case of death, when either is at liberty to marry again. (DC [1835 Edition] 101:4; RLDS DC [1950 Edition] 111:4b)

Bennett Named Women Whom He Claimed Joseph Tried to Seduce

Doctor Bennett charged that Joseph had tried to seduce several women who refused his advances. He named Sarah Pratt, wife of Apostle Orson Pratt; Martha Brotherton; Emeline White, a nonmember; and Nancy Rigdon, daughter of President Sidney Rigdon. The reader needs to remember that Sarah Pratt, Emeline White, and Nancy Rigdon had been subpoenaed by Chauncey Higbee as his witnesses when he was to be tried in the Carthage Circuit Court. Sarah Pratt and Nancy Rigdon had been a part of Bennett's clique in Nauvoo. Their cases, as well as the case of Martha Brotherton, will be treated in a later volume.

Conclusion

Bennett's efforts to have Joseph killed and the Saints scattered by military force failed to bring the Prophet's immediate death, as he had hoped. But those efforts had a lasting influence upon the Restoration Movement—both in the perpetuation of the polygamy doctrine among the Utah Mormons and in the misconception of the origin of polygamy in the Church. Bennett's sixth letter has helped shape the Mormon Church into what it is today. Bennett claimed that it was "Joe Smith's Love Letter To Nancy Rigdon" (*New York Herald* [August 31, 1842], 2). His efforts greatly aided the conspirators who brought about the death of the Prophet only two years later.

It is obvious that Joseph was not a polygamist, because he had no children by any woman other than Emma. The supposed purpose of polygamy was for a man to be the father of as many children as possible, to increase his kingdom and glory in the hereafter (see LDS DC 132:29–31). Bennett compared Joseph to Solomon, who had seven hundred wives (see Bennett, *History of the Saints*, 218). If this were true, Joseph would have had many children by other women. Members of the LDS Church in Utah have searched for over one hundred and fifty years to find a single descendant of Joseph from an alleged plural wife, and have found none. As Joseph proclaimed a month before his death, "What a thing it is for a man to be accused of . . . having seven wives, when I can only find one" (LDS *History of the Church* 6:411).

Chapter 16

Bennett's Polygamy Charges and the Saints' Responses

In order to grasp the full significance of Dr. John Bennett's attack on Joseph Smith and the Church, it is necessary to examine more of the details of his charges and the responses which the Saints made to them. General Bennett falsely declared in his infamous letters that Joseph introduced "a new degree of masonry [in the Nauvoo Masonic Lodge] called, 'Order Lodge' " (*Quincy Whig,* July 26, 1842), in which leading men of Nauvoo promoted their polygamous activities. In his third letter, written at Carthage on July 4, 1842, Bennett published:

> JOE's HOLY LODGE CALLED "ORDER." I alluded to this holy institution in one of my former letters. Joe says he has given them [members of the alleged lodge] the Master's word by revelation. In the preparation [to become members] they are stripped naked so as to see if they will pass the holy examination as required in Deuteronomy, 23d chapter and 1st verse. They are then clothed upon and the precious ointment poured upon the head, running down upon the beard, and the skirts of the garment. The ungodly oath, a part of which I gave you, is then administered in order to prepare them for SPIRITUAL WIFE operations, and save Joe from public disgrace and infamy. (*Sangamo Journal*, July 15, 1842; see also Bennett, *History of the Saints*, 275)

Such a claim by Bennett, a Mason, naturally caused many Masons to have great animosity against Joseph.

Joseph Likened to Matthias

Editor James Gordon Bennett of the *New York Herald* read the above statement in Dr. Bennett's third letter and commented through his paper that perhaps Joseph Smith had "a secret lodge of women" too. This suggestion by the *Herald* editor gave Dr. Bennett a new field of thought—so he invented another story. In Bennett's fourth letter, which was published in the *Louisville Journal*, the doctor wrote:

> "In the New York Herald, of the 26th inst., the editor says, 'This presents a strange and curious state of things for the centre of the nineteenth century; and the developments are the most remarkable we ever heard of. The initiatory proceedings at Joe's "Order Lodge" resemble those practised by Matthias at Pearson's house, only his members were females, and they danced around a stone, whilst Matthias anointed them. But, perhaps, after all, Joe Smith has a secret lodge of women! We shall see.' Yes [Dr. Bennett answered], Joe *has* a secret lodge of women! and the editor *will* see. Joe's female lodge (the Mormon inquisition, and seraglio) is the most singular thing of the age." (Bennett, *History of the Saints*, 217)

By republishing the response of the *Herald* editor to the "Order Lodge" claims, Dr. Bennett was likening Joseph to the highly publicized Matthias (see Dean C. Jessee, *The Papers of Joseph Smith*, 1:499–500; Whitney R. Cross, *The Burned-over District*, 39). Some of the Saints at Nauvoo had met Matthias personally at Kirtland in 1835. Matthias went to Kirtland, where he used a ficticious name and tried to palm himself off on Joseph and the Church as a Jewish priest. Joseph recorded:

> "Monday morning, 9th [November 1835]. . . .
> "While sitting in my house, between ten and eleven this morning, a man came in and introduced himself to me by the name of 'Joshua, the Jewish Minister'. . . . We soon commenced talking on the subject of religion. . . . Curiosity to see a man that was reputed to be a Jew, caused many to

call during the day, and more particularly in the evening.

Suspicions were entertained that the said Joshua was the noted Matthias of New York, spoken so much of in the public prints, on account of the trials he endured in that place, before a court of justice, for murder.... After some equivocating, he confessed that he really was Matthias.

After supper I proposed that he should deliver a lecture to us. He did so.... After the congregation dispersed, he conversed freely upon the circumstances that transpired at New York. His name is Robert Matthias. He says that Joshua is his priestly name....

Tuesday, 10th. I resumed conversation with Matthias .... I told him that his doctrine was of the devil.... He tarried until Wednesday, 11th, after breakfast, when I told him, that my God told me, that his god was the devil, and I could not keep him any longer, and he must depart. And so I, for once, cast out the devil in bodily shape, and I believe a murderer." (*Millennial Star* 15 [Saturday, June 18, 1853]: 396–397; ibid. 15 [Saturday, July 2, 1853]: 422; RLDS *History of the Church* 1:598–600; LDS *History of the Church* 2:304–307)

The reported activities of Matthias are another evidence that polygamy was practiced in early America.

Bennett Described the Fictitious Seraglio

In order to include women in his supposed "lodge," Bennett immediately began writing a story in which he charged that the Church's Ladies' Relief Society at Nauvoo, of which the Prophet's wife, Emma, was president, was a "seraglio." He stated that the Relief Society was composed of women who were practicing the doctrine of plural marriage for time and eternity with the high officials of the Church. In order to make his story sound more authentic, the shrewd doctor also published what he claimed was a copy of the plural marriage ceremony that was supposedly used in the lodge. Dr. Bennett declared:

> The most extraordinary and infamous feature of the

social and religious system established by the Mormon Prophet, and one in which he closely resembles his master and model, Mahomet [Muhammad], is the secret regulations he has formed for directing the relations of the sexes. . . .The Mormon seraglio is very strictly and systematically organized. It forms a grand lodge, as it were, and is divided into three distinct orders, or degrees. The first and lowest of these is styled the "*Cyprian Saints*;" the second, the "*Chambered Sisters of Charity*;" and the third and highest degree is called the "*Cloistered Saints*," or "*Consecratees of the Cloister*." (Bennett, *History of the Saints*, 218, 220)

In the above, Bennett was comparing Joseph with the polygamist, Muhammad, founder of the Islamic religion.

The Cyprian Saints

Bennett declared that the lowest degree in the lodge was made up of "many young and beautiful females," for the "gratification of the vilest appetites of the brutal Priests and Elders of the Mormon Church." He declared that the Relief Society through "secret and select council" either found girls who were guilty of promiscuity or those to whom they could attach guilt by gossip, and that the Relief Society members then brought them before a council called the "Inquisition." He asserted that the young women were harangued and terrorized until they agreed to be prostitutes for the leading officials of the Church. According to Bennett, after a girl made this agreement, she was called "a Cyprian" of the "White Veil" (see ibid., 220–221). According to the doctor, no marriage ceremonies occurred in the lower group. They were but concubines. Bennett then asked the question, "Was there ever known, in the history of the world, a more diabolical system than this?" (ibid., 221).

The Chambered Sisters of Charity

Bennett stated that in this middle group there also were

no marriage ceremonies. He wrote:

> This order comprises that class of females who indulge their sensual propensities, without restraint, whether married or single, by the express permission of the Prophet .... Provided the Holy Joe does not desire to monopolize any of them, they are at the service of each and all of the Apostles, High Priests, and Elders of Israel. (ibid., 221–222)

The Cloistered Saints

Bennett asserted that the highest degree in the seraglio consisted of women who actually married leading men of the Church for time and eternity—becoming plural wives. He wrote:

> Its ranks are filled up in the following manner: When an Apostle, High Priest, Elder, or Scribe, conceives an affection for a female, and he has satisfactorily ascertained that she experiences a mutual flame, he communicates confidentially to the Prophet his *affaire du coeur*, and requests him to inquire of the Lord whether or not it would be right and proper for him to take unto himself the said woman for his spiritual wife. It is no obstacle whatever to this spiritual marriage if one or both of the parties should happen to have a husband or wife, already united to them according to the laws of the land.
>
> The Prophet puts this queer question to the Lord, and, if he receives an answer in the affirmative, which is always the case where the parties are in favor with Joe, His Holiness, either in person or by a duly-authorized administrator, proceeds to concecrate the sacred sister in the following solemn manner . . . (ibid., 223)

After giving a purported marriage ceremony, Dr. Bennett assured his readers that,

> The above is a faithful and unexaggerated account of the most enormous and detestable system of depravity that was ever concocted by the corrupt heart of a human being. . . . by the arch villain. . . . this brutally sensual

wretch.... The imposture of Joseph Smith has never had its parallel.... I can only say that I have not told the tenth part of the Prophet's licentiousness. (ibid., 225)

Bennett Published an Alleged Plural-Marriage-for-Time-and-Eternity Ceremony

After publishing what he claimed was the men's Order Lodge in which Church leaders allegedly prepared for spiritual wifery, and the story of the women's lodge, Bennett carried the whole matter of the seraglio one step further by publishing a plural marriage ceremony that was supposedly used within the Church. Bennett stated:

> The parties [the man and woman] assemble in the lodge room, and place themselves kneeling before the altar; the administrator commences the ceremony by saying,—
> "You, separately and jointly, in the name of Jesus Christ, the Son of God, do solemnly covenant and agree that you will not disclose any matter relating to the sacred act now in progress of consummation, whereby any Gentile shall come to a knowledge of the secret purposes of this order, or whereby the Saints may suffer persecution; your lives being the forfeit."
> After the bow of assent is given by each of the pair, the administrator then proceeds—
> "In the name of Jesus Christ, and by the authority of the holy priesthood, I now consecrate you and set you apart by the imposition of my hands, as husband and wife, according to the laws of Zion, and the will of God our heavenly Father; for which especial favor you now agree to serve him with a perfect heart and a willing mind, and to obey his Prophet in all things according to his divine will."
> Again the nod of assent is given by the man and woman, and the administrator continues in a solemn and impressive manner—
> "I now anoint you with holy, consecrated oil, in the name of Jesus Christ, and by the authority of the holy

priesthood, that you may be fully and unreservedly consecrated to each other, and to the service of God, and that with affection and fidelity you may nourish and cherish each other, so long as you shall continue faithful and true in the fellowship of the Saints; and I *now pronounce upon you the blessings of Jacob*, whom God honored and protected in the enjoyment of like special favors; and may the peace of Heaven, which passeth all understanding, rest upon you in *time and in eternity!*"

The parties then rise and embrace each other, and the robe of investiture is placed upon and around them by the administrator, who says,—

"According to the prototype, I now pronounce you *one flesh*, in the name of the Father, and of the Son, and of the Holy Ghost. Amen."

The robe is then removed, and the parties leave the cloister, with generally a firm belief, at least on the part of the female, in the sacredness and validity of the ceremonial, and thereafter consider themselves as united in spiritual marriage, the duties and privileges of which are in no particular different from those of any other marriage covenant. (ibid., 223–224; italics added)

The Significance of the Plural Marriage Ceremony

Perhaps members of the Mormon Church will see a resemblance between Bennett's plural marriage ceremony published here, and that used in their temples. The second paragraph should be noted for the threat it carries, stating that the couple's lives will be forfeited if they disclose the secret nature of the ceremonies. Since the days of Brigham Young, threats have been a part of the LDS Church's temple ceremonies.

The middle paragraphs employ language found among the Saints, such as "according to the laws of Zion," which could have only been written by one who had been closely associated with the Church, as Bennett had been. The fact that he had been a member of the Church made the doctor all the more cunning and deceptive. The use of the term "the blessings of Jacob" is another example of the attempt by Bennett to make his marriage ceremony sound authentic, so it would appear that polygamy was practiced at Nauvoo under Joseph's guidance. It was a cunning move by the doctor to make reference to the Bible account of Jacob who had two wives and two concubines. It is true that Jacob was a polygamist, but his polygamy was never divinely approved. In fact, the practicing of polygamy in Old Testament times (the period in which Jacob lived) is strongly condemned in the Book of Mormon (RLDS Jacob 2:32–37; LDS Jacob 2:23–28).

The Significance of the "Time and Eternity" Phrase

In making his concocted story of an alleged plural marriage ceremony more realistic to the public, Dr. Bennett's evil mind made use of the phrase "time and eternity," which was a term familiar to members of the Church. As early as 1831 the Lord used these words in a revelation in which He stated that they who received His words "shall be gathered unto me in time and in eternity" (RLDS DC 39:5c; LDS DC 39:22).

Bennett's patriarchal blessing, pronounced upon his head by Hyrum Smith in 1840, states that if Bennett would be faithful, "Thou shalt have an inheritance among the Saints *in time and in eternity*, for this is the will of God" (Bennett, *History of the Saints*, 43; italics added). In order to make his plural marriage charges against Joseph sound more scriptural and convincing, Bennett maliciously wove the "in time and in eternity" phrase into them. His wordage gave the doctrine a "Latter Day Saint tone." Bennett's phraseology made it easier for Brigham Young and his associates to transfer plural marriage into the Church after Joseph's death.

The real significance of the phrase "time and eternity" was that it not only made plural marriage sound pious, but also the word *eternity*, in this case, meant that the marriages so contracted were to continue after death—throughout eternity. Here in one simple phrase was born a theology that has filled books, and has ruined the lives of many Saints and families in the LDS Church. From it came the idea of sex and childbearing in the hereafter—and the doctrine of endless dominions, exaltation, and godhood—which naturally spawned the doctrines of Adam-god and blood atonement.

Bennett's Charges Refuted by the Church

When Joseph, Hyrum, and other leading men and women of the Church read the seraglio story with its false marriage ceremony, they took action because they wanted the Saints and the world to know that no such marriage system existed within the Church. They knew that no such thing had ever been taught and practiced in Nauvoo with Joseph's consent. The Church's efforts at rebuttal included statements by Joseph and others which denied the doctor's accusations. In addition to the Prophet's efforts to stop the rumors, the Ladies' Relief Society came forth with a cerificate which stated that Joseph was innocent. A group of prominent men also made affidavit denying the existence of the seraglio, and affirming that they knew of no marriage system in the Church other than the one found in the Doctrine and Covenants. And Joseph's brother, Apostle William Smith, editor of the Nauvoo *Wasp,* was quick to deny Bennett's charges and exonerate Joseph.

Editor Joseph Smith Answered
the Plural Marriage Charges

It is surprising how much Joseph published to refute Bennett's evil stories when one considers that the Prophet was in hiding much of the time and was always burdened with Church affairs. As editor of the *Times and Seasons*, Joseph denounced polygamy over and over and printed affidavits declaring his innocence. When the July 8 and July 15 issues of the *Sangamo Journal* reached Nauvoo, containing some of Dr. Bennett's letters, Joseph published eleven pages of statements and affidavits to prove Bennett's declarations false (see *Times and Seasons* 3 [August 1, 1842]: 868-878). William Smith responded likewise with lengthy rebuttals in the *Wasp*.

Joseph wrote of Bennett:

> He professed to be virtuous and chaste, yet did he pierce the heart of the innocent, introduce misery and infamy into families, reveled in voluptuousness and crime, and led the youth that he had influence over to tread in his unhallowed steps;—he professed to fear God, yet did he desecrate his name, and prostitute his authority to the most unhallowed and diabolical purposes; even to the seduction of the virtuous, and the defiling of his neighbor's bed. . . . [H]e has published that the conduct of the Saints was bad—that Joseph Smith and many others were adulterers, murderers . . . *that we believed in and practiced polygamy.* (*Times and Seasons* 3 [August 1, 1842]: 868-869; italics added)

It is most important to note that Joseph stated that the devious doctor had accused him of practicing *polygamy*, and that Joseph devoted most of this issue of the *Times and Seasons* to prove that Bennett's charges in this regard were false. If Joseph had been guilty of polygamy and yet published all this evidence claiming that he was not, then he was the greatest liar in history. But there is ample evidence that he was innocent, just as he claimed to be.

Within the eleven pages which Joseph published he mentioned "a meeting of the citizens of the city of Nauvoo" which was held at the "meeting ground" on July 22, 1842. At this gathering "about a thousand men" voted that Joseph was innocent of Bennett's charges, which included polygamy. Another petition was also signed by many nonmembers who declared the same (ibid., 869). Included in Joseph's eleven pages were affidavits and certificates (some of which have been previously quoted) made by Hyrum Smith, William Law, Daniel Wells, Elias and Francis Higbee, Pamela Michael, Sidney Rigdon, and William and Henry Marks— exposing Bennett's evil and upholding Joseph's innocence.

Of this list, all but Hyrum had been called upon by Bennett to "come out" and publish a statement against Joseph in the newspapers. Instead, they all wrote statements exonerating the Prophet.

On September 1, 1842, thirty days after Bennett's seraglio story was published, Joseph wrote a letter "To All the Saints in Nauvoo." In this letter (now a part of the Doctrine and Covenants), the Prophet assured the Saints that he was innocent of all the plural marriage charges against him by writing:

> Forasmuch as the Lord has revealed unto me that my enemies, both in Missouri and this state, were again on the pursuit of me; and inasmuch as they pursue me without a cause, and have not the least shadow or coloring of justice or right on their side in the getting up of their prosecutions against me; and inasmuch as *their pretensions are all founded in falsehood of the blackest dye*, I have thought it expedient and wisdom in me to leave the place for a short season, for my own safety and the safety of this people. (RLDS DC 109:1a–b; LDS DC 127:1; italics added)

By stating that "their pretentions are all founded in falsehood," the Prophet was once again declaring that the charges of polygamy against him were false. In order to make his denial of that doctrine more emphatic, Joseph also published the Church's law of marriage which he had caused to be written in the Doctrine and Covenants in 1835. (The concept of monogamy and the outlawing of polygamy were plainly written into the basic Scriptures of the Restoration long before the arrival of Dr. Bennett.) Therefore, in the September 1, 1842, issue of the *Times and Seasons*, Editor Joseph Smith republished the following from the Doctrine and Covenants:

> Inasmuch as the public mind has been unjustly abused through the fallacy of Dr. Bennett's letters, we make an extract on the subject of marriage, showing the rule of the church on this important matter. The extract is from the Book of Doctrine and Covenants, and is the *only* rule al-

lowed by the church. All legal contracts of marriage made before a person is baptized into this church, should be held sacred and fulfilled. Inasmuch as this church of Christ has been reproached with the crime of fornication, and *polygamy*: we declare that we believe, that one man should have one wife; and one woman, but one husband, except in case of death, when either is at liberty to marry again. (*Times and Seasons* 3:909; see also RLDS DC 111:4a–b; italics added)

(As previously explained, the article on Marriage was Section 101 in the 1835 Edition, but was removed from the Mormon Church's Doctrine and Covenants in 1876 when Brigham Young inserted Section 132 on polygamy. This is a prime example of how Brigham and his associates changed basic doctrines of the Church—which made their church a different denomination than the original Restoration Movement.)

A month later, on October 1, 1842, to further emphasize the law against polygamy and the Church's stand for monogamy, Joseph reprinted more of the law of the Church on Marriage in the *Times and Seasons*. He published:

> From the Book of Doctrine & Covenants of the
> Church of Jesus Christ of Latter-Day Saints.
> ON MARRIAGE.
>
> According to the custom of all civilized nations, marriage is regulated by laws and ceremonies: therefore we believe, that *all* marriages in this church of Christ of Latter Day Saints, should be solemnized in a *public meeting*, or feast, prepared for that purpose: and that the solemnization should be performed by a presiding high priest, high priest, bishop, elder, or priest, not even prohibiting those persons who are desirous to get married, of being married by other authority.—We believe that it is not right to prohibit members of this church from marrying out of the church, if it be their determination so to do, but such persons will be considered weak in the faith of our Lord and Savior Jesus Christ.
>
> Marriage should be celebrated with prayer and thanks-

giving; and at the solemnization, the persons to be married, *standing together*, the man on the right, and the woman on the left, shall be addressed, by the person officiating, as he shall be directed by the holy Spirit; and if there be no legal objections, he shall say, calling each by their names: "You both mutually agree to be each other's companion, husband and wife, observing the legal rights belonging to this condition; that is, keeping yourselves wholly for each other, and from all *others*, during your lives." And when they have answered, "Yes," he shall pronounce them "husband and wife" in the name of the Lord Jesus Christ, and by virtue of the laws of the country and authority vested in him: "may God add his blessings and keep you to fulfill your covenants from henceforth and forever. Amen."

The clerk of every church [branch] should keep a record of all marriages, solemnized in his branch.

All legal contracts of marriage made before a person is baptized into this church, should be held sacred and fulfilled.

Inasmuch as this church of Christ has been reproached with the crime of fornication, and polygamy: we declare that we believe, that one man should have one wife; and one woman, but one husband, except in case of death, when either is at liberty to marry again....

We have given the above rule of marriage as the *only* one practiced in this church, to show that Dr. J. C. Bennett's "secret wife system" is a matter of his own manufacture; and further to disabuse the public ear, and shew that the said Bennett and his misanthropic friend Origen Bachelor [who lectured with Bennett], are perpetrating a foul and infamous slander upon an innocent people, and need but be known to be hated and despised. (*Times and Seasons* 3:939; italics added)

Note again that Joseph published that this marriage law was the *only* rule of marriage in the Church. If Joseph were truthful, then he was a monogamist and was honest in declaring polygamy a false doctrine. If he were lying, he was a sinner, a coward, and a fallen prophet. Section 101 (of the 1835 Edition of the Doctrine and Covenants) stated that "this church of Christ has been reproached with the *crime of fornication, and polygamy*," and that "one man should have one wife." Joseph's republishing of the Church's marriage law twice is evidence that he did not believe, teach, nor countenance plural marriage in the Church, and that he went to great lengths to make that fact a matter of public record.

Other differences, between the Church's official marriage law and Bennett's fabrication, are that the marriage law states:

1. That "all marriages in this church of Christ of Latter Day Saints, should be solemnized in a *public meeting*." According to Bennett's alleged plural marriage ceremony, marriages were not conducted in a public meeting, but in the secret Order Lodge;

2. That the couple to be married should be "standing together," while Bennett's plural marriage document had them kneeling for the ceremony;

3. That the couple should keep "yourselves wholly for each other, and from all others, during your lives." This precludes any possibility of the husband being a polygamist, for he too vows to keep himself "from all others";

4. That the clerk of every congregation should "keep a record of *all* marriages." If Joseph had been married to twenty-seven wives (as declared by LDS Church authorities), then twenty-seven primary marriage records would still exist—and the Mormon Church would have published them far and wide. It is a fact that not one primary marriage record can be found for Joseph Smith, other than the record of his marriage to Emma Hale in 1827.

Joseph, as editor, concluded the article in the *Times and Seasons* by repeating that the above "rule of marriage" was "the only one practiced in this church" (ibid.). This was another definite statement by him which upholds monogamy and disproves polygamy.

In that same issue of the *Times and Seasons* Joseph published:

> We have two presses doing as much as can be expected from the limited resources of a people twice plucked up by the roots, and plundered, even to their clothes, besides the loss of a good printing establishment. As far as truth can be spread and lies contradicted by two presses, against several thousand [presses], *it is done!* and we have the gratification of saying that things seem to work together for good to them that look for the second appearing of our Lord Jesus Christ.... [A]nd we do sincerely hope, that we as children of the kingdom, may keep the law of God, and the law of the land. (ibid. 937)

When "several thousand" presses throughout America, and major cities in England and France, published Bennett's seraglio story and the supposed plural marriage ceremony, Joseph did not fight the battle alone. Leading men and women at Nauvoo promptly published certificates denying Bennett's claims and upholding Joseph's innocence.

Leading Men and Women Denounced Bennett's Polygamy Story

In the same issue of the *Times and Seasons* in which he republished the marriage law the second time, Joseph also published two certificates to show that "Dr. J. C. Bennett's 'secret wife system' is a matter of his own manufacture." The certificate by leading men stated:

> We the undersigned members of the church of Jesus Christ of Latter-Day Saints and residents of the city of Nauvoo, persons of families do hereby certify and declare that we know of no other rule or system of marriage than the one published from the Book of Doctrine and Covenants, and we give this certificate to show that Dr. J. C. Bennett's "secret wife system" is a creature of his own make as we know of no such society in this place nor never did.
>
> S. Bennett,   N. K. Whitney,
> George Miller,   Albert Pettey,

Alpheus Cutler,   Elias Higbee,
Reynolds Cahoon,   John Taylor,
Wilson Law,   E. Robinson,
W. Woodruff,   Aaron Johnson.
(*Times and Seasons* 3 [October 1, 1842]: 939–940)

These were men of prominence who were closely associated with Joseph, who knew whether or not there was such a doctrine as plural marriage being taught within the Church. The name of Brigham Young, who was enroute east on a mission, is missing from this list. In June of 1842, four months before this certificate was published, Brigham, who had a living wife, secretly married Mrs. Lucy Ann Decker Seely as his first plural wife (see Stewart, *Brigham Young and His Wives*, 85).

The signature of Judge Elias Higbee, stating that he knew of no such doctrine as plural marriage for time and eternity, is strong evidence in Joseph's behalf—for his sons, Francis and Chauncey, had practiced spiritual wifery with Bennett, as previously shown. Only truth could have caused this venerable brother to stand for the Prophet and against his two sons. The list includes the names of Bishop George Miller and Bishop Newel K. Whitney. The names of Aaron Johnson and Alpheus Cutler also appear—they were members of the Church's High Council. Apostle John Taylor and Apostle Wilford Woodruff, who both later became presidents of the Church in Utah, also signed the above. The signatures of these leaders are testimonies that the plural marriage charges were false—and that "Dr. J. C. Bennett's 'secret wife system' is a creature of his own make as we know of no such society in this place nor never did."

The Relief Society's Certificate against the Polygamy Charges

The Ladies' Relief Society was only a few months old, having had its first meeting on March 24, 1842 (*Times and Seasons* 3 [April 1, 1842]: 743). Imagine the extreme disgust with which the ladies of Nauvoo viewed the story that Bennett had written about their being a part of a harem! The seraglio story incriminated them as much as it did the Prophet, since Bennett had claimed that the chief purpose of the Relief Society was to provide women for the plural marriage system. Accordingly, these women came forward to declare that plural marriage was not taught by Joseph, nor by the Church; neither was it a part of their organization, but that it was a falsehood invented by John Bennett. Their certificate read:

> We the undersigned members of the ladies' relief society, and married females do certify and declare that we know of no system of marriage being practised in the church of Jesus Christ of Latter Day Saints save the one contained in the Book of Doctrine and Covenants, and we give this certificate to the public to show that J. C. Bennett's "secret wife system" is a disclosure of his own make.
>
> Emma Smith, President,
> Elizabeth Ann Whitney, Counsellor,
> Sarah M. Cleveland, Counsellor,
> Eliza R. Snow, Secretary,
>
> Mary C. Miller, Catharine Pettey,
> Lois Cutler, Sarah Higbee,
> Thirza Cahoon, Phebe Woodruff,
> Ann Hunter, Leonora Taylor,
> Jane Law, Sarah Hillman,
> Sophia R. Marks, Rosannah Marks,
> Polly Z. Johnson, Angeline Robinson,
> Abigail Works.

(*Times and Seasons* 3 [October 1, 1842]: 940)

These leaders of the Ladies' Relief Society were in most instances wives of the Church's most prominent men. They knew there was not a plural marriage system in the Church headed by Joseph. Their signatures included the names of Emma Smith, wife of the Prophet; Jane Law, wife of President William Law; Phebe Woodruff, wife of Apostle Wilford Woodruff; Leonora Taylor, wife of Apostle John Taylor;

Rosannah Marks, wife of Nauvoo Stake President William Marks; and Sarah Higbee, wife of Judge Elias Higbee and the mother of Francis and Chauncey Higbee. Also signing the certificate was Mary C. Miller, wife of Bishop George Miller; and Elizabeth Ann Whitney, wife of Bishop Newell K. Whitney. Of great importance is the name "Eliza R. Snow, Secretary," showing that the statement she made in later years (that she was married to Joseph Smith) was false. Eliza's signature attests to the fact that she knew of "no system of marriage being practised in the church of Jesus Christ of Latter Day Saints save the one contained in the Book of Doctrine and Covenants."

Conclusion

Joseph's frank and extensive sermons and writings against polygamy, and his publishing of the Church's law of Marriage twice in 1842, were positive evidences that he strongly opposed the doctrine of polygamy in all forms. The certificates of leading men and women, who associated daily with Emma and Joseph, are more proof that Joseph was a monogamist. Their testimonies, and the fact that Joseph fathered no children by any woman other than Emma, would have convinced even the Utah Saints and the world that Joseph was telling the truth, if Brigham had not secretly begun to put Bennett's plural marriage system into practice before Joseph's death, and made polygamy a cardinal doctrine following the martyrdom.

Chapter 17

Isaac Sheen Was Not a Credible Witness Concerning Polygamy

Writers in the Mormon Church often use statements by RLDS Editor Isaac Sheen in an effort to prove that Joseph Smith taught and practiced polygamy. Isaac Sheen, editor of the *True Latter Day Saints' Herald* for January 1860, indicated that it was his (Sheen's) opinion that Joseph had been involved in polygamy, but had "repented of his connection with this doctrine" before his death.

Editor Sheen's statement has no foundation, however, because:

1. He gave no evidence nor documentation to support his allegations;
2. He did not live close enough to Joseph to know personally whether or not the Prophet practiced polygamy;
3. He had associated with polygamists and had received his information from them;
4. The leaders of the Reorganized Church, who were sponsoring Editor Sheen and the *Herald*, believed that Joseph was not a polygamist—therefore Sheen's statement did not represent the official beliefs of the Church, then or now. Joseph Smith III had not yet taken his place as prophet of the Church. There was no Church presidency, no presiding bishop; nor had all the quorums been set in order. Therefore, Sheen expressed only his own undocumented opinion.

Editor Sheen's Statement in the *Herald*

Isaac Sheen learned that a group of Saints were having a

conference in October 1859 at the home of Israel Rogers near Plano, Illinois. Sheen attended the conference and was pleased to find the Saints preaching and teaching the original gospel, and enjoying the spiritual gifts. He also found them eager to publish a Church paper and in need of an editor. Among the Saints at that conference, Isaac, no doubt, was the most qualified person for the editorial position. Accordingly, he was chosen to edit the *True Latter Day Saints' Herald* (see *True Latter Day Saints' Herald* 21 [April 15, 1874]: 240–241). He published the first issue in January 1860 in Cincinnati, Ohio.

The Saints read the little *Herald* and rejoiced about most of its contents. However, they were shocked to find that Editor Sheen had reprinted a letter which he had written and published seven years earlier concerning the Mormon Church in Utah and plural marriage. What made it so shocking was that in his letter Sheen had implicated Joseph in polygamy. His letter was dated September 20, 1852, and had been published in the *Cincinnati Commercial* and also in the *Saturday Evening Post* for October 9, 1852 (ibid. 1 [January 1860]: 26; *Saint's Herald* 57 [January 26, 1910]: 95).

The quotation from Sheen's letter which LDS missionaries often use when trying to undermine the RLDS position is:

> Joseph Smith repented of his connection with this doctrine [polygamy], and said it was of the devil. He caused the revelations* on that subject to be burned, and when he voluntarily came to Nauvoo [returned from Iowa] and resigned himself into the arms of his enemies, he said that he was going to Carthage to die. At that time he also said, that if it had not been for that accursed spiritual wife doctrine, he would not have come to that. (*True Latter Day Saint's Herald* 1 [January 1860]: 27)

The portion of Sheen's statement which the Mormons have stressed so heavily is "Joseph Smith repented of his connection with this doctrine." This statement alone, taken as

---

* In the January 1860 *Herald*, the typesetter added the letter "s" to the word "revelation" making it plural. Sheen's original letter in the *Saturday Evening Post* said "revelation" (*Saints' Herald* 89 [December 12, 1942]: 5).

fact, would mean that Joseph did teach and practice polygamy. Here they think that they have an authoritative statement right from the RLDS leaders of 1860 that Joseph was a polygamist. But this is untrue—Isaac Sheen was not a primary witness. Furthermore, Edmund Briggs and other leaders at that time did not believe as Sheen did.

If the Mormons are going to accept Sheen's statement as authoritative about Joseph having had a "connection with this," then they must also accept his declaration that Joseph "repented of his connection with this doctrine." In other words, if the Mormons accept Sheen as an absolute authority, then they must agree also that Joseph denounced polygamy and that it is a false doctrine.

There is truth to the final part of Sheen's statement, however, that "if it had not been for that accursed spiritual wife doctrine, he [Joseph] would not have come to that [arrest and martyrdom]." As has been previously shown, Brigham Young and others in high Church offices were secretly practicing "the accursed doctrine" of polygamy before Joseph's death, and were using John C. Bennett's lies that Joseph and "others of the authorities of the church" were practicing it, and "there would be no harm if they should not make it known" (*Times and Seasons* 3 [July 1, 1842]: 840; RLDS *History of the Church* 2:586).

While Joseph was publicly denouncing polygamy, Brigham was secretly living with four wives by 1844: Mary Ann Angell, Lucy Ann Decker Seely, Harriet Elizabeth Cook, and Augusta Adams Cobb (Stewart, *Brigham Young and His Wives*, 84–86).

Joseph rightly called it "a cursed doctrine" (*True Latter Day Saints' Herald* 1 [January 1860]: 26; RLDS *History of the Church* 2:733).

Editor Sheen's Background

Sheen was closely associated with polygamist Almon Babbitt and had some contact with Utah Apostle Orson Pratt. This helps to account for Sheen's belief that Joseph was connected with polygamy.

Isaac Sheen was born December 22, 1810, at Littlethorpe, Leicestershire, England, and emigrated to America in 1830. A devout Christian, who had been reared under the influence of the Baptist Church, he settled in Pennsylvania, living for almost ten years in the vicinity of Philadelphia and Germantown. During this period he was associated mainly with the Quakers, for whom he "formed a strong attachment." From them he came to have a deep interest in the universal freedom of every individual and to embrace the doctrine that "all men are created free and equal." This doctrine led him to become an abolitionist who openly opposed slavery and published an antislavery paper (see *True Latter Day Saints' Herald* 21 [April 15, 1874]: 240; ibid. 57 [January 26, 1910]: 95; Inez Smith Davis, *The Story of the Church*, 436).

Although he had received only six months of formal schooling, Sheen became known as an outstanding speller and prolific writer. In Philadelphia he worked as a newpaper carrier—an occupation that gave him the opportunity he craved to become better educated. He was able to observe how articles were written and newspapers produced. His style of penmanship was known to printers as "Scotchface." His talent for writing was so advanced that he invented a shorthand system and sold it to *Harpers* of New York for one hundred dollars—a large amount for that period. One day in 1840 in the city of Philadelphia, Isaac noticed a crowd of people entering a hallway, and out of curiosity followed them. They were Saints assembling for worship. He stayed and listened and believed. His life was changed forever. In 1840 he was baptized and confirmed (see *Saints' Herald* 57 [January 26, 1910]: 76, 94–95).

Isaac Sheen Did Not Live near Joseph

In 1841 Sheen traveled with Seventy Almon W. Babbitt to Kirtland, where the congregation of Saints numbered between three and four hundred members. A Church conference convened at Kirtland on May 22, 1841, and Elder Almon Babbitt was elected "president or presiding elder of the stake in Kirtland" (*Times and Seasons* 2 [July 1, 1841]: 458). Sheen was ordained to the office of elder in 1841, and that same year married Almon's sister, Drusilla Babbitt, with Almon performing the wedding ceremony (see *Saints' Herald* 57 [January 26, 1910]: 95).

Sheen did not know Joseph at Kirtland, for by the time Sheen moved there, Joseph was living in Nauvoo. When Sheen moved to Nauvoo he only stayed there briefly. Joseph Smith III said of him:

> In August, 1842, he went to Nauvoo, Illinois, and thence to Macedonia, Hancock County, Illinois, where himself and family remained until January, 1846. (*True Latter Day Saints' Herald* 21 [April 15, 1874]: 240)

Macedonia was also known by two other names: Webster and Ramus. It was a settlement about twenty-five miles east of Nauvoo—nearly a day's journey then. Isaac did not live close enough to Joseph to be intimately acquainted with him, and therefore he was not a primary witness in this case.

Isaac Sheen Separated from Brigham Young

After Joseph's death, Brigham Young emerged as leader and Sheen would neither accept polygamy as a true doctrine nor follow Brigham. In contrast, Babbitt gave his allegiance to Brigham, and although Babbitt had a living wife, he married three plural wives at Nauvoo (see *Regional Studies in Latter-day Saint History: Illinois*, 47). In February 1846, Brigham directed the majority of the Saints in an exodus from Nauvoo by crossing the Mississippi River to find a new home in the West. Sheen borrowed a carriage from Babbitt to convey his family across the frozen Mississippi River. Then Sheen separated from the main body.

Years later Isaac's son, John Kirk Sheen, wrote of those days:

> [With] Joseph and Hyrum dead and the Twelve Apostles sitting upon the throne, the exodus came and Isaac Sheen said, "Brigham, go thy way and I will go mine." Placing his wife, daughter, and baby boy [John Kirk] in Almon Babbitt's

carriage, in February, 1846, he crossed the frozen Mississippi and headed for Booneville, Missouri. Leaving his family here with relatives he went to Cincinnati, Ohio, and engaged again in newspaper carrying and shortly was enabled to send for his family and located them in Covington, Kentucky, in 1847. (*Saints' Herald* 57 [January 26, 1910]: 95)

Sheen United with William Smith

Sheen went to Ohio and found employment in Cincinnati—but he made his home in Covington, Kentucky, which is located directly across the Ohio River. Sheen still strongly believed in the truthfulness of the Church, but he did not believe that Brigham had the right to lead it. In an attempt to discover whose right it was to be the Martyr's successor, he began a serious study of the law of lineage as found in the Scriptures. This led him to believe that Joseph's only living brother, William Smith, had the right to lead the Church until Joseph III should come of age. John Kirk Sheen stated of his father:

> Here he discovered the lineal priesthood doctrine and made a synopsis along that line from the Book of Mormon, and that synopsis is now before me. He wrote William Smith along that line and William and himself got together, first by letter, then personally. Isaac published a small paper for several months while William preached in Lee County, Illinois, and Cincinnati. . . . A conference was held in Covington in June, 1847, and although I was only about four and one half years of age I have distinct memory of the hall and gathering and it was there resolved that it was "young Joseph's right by lineage," etc., and that William should stand in his stead until Joseph should come of age. (ibid.)

William declared himself president of the Church of Jesus Christ of Latter Day Saints, and Isaac became a member of his First Presidency. Proof of this relationship is found in the fact that William and Isaac sent a petition dated December 31, 1849, "To the Honorable Senate of the United States of America in Congress assembled." The document was "against the admission of the Salt Lake Mormons into the Union as a State." The petition was signed by:

> William Smith
> Isaac Sheen
> Presidents of the church of Jesus Christ of Latter Day Saints.
> (National Archives, Record Group #46, Petition, p. 4)

Brigham's Polygamy Document Influenced Sheen

On August 29, 1852, at a special conference in Salt Lake City, a polygamous document was publicly introduced. The document was published in the *Deseret News Extra*, September 14, 1852. (It was later placed in the LDS Doctrine and Covenants as Section 132.) Brigham Young was assisted by Apostle Orson Pratt in forcing that document upon the Saints. Brigham boldly admitted that the document was not the original, but assured the Saints that what they heard read was a *copy* of a revelation given to Joseph Smith before his death. Brigham declared:

> The original copy of this revelation was burnt up. . . . Sister Emma burnt the original. (Supplement to *Millennial Star* 15 [1853]: 31; RLDS *History of the Church* 3:348)

Soon after Brigham and Orson introduced the polygamy document, Isaac Sheen was notified concerning it. On September 20 he wrote his letter condemning polygamy and sent it to the *Cincinnati Commercial* and the *Saturday Evening Post*. He wrote:

> They announce that polygamy is a doctrine "sent forth as a Standard of Universal Restoration for the Tribes of Israel, and for all nations". . . . A specimen of this kind of sophistry is presented by Mr. Pratt in his communication. (*True Latter Day Saints' Herald* 1 [January 1860]: 26)

Even though Sheen bitterly opposed Pratt's polygamous teachings, they stayed in contact with one another. Orson's teachings no doubt influenced Isaac's belief that Joseph had connections with polygamy, as the following shows:

When, in September, 1852, Apostle Orson Pratt went on a mission to England, he called on Mr. Sheen on his way East. (Editors Scott Facer Proctor and Maurine Jensen Proctor, *The Revised and Enhanced History of Joseph Smith By His Mother*, xxiii)

During Orson's visit, Isaac sold him a valuable manuscript—that of Lucy Mack Smith's history of Joseph Smith the Prophet. Sheen had evidently obtained the manuscript from William Smith or Almon Babbitt. Orson took the manuscript to England, where he published it in 1853 under the title of *Biographical Sketches of Joseph Smith, the Prophet, and His Progenitors for Many Generations* (see ibid., xxiii–xxiv; also Jan Shipps, *Mormonism—The Story of a New Religious Tradition*, 99–100).

Sheen and Pratt must have discussed polygamy during Orson's visit. Pratt, the husband of six wives, undoubtedly had a copy of the polygamous document in his possession, and would have shown it to Sheen. Pratt was on his way to Washington, D.C., to publish a paper called *The Seer*. The first issue was published January 1853, with the polygamous document on pages 7 to 11.

Babbitt Continued to Influence Sheen

Isaac's polygamous brother-in-law, Almon Babbitt, moved to Utah, where he became a delegate to Congress and Secretary of the Territory of Utah. He made several trips to Washington, D.C. (see LDS *Biographical Encyclopedia* 1:284). No doubt Almon visited his sister, Drusilla, and Isaac at every opportunity while traveling back and forth. In conversing with Isaac, Babbitt would have justified his own polygamy by assuring Sheen that Joseph had been a polygamist. The seemingly sincere testimonies of men such as Orson Pratt and Almon Babbitt evidently caused Sheen to continue to hold the wrong opinion about Joseph and the false doctrine of polygamy.

Edmund Briggs Speaks out against Sheen's Statements

Many in the Reorganization did not agree with the position Sheen took in the *Herald*. Apostle Edmund Briggs recorded his disappointment in these words:

> Gallands Grove, Iowa, January 30, 1860. I arrived at Bro. J. A. McIntosh's after a tedious ride in the cold. Found him in the best of spirits and hope in the reorganization of the church. And to my surprise here is the first number of the TRUE LATTER DAY SAINTS' HERALD. Have read it with much interest, though disappointed and sorry to find the letter of Elder I. Sheen of October 9, 1852, taken from the *Cincinnati Commercial*. He [Sheen] says . . . ["]The Salt Lake apostles also excuse themselves by saying that Joseph Smith taught the spiritual wife doctrine [polygamy]. . . . Joseph Smith repented of his connection with this doctrine and said it was of the Devil. He caused the revelation on this subject to be burned.["]
>
> Every public utterance and printed statement of Joseph, and Hyrum, his brother, before their cruel martyrdom, attests the fact that they never favored it in the least degree. But Bro. Sheen's letter in this first number of the HERALD will be used by our enemies against the true position of the Reorganization in relation to Joseph being responsible for that accursed doctrine. Bro. Sheen must have given credence to Young's lie, when he said, "Emma burned it." Emma told me she never saw such a revelation until it was published by [Orson] Pratt in the *Seer* [January 1853]. Young says she burned it; and now Elder Sheen says Joseph had it burned. That is a new statement and the first I had heard of it.
>
> I have met thousands of the old members of the church who were well acquainted with Joseph, and yet I never saw a man who heard Joseph teach polygamy; but they said that they had heard him denounce it as a corrupt doctrine.
>
> In the *Times and Seasons* for two years we had been warned against that abomination [polygamy] by Joseph and Hyrum Smith; and they took great pains to denounce it as a corrupt and wicked practice. And it is evident from Elder Marks' letter in this same HERALD that Joseph never had any

affiliation with it; and proposed immediately to make a thorough investigation and find out who were in any way favoring it, and cut them off from the church. Bro. Marks said this to me personally, referring to his talk with President Smith upon this conversation set out in this HERALD. He has not given it in full as he did to me.

I said to him, "Did you, when you had that conversation with Bro. Joseph, think he had been in any way mixed up in polygamy, or had favored it?"

He replied, "No. I had more confidence in him at that time than I ever had in all my life before, and was satisfied that he was pure from that gross crime. I had been troubled over the condition of the church for some time, and been fearful that Joseph did not bring the pressure against some men in the church that he should have done. You see from John C. Bennett's time there had been so many rumors going the rounds, I was fearful that there might be something in the stories afloat that might implicate Joseph. But Joseph was so free and positive in his denunciation of polygamy in every form, that I took courage; and I could see Joseph was in earnest and felt just as I did about it. But before the Sunday following our conversation, Joseph was having his suit [the lawsuit], and he was killed before he had a chance to commence his investigation against those whom he had suspicioned of teaching it privily. But I thought he had been deceived in some of the men and elders of the church, and had too much confidence in some of them. But I guess it was to be so to fulfill the Scriptures in relation to the latter-day apostasy."

I then said, "Bro. Marks, did you ever see the revelation on polygamy before it was published in 1852 [in the *Seer*] by Mr. Pratt?" Marks emphatically replied, "No, never."

"You were president of the stake at Nauvoo, and if Joseph had such a revelation, would you not have been privileged, according to custom, to have seen it, or heard of it?"

He replied, "Yes, without a doubt. There was no such revelation in existence during Joseph's life. Brigham Young and his clique got that up after Joseph's death; for if there had been any such revelation in existence when I lived in Nauvoo, just after Joseph's death, Brigham Young would have showed it to me when I opposed his measures. But he never pretended to any such thing to me, that there was such a revelation on the subject from Joseph". . . .

I am sorry on account of these errors. They are evidently the errors of Bro. Sheen, who has but lately united with the church. But I am really sorry that they are in the first HERALD. Our enemies will take advantage of them to do us an injury, if possible. May God help us is my fervent prayer. For the sake of the lambs of the church, right, only right, is all I want. By the grace of God helping me, for that will I ever contend while God gives me breath, in all these matters that affect our glorious church. Amen. (*Saints' Herald* 50 [April 22, 1903]: 363–364)

Joseph Smith III and Sheen Had Different Views

Isaac Sheen was editor for five years before Joseph III took editorial control of the *Herald*. Joseph had this to say about Sheen's editorial policies:

> had I been in control of the HERALD in its incipiency, I could not have subscribed to some of the views expressed and maintained in its opening issues. It seemed to me that they were based upon insufficient foundation. They were advanced by men older than myself and were held to tenaciously, and it seemed to them that the stability of the fabric which we were building depended upon these theories, and that a divergence from them would result disastrously. Under these conditions all I could do was to wait, watch, and pray, which I did, until better conditions prevailed. (ibid. 57 [January 26, 1910]: 77)

Conditions are even better today than they were in the days of Joseph III, for many documents which were not obtainable then are now available. These documents are proving, and will continue to reveal, that Joseph the Martyr was innocent of polygamy—and that that evil doctrine was brought into the Church by Brigham Young and his coconspirators.

Chapter 18

The Book of Mormon Condemns Polygamy
(A Study of the "Righteous Seed" Theory)

When many people first hear about the Book of Mormon, they assume that it is a history of Joseph Smith and that it teaches that polygamy is a doctrine of the Church. These are false assumptions, for the Book of Mormon is a history of God's dealings with the people of Ancient America, and it condemns polygamy most severely.

If this is true, one may ask, How is it that the Church of Jesus Christ of Latter-day Saints believes in polygamy? The answer is that the Mormon Church leaders of over a century ago practiced polygamy—but they did it in spite of the Book of Mormon's warnings against it. They did this by misinterpreting one statement in the book. They taught that polygamy was wrong—unless God gave the command to practice it, and then it became mandatory and a cardinal doctrine of their faith. They then proceeded to practice polygamy, claiming that God had commanded Joseph Smith to practice it and teach others to do so.

The Book of Mormon's Condemnation of Polygamy

There are a number of references in the Inspired Version of the Bible and the Doctrine and Covenants which condemn polygamy, and none which command it to be practiced—but the most scathing denunciation of polygamy in Joseph's writings is found in the Book of Jacob in the Book of Mormon. There the Lord gives an inspired message through His Nephite prophet, Jacob, more than three pages in length, which definitely forbids polygamy. It prophetically warns the Nephites that if they do not choose the Lord as their commander, they will choose to do *otherwise*—the *otherwise* being that they would degenerate into the sinful practice of polygamy.

It is important to review the circumstances under which the Prophet Jacob received this divine revelation forbidding polygamy. Years earlier, under God's direction, Jacob's older brother, Nephi, had directed the Nephites in building a temple. After Nephi's death, Jacob became the prophet-leader. The Lord commanded Jacob to go into the temple where the Nephites would be at worship, and bring to them a revelation condemning polygamy. In that revelation Jacob gave a stern condemnation of that dogma—and since Joseph Smith published the Book of Mormon and proclaimed that it contained the fullness of the gospel, the Lord's denouncement of polygamy through Jacob is also Joseph's testimony against that false doctrine. Jacob declared:

> the people of Nephi . . . began to grow hard in their hearts, and indulge themselves somewhat in wicked practices, such as like unto David of old, desiring many wives and concubines, and also Solomon, his son. . . . Wherefore, I, Jacob, gave unto them these words as I taught them in the temple, having firstly obtained mine errand from the Lord. (RLDS Jacob 1:15–17; LDS Jacob 1:15–17)

Below is a condensed portion of the Prophet Jacob's inspired message to his people in which he so strongly condemned polygamy:

> Now, my beloved brethren, I, Jacob, according to the responsibility which I am under to God . . . come up into the temple this day, that I might declare unto you the word of God. . . . [B]y the help of the all-powerful Creator of heaven and earth, I can tell you concerning your thoughts, how that ye are beginning to labor in sin, which sin appeareth very . . . abominable unto God. . . .
>
> Wherefore, it burdeneth my soul, that I should be constrained because of the strict commandment which I have received from God, to admonish you, according to your crimes. (RLDS Jacob 2:2–9; LDS Jacob 2:2–9)

This rebuke concerning other sins was sharp; however, the Lord gave Jacob words which were even more harsh in condemning the sin of polygamy:

> I must speak unto you concerning a *grosser crime*. . . . [T]he word of God burthens me because of your grosser crimes. For behold, thus saith the Lord, This people begin to wax in iniquity; they understand not the scriptures: for they seek to excuse themselves in committing whoredoms, because of the things which were written concerning David, and Solomon his son.
>
> *Behold, David and Solomon truly had many wives, and concubines, which thing was abominable before me, saith the Lord*, wherefore, thus saith the Lord, I have led this people forth out of the land of Jerusalem, by the power of mine arm, that I might raise up unto me a righteous branch from the fruit of the loins of Joseph. Wherefore, I, the Lord God, will not suffer that this people shall do like unto them of old.
>
> Wherefore, my brethren, hear me, and hearken to the word of the Lord: *For there shall not any man among you have save it be one wife; and concubines he shall have none: For I, the Lord God, delighteth in the chastity of women.* . . .
>
> Wherefore, this people shall keep my commandments, saith the Lord of hosts, or cursed be the land for their sakes. For if I will, saith the Lord of hosts, raise up seed unto me, I will command my people: *otherwise*, they shall hearken unto these things.
>
> For behold, I, the Lord, have seen the sorrow, and heard the mourning of the daughters of my people in the land of Jerusalem; yea, and in all the lands of my people, because of the wickedness and abominations of their husbands.
>
> And I will not suffer, saith the Lord of hosts, that the cries of the fair daughters of this people, which I have led out of the land of Jerusalem, shall come up unto me, against the men of my people, saith the Lord of hosts; for they shall not lead away captive, the daughters of my people . . . save I shall visit them with a sore curse, even unto destruction; for they shall not commit whoredoms, like unto them of old [David, Solomon, and others], saith the Lord of hosts. . . . [T]hese commandments were given to our father Lehi; wherefore, ye have known them before; and ye have come unto great condemnation. . . .[Ye] have done greater iniquity than the

Lamanites, our brethren. Ye have broken the hearts of your tender wives, and lost the confidence of your children . . . and the sobbings of their hearts ascend up to God against you . . . .

[W]o, wo, unto you that are not pure in heart. . . . [E]xcept ye repent, the land is cursed for your sakes; and the Lamanites . . . shall scourge you even unto destruction. . . . [T]he Lamanites . . . are more righteous than you; for they have not forgotten the commandments of the Lord, which were given unto our fathers, that they should have, save it were one wife: and concubines they should have none. . . . [T]his commandment they observe to keep; wherefore because of this observance in keeping this commandment [of one wife each], the Lord God will not destroy them, but . . . they shall become a blessed people. (RLDS Jacob 2:30-56; LDS Jacob 2:22-35; 3:1-6; italics added)

Mormon Church Misinterprets the Prophet Jacob's Statement

At the time of Joseph Smith's death, several of the apostles and other leaders (including some who had performed missionary work among the polygamous Cochranites in the state of Maine) were secretly involved in polygamy, as previously noted. During the last two years of Joseph's life, he was continuously engaged in attempting to stamp out the practice of polygamy in the Church. In the spring of 1844 Joseph decided to expose the polygamists openly, in spite of the fact that a number of high Church officials were involved in that practice. Joseph sought out the Nauvoo Stake President, High Priest William Marks, and asked his help in expelling from the Church those in transgression. Within a few weeks Joseph and Hyrum were killed (see *True Latter Day Saints' Herald* 1 [January 1860]: 26; RLDS *History of the Church* 2:733-734).

By June 27, 1844, the date of Joseph's death, Brigham Young was married to four women—his legal wife, Mary Ann Angell Young, Mrs. William Seely (Lucy Ann Decker Seely Young), Mrs. Henry Cobb (Augusta Adams Cobb Young), and Mrs. Harriet Elizabeth Cook Campbell Young (see Kate B.

Carter, *Brigham Young—His Wives and Family*, 12–15; Stewart, *Brigham Young and His Wives*, 84–86; *Utah Genealogical Magazine* 11 [April 1920]: 52–54). (For confirmation of Lucy Ann Decker's marriage to William Seely, see records of Isaac Perry Decker and Harriet Page Wheeler Decker in the Genealogical Society Library in Salt Lake City, Utah.)

On August 29, 1852, eight years after Joseph's death, Brigham publicly proclaimed polygamy by introducing a polygamous document (now Section 132 in the LDS Doctrine and Covenants), and placed the responsibility for that practice on Joseph (LDS DC 132, Introduction; Supplement to *Millennial Star* 15 [1853]: 31; RLDS *History of the Church* 3:348–349).

In the years which followed introduction of the polygamy document in Utah in 1852, there was a tremendous effort made by LDS Church leaders to find support for their polygamy. Like the Nephites of old, they justified their polygamy because of what the Old Testament states about David and Solomon. They were commanded by Section 132 to do as David and Solomon had done (which is contrary to the Scriptures). Many statements appear in their early publications which demonstrate how their leaders twisted biblical passages to give credence to the doctrine of polygamy. A prime example of how far they went is found in "A Lecture by President Orson Hyde, delivered at the General Conference, in the Tabernacle, Great Salt Lake City, October 6, 1854." The title of his lecture was "The Marriage Relations." Hyde tried to justify Mormon polygamy by declaring that "Jesus was the bridegroom at the marriage of Cana of Galilee," that Christ physically fathered children, that He was a polygamist, and that Mary Magdalene was one of His wives. Hyde also declared that when Mary Magdalene visited Christ's tomb and found it empty, she began to weep, and when the gardener asked her why she was weeping, Mary Magdalene replied, " 'Because they have taken away my Lord,' or husband" (*Journal of Discourses* 2 [1855]: 81–82).

Apostle Orson Pratt was another LDS Church leader who made a tremendous effort to support polygamy by wresting the Scriptures. He gave the initial sermon which announced polygamy as a doctrine, which he delivered in the Tabernacle, in Salt

Lake City, August 29, 1852, entitled "Celestial Marriage." He argued that (1) God has a vast number of human spirits in Heaven who are to be sent to earth and given bodies, (2) that God wants the more intelligent portion of them to be born into Mormon homes, and (3) that polygamy is necessary in order to have them born into those homes. Orson declared:

> among them are many spirits that are more noble, more intelligent than others, that were called the great and mighty ones, reserved until the dispensation of the fulness of times . . . . This is the reason why the Lord is sending them here, brethren and sisters; they are appointed to come and take their bodies here. . . .Then is it not reasonable, and consistent that the Lord should say unto His faithful and chosen servants . . . take unto yourselves more wives?" (*Journal of Discourses* 1 [1854]: 62–63)

The belief that God wants to use polygamy as a means to bring these souls into the world is a false doctrine, however, for the Lord has instructed that monogamy is to be used to "fill the measure of man." The scripture states:

> marriage is ordained of God unto man; wherefore it is lawful that he should have one wife, and they twain shall be one flesh, and all this that the earth might answer the end of its creation; and that it might be filled with the measure of man, according to his creation before the world was made. (RLDS DC 49:3a–c; LDS DC 49:15–17)

This scripture shows that a certain number of human spirits were created "before the world was made," and that when they all have been born into the world, the earth shall have been "filled with the measure of man." It is important to note that the Lord has declared that in order to do this, *each man is to have one wife*. Therefore, once again Mormon theology fails and polygamy is shown to be a false doctrine.

The speculation and unfounded interpretation of the Scriptures increased as the Mormon leaders, such as Hyde and Pratt, continued to justify polygamy and lay the blame for its entry into the Church upon the dead prophet, Joseph. In time the leaders of the Mormon Church tampered with the Doctrine and

Covenants by adding Section 132 in 1876, which commanded that polygamy must be practiced, as previously mentioned. They also deleted from their Doctrine and Covenants the section that is entitled "Marriage," which forbids polygamy (see RLDS DC 111; 1835 Kirtland Edition, Section CI; 1844 Nauvoo Edition, Section CIX; and the 1866 Liverpool [England] Edition (published by Brigham Young, Jun.), Section CIX).

The Mormon Church Tried to Use the "Righteous Seed" Theory to Justify Polygamy

The LDS Church also added an introduction to the second chapter of Jacob in the Book of Mormon which stated, "Plurality of wives forbidden because of iniquity" (LDS Jacob, chapter 2, heading). Joseph Smith did not place those words there. It was done after his death. A careful reading of the chapter reveals that the chapter heading which Mormon leaders added is a false statement, because the chapter does not say that God was withholding polygamy because the Saints were sinful. It says that polygamy was a "grosser" crime—worse than the other sins. The heading should read, "The people condemned for practicing polygamy and other sins." Again, it must be noted that Joseph Smith did not place that heading at the beginning of the chapter. The original Book of Mormon had no titles at the heads of chapters. The LDS Book of Mormon, copyrighted in 1948, states on the copyright page, "First issued . . . with chapter headings . . . in 1920."

During all of the theological struggles over the question of polygamy, Jacob's stern denunciation of it in the Book of Mormon has stood like a fortress against polygamy. Somehow the LDS polygamists had to find a way to invalidate it. At last they found a way which would at least placate their followers. It was to misinterpret one sentence in the revelation which came through the Prophet Jacob. That passage was:

> For if I will, saith the Lord of hosts, raise up seed unto me, I will command my people: otherwise, they shall hearken unto these things. (RLDS Jacob 2:39; LDS Jacob 2:30)

The "Righteous Seed" Theory

The Mormon Church leaders and missionaries still use the above passage to claim that God commanded them to practice polygamy to "raise up a righteous seed"—with the theory that children born of polygamy are more righteous than children born of monogamy, and that when God decides to establish an especially righteous people, He will command that they must practice polygamy.

They interpret this passage:

> For if I will, saith the Lord of hosts, raise up [righteous] seed [or people] unto me, I will command my people [to practice polygamy]: otherwise [if the Lord does not give the commandment to practice polygamy], they shall hearken unto these things [Jacob's instruction to not practice it].

This interpretation makes this passage completely out of harmony with all the rest of Jacob's revelation against polygamy, and all of Joseph Smith's writings which were printed before his death.

The true interpretation of the passage shows that it is definitely monogamous, and that it is in harmony with all the rest of the revelation which the Lord gave through Jacob. The true interpretation is:

> For if I will, saith the Lord of hosts, raise up [righteous] seed unto me, I will command my people [the Lord will be their commander—He will give them commandments to obey]: otherwise [if the Lord is not their commander; or they do not obey His commandments], they shall hearken unto these things [they shall practice the sins of polygamy].

This is the true meaning of this passage—and therefore it condemns polygamy, rather than justifying it as the Mormon Church leaders claim.

God Always Uses Monogamy to "Raise Up a Righteous Seed"

Since there are two ways to interpret the meaning of this

passage, it is necessary to discover which method God uses to raise up a "righteous seed" or generation. The Mormon Church leaders have strongly emphasized the "righteous seed theory" to justify their practice of polygamy, but it actually destroys their theological basis—for God always uses monogamy, and not polygamy, when He starts a new nation or civilization. When God chose in various dispensations to "raise up a righteous seed," in every instance He provided only one wife for one man.

Adam and Eve—the first example. When God and Christ created the first man, Adam, one woman (Eve) was created to be his wife. Centuries later God explained, "And did not he make one? . . . And wherefore one? *That he might seek a godly seed.* Therefore take heed to your spirit, and let none deal treacherously against the wife of his youth" (Malachi 2:15; italics added). Why then did God provide only one wife for Adam? *That he might raise up a righteous seed!* This is a most important point.

Noah and his three sons. During the days of Noah, wickedness abounded and the Lord destroyed all but eight people. Those eight were Noah, his three sons, and four women—one wife for each man. Now "Noah was a just man, and perfect in his generation; and he walked with God, and also his three sons, Shem, Ham, and Japheth" (Genesis 8:16, Inspired Version). If ever there was a time since Adam to "raise up a righteous seed," it was after the flood. Yet God chose monogamy as the way.

Lehi and his colony. The story of Lehi and those who accompanied him to Joseph's land, the Land of Promise, is another example of monogamy being God's law. Lehi and his people were divinely led to the Western Hemisphere. God's purpose in doing so was specifically to "*raise up unto me a righteous branch* from the fruit of the loins of Joseph [who was sold into Egypt]" (RLDS Jacob 2:34; LDS Jacob 2:25; italics added). Since that was the purpose, this would have been the perfect time for the Lord to have commanded the practice of polygamy, if the LDS theory were true. Yet, Lehi and all the males in his group had only one wife, which was in keeping with the law that God had given to him (RLDS Jacob 2:44; LDS Jacob 2:34).

In Lehi's company there were four single adult sons and Zoram—and no single women. Nephi records that "the Lord spake unto him [Lehi] again, saying, that it was not meet for him, Lehi, that he should take his family into the wilderness alone; but that his sons should take daughters to wife, *that they might raise up seed unto the Lord* in the land of promise. And it came to pass that the Lord commanded him [Lehi] that I, Nephi, and my brethren, should again return unto the land of Jerusalem, and bring down Ishmael and his family." There were five unmarried daughters in Ishmael's family. "And it came to pass that I, Nephi, took one of the daughters of Ishmael to wife; and also, my brethren took of the daughters of Ishmael to wife; and also, Zoram took the eldest daughter of Ishmael to wife" (RLDS 1 Nephi 2:7–8; 5:7–8; LDS 1 Nephi 7:1–2; 16:7–8; italics added).

A modern-day example. When God restored His Church to the earth for the last time through the Prophet Joseph Smith, He once again moved to establish a righteous people. The Lord spoke through Joseph in 1831, saying:

> And that ye might escape the power of the enemy, and be gathered unto me *a righteous people*, without spot and blameless: wherefore, for this cause I gave unto you the commandment, that ye should go to the Ohio; and there I will give unto you my law. (RLDS DC 38:7; LDS DC 38:31–32; italics added)

The Saints gathered to Kirtland as a result of this revelation and were blessed with receiving the law of God—the revelation of February 9, 1831. And what was in the law concerning marriage which the Almighty gave the Saints when they arrived at Kirtland, that they might become *a righteous people* (branch or seed)? It was:

> Thou shalt love thy wife with all thy heart, and shall cleave unto her and *none* else; and he that looketh upon a [another] woman to lust after her, shall deny the faith, and shall not have the Spirit; and if he repents not, he shall be cast

out. (RLDS DC 42:7d; LDS DC 42:22–23; italics added)

Summary

Joseph Smith brought forth the Inspired Version of the Bible and the revelations in the Doctrine and Covenants. They too support the Book of Mormon's position condemning polygamy. In addition to these Three Standard Books, under Joseph's leadership the following periodicals were produced: the *Evening and the Morning Star*, the *Messenger and Advocate*, the *Elders' Journal*, and the *Times and Seasons*. A careful reading of these Church papers published during Joseph's lifetime shows that they all support the Book of Mormon's testimony against polygamy. There is not even a faint hint in any Church publication before Joseph's death on June 27, 1844, that polygamy could be right under any condition or circumstance.

God's use of monogamy in the days of Adam, Noah, Lehi, and Joseph Smith is proof that when God desires to raise up a righteous seed, He uses only monogamy to do so. It proves beyond all doubt that the LDS Church's "righteous seed" theory to justify polygamy is utterly false. God is the great Commander, and the people must follow His commands—otherwise they go against His law and fall into polygamy and similar sins, as Jacob warns.

It is time to put the words *otherwise* and *righteous seed*, as found in the Book of Jacob, into their proper context and proclaim that polygamy is a false doctrine, and that the Book of Mormon, brought forth through the Prophet Joseph Smith, is a conclusive witness against this false doctrine. Truly, the Book of Mormon condemns polygamy!

Chapter 19

Joseph's Sermon against Polygamy

Joseph Smith's sermon in which he denied being a polygamist is a fitting closing for this volume, even though there are many more conclusive proofs of his innocence in the long and complicated story of Utah Mormon polygamy. The additional proofs are to be treated in later volumes.

In 1844 William Law, a former member of the First Presidency at Nauvoo, formed a conspiracy along with others to depose Joseph and take the leadership of the Church from him. This group of conspirators went so far as to organize a new church called the "Reformed Mormon Church" and issue a call to the Saints to reject Joseph and join the new church (see the *Nauvoo Expositor*, Friday, June 7, 1844). William Law and others also went to the county seat at Carthage and gave testimonies which resulted in three indictments being brought against Joseph. One accused him of being guilty of polygamy. The story of this conspiracy will take several chapters in a later volume to discuss in detail, but Joseph's sermon in answer to the polygamy charge is of utmost value here.

William Marks, a member of the grand jury, and Joseph's devoted friend, made him aware of the grand jury's indictments. The news of the indictments arrived in Nauvoo on Saturday, May 25, a month before Joseph's martyrdom, and spread like a prairie fire. By ten o'clock the next morning when the Sunday worship services began, thousands of Saints gathered at the Stand (an outdoor meeting place near the Temple) to hear the Prophet discuss the indictments. Thomas Bullock, one of Joseph's secretaries, recorded the sermon, which appears today in the LDS Church history under the title, "Address of the Prophet—His Testimony Against the Dissenters at Nauvoo."

Excerpts from that sermon are given below. (It is recommended that the reader study the entire sermon in the LDS *History of the Church, Period I,* 6:408–412.)

Joseph declared:

> Another indictment has been got up against me [the polygamy indictment]. It appears a holy prophet [William Law] has arisen up, and he has testified against me [causing the polygamy indictment to be brought forth]. . . . God knows, then, that the charges against me are false.
>
> *I had not been married scarcely five minutes, and made one proclamation of the Gospel, before it was reported that I had seven wives.* I mean to live and proclaim the truth as long as I can.
>
> This new holy prophet [William Law] has gone to Carthage and swore that I had told him that I was guilty of adultery. *This spiritual wifeism! Why, a man dares not speak or wink, for fear of being accused of this.* . . .William Law . . . swears that I have committed adultery. I wish the grand jury would tell me who they [the alleged wives] are—whether it will be a curse or blessing to me. . . .
>
> A man asked me whether the commandment [revelation] was given that a man may have seven wives; and now the new prophet has charged me with adultery. . . . Wilson Law [William's brother] also swears that I told him I was guilty of adultery. . . . I have rattled chains before in a dungeon for truth's sake. *I am innocent of all these charges, and you can bear witness of my innocence, for you know me yourselves . . . .What a thing it is for a man to be accused of committing adultery, and having seven wives, when I can only find one.*
>
> I am the same man, and as innocent as I was fourteen years ago [when charged with polygamy shortly after his marriage to Emma Hale]; and I can prove them all perjurers. (LDS *History of the Church* 6:410–411; italics added)

This sermon is extremely important because in it Joseph Smith declared, just one month and one day before his martyrdom, that he had only one wife. In other words, he declared that he was not a polygamist. It is significant that this sermon is published by the LDS Church itself, in its most important history. The sermon alone proves that Joseph was not a polygamist.

There are a number of points in the sermon which deserve close analysis:

1. *I had not been married scarcely five minutes . . . before it was reported that I had seven wives.* Joseph was plagued with polygamy rumors all his public life and always denied being a polygamist. Either he told the truth and was a true prophet; or he was a polygamist who was a liar and base deceiver, and was therefore a fraud and a false prophet. There is no half-way situation in this matter. As previously stated, he never hesitated to tell the truth about any other doctrine, in spite of persecution—which is evidence that he was also telling the truth in this case.

2. *This spiritual wifeism! Why, a man dares not speak or wink, for fear of being accused of this.* This is a reference to Dr. Bennett's teachings two years earlier that Joseph taught that "promiscuous intercourse between the sexes, was a doctrine believed in by the Latter-Day Saints . . . that myself and others of the authorities of the church not only sanctioned, but practiced the same wicked acts" (*Times and Seasons* 3 [July 1, 1842]: 839–840). Joseph is declaring that spiritual wifery rumors are still prevalent in Nauvoo, and that they are all false.

3. *A man asked me whether the commandment was given that a man may have seven wives.* If Joseph had been guilty of polygamy, and was trying to keep it secret as the Utah polygamists claim, he certainly would not have made this statement. The truth is that he wanted to get the whole matter out in the open and to put a stop to the polygamous activities which some of the apostles and their friends were practicing at the time.

4. *What a thing it is for a man to be accused of . . . having seven wives, when I can only find one.* Here is a definite declaration by the Prophet that he had only one wife—Emma. This statement alone answers the question of whether or not

he was guilty of polygamy. Those who later claimed that he had more wives were polygamists themselves, who used his name to cover their own crimes of polygamy. Or, like William Law, claimed Joseph was a polygamist in order to depose him.

5. *I can prove them all perjurers.* Joseph's statement that "I can prove them all perjurers" was very significant, for it meant that he had foreseen the coming problem of being accused of polygamy and had taken the measures to be able to prove that he was innocent. He declared in the same sermon:

> For the last three years I have a record of all my acts and proceedings, for I have kept several good, faithful, and efficient clerks in constant employ; they have accompanied me everywhere, and carefully kept my history, and they have written down what I have done, where I have been, and what I have said; therefore my enemies cannot charge me with any day, time, or place, but what I have written testimony to prove my actions; and my enemies cannot prove anything against me. (LDS *History of the Church* 6:409)

Unfortunately, Joseph's carefully laid plans to prove his innocence were thwarted by Brigham Young and his followers—for they took Joseph's papers with them to Utah and kept them from the public.

Joseph Smith III (son of the Martyr) explained:

> At the death of my father, Joseph W. Coolidge was appointed administrator of the estate. . . . The private and personal correspondence of my father, many books and some other matters of personal character were in his office in care of [Apostle] Willard Richards, and others, clerks and officials. These were either retained by the administrator upon his own responsibility; or were refused to my mother's demand at the direction of the Twelve; the latter we were at the time led to believe. . . . In answer to repeated demands for my father's private papers, journal and correspondence, made by my mother, there was an invariable denial. (Edward W. Tullidge, *Life of Joseph the Prophet*, 744–745)

In another account Joseph III stated concerning the LDS leaders' refusal to return his father's private papers to Emma:

> His private records, biography, portions of history—family and general—manuscripts, memoranda, and parts of his library were all included in this refusal to comply with Mother's request. (*Saints' Herald* 82 [January 29, 1935]: 144)

Most of the "good, faithful, and efficient clerks" were not good and faithful to Joseph. Some were polygamists themselves, and they rewrote Joseph's history under Brigham's direction to make it appear that Joseph was the author of polygamy. The Mormon Church has published, "Moreover, since the death of the Prophet Joseph, the history has been carefully revised under the strict inspection of President Brigham Young, and approved by him" (LDS *History of the Church* 1:v–vi).

Elder Charles Wandell, upon reading Joseph's history as published by the LDS Church, declared that Joseph's history had been changed. He asserted:

> I notice these interpolations because having been employed (myself) in the Historian's office at Nauvoo by Doctor Richards, and employed, too, in 1845, in compiling this very autobiography, I know that after Joseph's death his memoir was "doctored" to suit the new order of things, and this, too, by the direct order of Brigham Young to Doctor Richards and systematically by Richards. (RLDS *History of the Church* 4:97)

After Joseph's death, Brigham Young expanded his polygamous base by bringing more and more Saints into the polygamy fold. After he had led his followers to Utah and Joseph had been dead for eight years, Brigham publicly presented to the Saints a mysterious document (Section 132 of the LDS Doctrine and Covenants). He claimed that it was only a copy of an original revelation which Joseph had received. Brigham claimed that he had kept the copy secretly hidden in his desk. He declared:

> This revelation has been in my possession many years; and who has known it? None but those who should know it.

I keep a patent lock on my desk, and there does not anything leak out that should not. (Supplement to *Millennial Star* 15 [1853]: 31; RLDS *History of the Church* 3:349)

The mystery which was "had in secret chambers" for years was now made public. That mystery was polygamy! Joseph Smith fought against polygamy all of his public life, but Brigham Young managed to bring it into the Church in spite of Joseph's efforts to keep it out.

Joseph Smith Fought Polygamy
Is to Be Continued

This present volume documents the story of Joseph's struggle to keep polygamy out of the Church up to the summer months of 1842, but there is much more important information concerning the problem as it transpired after that date. During the two years that preceded Joseph's death, he continued his efforts—ever trying to eradicate the doctrine and practice. Eight years after Joseph's death Brigham Young and his polygamous associates made polygamy a cardinal doctrine by falsely declaring that Joseph had received a revelation commanding its practice. There is much evidence that Joseph gave no such revelation, and that the instituting of the dogma was a fraudulent act upon the part of the Mormon Church leaders, who were themselves the instigators.

Further information on this subject is being published serially in the *Vision* magazine, which is available from Price Publishing Company, 915 E. 23rd. St., Independence, MO 64055. It is planned that this additional material will be compiled in future volumes.

Selected Bibliography

Affidavits and Certificates Disproving the Statements and Affidavits Contained in John C. Bennett's Letters. Two-sided broadside published in Nauvoo, Illinois, August 31, 1842. Published under the direction of Joseph Smith.

American Heritage. New York, N. Y.: American Heritage Publishing Co., 1965.

An American Prophet's Record: The Diaries and Journals of Joseph Smith. Edited by Scott H. Faulring. Salt Lake City, Utah: Signature Books in association with Smith Research Associates, 1989.

Arrington, Leonard J. *Brigham Young: American Moses.* New York: Alfred A. Knopf, 1985.

Autumn Leaves: Published for the Youth of the Reorganized Church of Jesus Christ of Latter Day Saints. Marietta Walker, founder and first editor. Lamoni, Iowa, 1888–1928.

Barron, Howard H. *Orson Hyde—Missionary, Apostle, Colonizer.* Bountiful, Utah: Horizon Publishers, 1977.

Beecher, Maureen Ursenbach. *Eliza and Her Sisters.* Salt Lake City, Utah: Aspen Books, 1991.

Bennett, John C. *The History of the Saints; or, An Exposé of Joe Smith and Mormonism.* Boston: Leland & Whiting; New York: Bradbury, Soden, & Co.; Cincinnati: E. S. Norris & Co., 1842.

Book of Mormon, The. Translated by Joseph Smith, Jr. Independence, Missouri: Herald Publishing House for the Reorganized Church of Jesus Christ of Latter Day Saints, 1908.

Book of Mormon, The. Translated by Joseph Smith, Jun. Salt Lake City, Utah: Published by the Church of Jesus Christ of Latter-day Saints, 1952.

Bourne, Edward E. *The History of Wells and Kennebunk* [Counties, Maine]. Salt Lake City, Utah: Utah Genealogical Society, 1875.

Brodie, Fawn. *No Man Knows My History: The Life of Joseph Smith, the Mormon Prophet.* New York: Alfred A. Knopf, 1971.

Cannon, George Q. *The Life of Joseph Smith the Prophet.* Salt Lake City, Utah: The Deseret News, 1907.

Carter, Kate B. *Brigham Young—His Wives and Family.* Salt Lake City, Utah: Utah Printing Company; published by Daughters of Utah Pioneers.

———, comp. *Our Pioneer Heritage.* Salt Lake City, Utah: Utah Printing Company, 1973; published by Daughters of Utah Pioneers.

Chamberlain, Ralph V. *The University of Utah: A History of Its First Hundred Years, 1850–1950.* Edited by Harold W. Bentley. Salt Lake City, Utah: University of Utah Press, 1960.

"Cochran Fanaticism in York County, The." [Typed manuscript, dated August 3, 1867; compiler quotes "From the manuscript letter of P. Huntoon, Esq., . . . of Enfield, N. H. . . . July 1866"]. Maine Historical Society.

Complainant's Abstract of Pleading and Evidence in the Circuit Court of the United States, Western District of Missouri, Western Division of Kansas City. The Reorganized Church of Jesus Christ of Latter Day Saints, Complainant, vs. The Church of Christ at Independence, Missouri . . . Respondents. Lamoni, Iowa: Herald Publishing House and Bindery, 1893 (see *Temple Lot Case*).

Cross, Whitney R. *The Burned-Over District: The Social and Intellectual History of Enthusiastic Religion in Western New York, 1800–1850.* Ithaca and London: Cornell University Press, 1950.

DC (see Doctrine and Covenants).

Davis, Inez Smith. *The Story of the Church.* Independence, Missouri: Herald Publishing House, 1955.

Deseret News. Salt Lake City, Utah: Church of Jesus Christ of Latter-day Saints, 1850–1898.

Deseret News (weekly). Salt Lake City, Utah: Church of Jesus Christ of Latter-day Saints.

Deseret Semi-Weekly News. Salt Lake City, Utah: Church of Jesus Christ of Latter-day Saints.

Dixon, William Hepworth. *Spiritual Wives.* 2 vols. London: Hurst and Blackett, Publishers, 1868.

Doctrine and Covenants of the Church of the Latter Day Saints. Kirtland, Ohio: Printed by F. G. Williams & Co., 1835.

Doctrine and Covenants of the Church of Jesus Christ of Latter Day Saints, The. Second Edition. Nauvoo, Illinois: Printed by John Taylor, 1844.

Doctrine and Covenants of the Church of Jesus Christ of Latter-Day Saints, The Book of. Fifth European Edition. Stereotyped. Liverpool [England]: Published by Brigham Young, Jun., 1866.

Doctrine and Covenants, Book of. Independence, Missouri: Herald Publishing House for the Reorganized Church of Jesus Christ of Latter Day Saints, 1950 (see RLDS DC).

Doctrine and Covenants of the Church of Jesus Christ of Latter-day Saints, The. Salt Lake City, Utah: Published by the Church of Jesus Christ of Latter-day Saints, 1952 (see LDS DC).

Doctrine and Covenants Student Manual, The. Salt Lake City, Utah: The Church of Jesus Christ of Latter-day Saints, 1981.

Elders' Journal of the Church of Latter Day Saints. Kirtland, Ohio, October 1837–November 1837; *Elders' Journal of the Church of*

Jesus Christ of Latter Day Saints. Far West Missouri, July 1838–August 1838.

Encyclopedia Americana. New York: Americana Corporation, 1954.

England, Breck. *The Life and Thought of Orson Pratt.* Salt Lake City, Utah: University of Utah Press, 1985.

Ensign of the Church of Jesus Christ of Latter Day Saints, The. Salt Lake City, Utah.

Evans, R. C. *Autobiography of Elder R. C. Evans: One of the First Presidency of the Reorganized Church of Jesus Christ of Latter Day Saints.* London, Ont.: Advertiser Printing Co., 1907.

Evening and the Morning Star, The. Independence, Missouri: W. W. Phelps & Co., June 1832–July 1833; Kirtland, Ohio: F. G. Williams & Co., December 1833–September 1834.

Gates, Susa Young. *The Life Story of Brigham Young.* New York: The MacMillan Company, 1930.

Historical Record, The: A Monthly Periodical. Devoted Exclusively to Historical, Biographical, Chronological and Statistical Matters. Edited and Published by Andrew Jenson. Salt Lake City, Utah, May 1887.

History of the Church of Jesus Christ of Latter-day Saints, Period I. 6 vols. Salt Lake City, Utah: The Deseret Book Company, 1978 (see LDS *History of the Church*).

History of the Reorganized Church of Jesus Christ of Latter Day Saints, The. 8 vols. Independence, Missouri: Herald House, 1951 (see RLDS *History of the Church*).

Holy Scriptures, The. Translated and Corrected by Joseph Smith, Jr. Plano, Illinois: Herald Publishing House, 1867 (see Inspired Version).

Illinois State Register. Periodical. Springfield, Illinois.

Inspired Version. Published by the Reorganized Church of Jesus Christ of Latter Day Saints (see Holy Scriptures, The).

Jacob. The Book of Jacob in the Book of Mormon.

Jenson, Andrew. *LDS Biographical Encyclopedia.* 4 vols. Salt Lake City: Andrew Jenson Historical Co., 1901–1936.

Journal of Discourses. 26 vols. London: Latter-Day Saints' Book Depot, 1854–1886.

Journal of History. 18 vols. 1908–1921, Lamoni, Iowa; April 1921–1925, Independence, Missouri: Published by the Reorganized Church of Jesus Christ of Latter Day Saints.

Journal of Orson Hyde (February 1832–December 1832). Salt Lake City, Utah: Church of Jesus Christ of Latter-day Saints Archives [typescript].

Journals of William E. McLellin, 1831–1836, The. Edited by Jan Shipps and John W. Welch. Provo, Utah: *BYU Studies*, Brigham Young University; Urbana and Chicago: University of Illinois Press, 1994.

Kimball, Stanley B. *Heber C. Kimball—Mormon Patriarch and Pioneer.* Urbana, Chicago, London: University of Illinois Press, 1981.

Kirtland Elders' Quorum Record: 1836–1841. Edited by Lyndon W. Cook and Milton V. Backman, Jr. Provo, Utah: Grandin Book Company, 1985.

LDS (Church of Jesus Christ of Latter-day Saints—Mormon).

LDS DC (see Doctrine and Covenants of the Church of Jesus Christ of Latter-day Saints, The. Salt Lake City, Utah).

LDS *History of the Church* (see *History of the Church of Jesus Christ of Latter-day Saints.* Salt Lake City, Utah).

Lamoni Gazette "Supplement." Periodical. Lamoni, Iowa.

Latter Day Saints' Messenger and Advocate. 3 vols. Kirtland, Ohio: F. G. Williams & Co., 1834–1837.

Latter-Day Saints' Millennial Star, The. Manchester and Liverpool, England, 1840–1970.

McConkie, Bruce R. *Mormon Doctrine.* Salt Lake City, Utah: Bookcraft, 1979.

Magill, Frank N., Editor. *Critical Survey of Drama: Foreign Language Series.* Englewood Cliffs, N. J.: Salem Press.

Messenger and Advocate (see *Latter Day Saints' Messenger and Advocate*).

Messenger of the Reorganized Church of Jesus Christ of Latter Day Saints, The. Edited by Jason W. Briggs. Salt Lake City, Utah, 1874–1877.

Millennial Star (see *Latter-Day Saints' Millennial Star*).

Missionary Journal of Samuel Harrison Smith—1832. Provo, Utah: Brigham Young University Library [typescript].

Nauvoo Expositor. Nauvoo, Illinois, Friday, June 7, 1844 (one issue only). Publishers: William Law, Wilson Law, Charles Ivins, Francis M. Higbee, Chauncey L. Higbee, Robert D. Foster, Charles A. Foster.

Nauvoo Neighbor. Weekly periodical edited by John Taylor. Nauvoo, Illinois, 1843–1845.

Nephi, 1. The Book of 1 Nephi in the Book of Mormon.

Newell, Linda King, and Valeen Tippetts Avery. *Mormon Enigma: Emma Hale Smith.* Garden City, New York: Doubleday & Company, Inc., 1984.

New York Herald. Periodical edited by James Gordon Bennett. New York City, New York.

Papers of Joseph Smith: Autobiographical and Historical Writings, The. Volume 1. Edited by Dean C. Jessee. Salt Lake City, Utah: Deseret Book Company, 1989.

People vs. Chauncey L. Higbee, The (court case). Hancock County Courthouse, Carthage, Illinois.

Personal Writings of Eliza Roxcy Snow, The. Edited by Maureen Ursenbach Beecher. Salt Lake City, Utah: University of Utah Press, 1995.

Pratt, Parley P. *Autobiography of Parley Parker Pratt.* Salt Lake City, Utah: Deseret Book Company, 1970.

Quincy Whig. Periodical. Quincy, Illinois. Illinois State Historical Library, Springfield, Illinois.

RLDS (Reorganized Church of Jesus Christ of Latter Day Saints).

RLDS DC (see Doctrine and Covenants, The Book of. Independence, Missouri).

RLDS *History of the Church* (see *History of the Reorganized Church of Jesus Christ of Latter Day Saints, The.* Independence, Missouri).

Red Brick Store Daybook. Record kept at Joseph Smith's Red Brick Store, Nauvoo, Illinois.

Regional Studies in Latter-day Saint History: Illinois. Edited by H. Dean Garret. Provo, Utah: Brigham Young University, 1995.

Remich, Daniel. *History of Kennebunk from Its Earliest Settlement to 1890: Including Biographical Sketches.* Salt Lake City, Utah. Genealogical Society of Utah Library.

Revised and Enhanced History of Joseph Smith By His Mother, The. Edited by Scot Facer Proctor and Maurine Jensen Proctor. Salt Lake City, Utah: Bookcraft, Inc., 1996.

Ridlon, Sr., G. T. *Saco Valley Settlements and Families: Historical, Biographical, Genealogical, Traditional, and Legendary.* Portland, Maine: Published by the author, 1895. Genealogical Society of Utah Library.

Saints' Herald (see *True Latter Day Saints' Herald, The*).

Sangamo Journal. Periodical edited by Simeon Francis. Springfield, Illinois.

Seer, The. 2 vols. Edited by Orson Pratt. Washington City, D.C., January 1853–August 1854.

Shipps, Jan. *Mormonism: The Story of a New Religious Tradition.* Urbana and Chicago: University of Illinois Press, 1985.

Smith, Alexander H. *Polygamy: Was It an Original Tenet of the Church of Jesus Christ of Latter Day Saints?* [tract]. Lamoni, Iowa: Published by the Reorganized Church of Jesus Christ of Latter Day Saints.

Smith, Andrew F. *The Saintly Scoundrel: The Life and Times of Dr.*

John Cook Bennett. Urbana and Chicago: University of Illinois Press, 1997.

Smith, Esq., Gamaliel E. *Report of the Trial of Jacob Cochrane on Sundry Charges of Adultery and Lewd and Lascivious Conduct Before the Supreme Judicial Court.* Kennebunk [Maine]: Printed by James K. Remich, 1819. New York City Public Library.

Smith III, Joseph. *Reply to Orson Pratt* [tract]. Lamoni, Iowa: Published by the Reorganized Church of Jesus Christ of Latter Day Saints.

Smith, Lucy. *Biographical Sketches of Joseph Smith the Prophet and His Progenitors for Many Generations.* Lamoni, Iowa: Herald Publishing House for the Reorganized Church of Jesus Christ of Latter Day Saints, 1908.

Smith-Sheen Petition (31 Congress, 1st Session). National Archives, Record Group #46.

Spencer, Clarissa Young. *Brigham Young at Home.* Salt Lake City, Utah: Deseret Book Company, 1961.

Statutes of Illinois, Criminal Code. Section 121–122.

Stewart, John J. *Brigham Young and His Wives: And the True Story of Plural Marriage.* Salt Lake City, Utah: Mercury Publishing Company, Inc., 1961.

Stinchfield, Ephraim (A Watchman). *Cochranism Delineated: or, a Description of, and Specific for a Religious Hydrophobia, Which Has Spread, and Is Still Spreading, in a Number of the Towns in the Counties of York and Cumberland: District of Maine.* Boston: Printed for N. Coverly, Milk-Street, 1819. Library of Congress.

Temple Lot Case (see *Complainant's Abstract of Pleading and Evidence*).

Testament of the Twelve Patriarchs, the Sons of Jacob, The. Manchester, England: Published by Elder Samuel Downes, 1843.

Times and Seasons. 6 vols. Commerce-Nauvoo, Illinois: Church of Jesus Christ of Latter Day Saints, November 1839–February 1846.

True Latter Day Saints' Herald, The. Cincinatti, Ohio (January 1860–March 1863); Plano, Illinois (April 1863–October 1881); Lamoni, Iowa (November 1881–April 1921); Independence, Missouri (May 1921–Present): Reorganized Church of Jesus Christ of Latter Day Saints (see *Saints' Herald*; name changed to *Saints' Herald* on January 1, 1877).

Tullidge, Edward W. *Life of Joseph the Prophet.* New York, 1878.

———. *The Women of Mormondom.* New York, 1877.

Utah Genealogical and Historical Magazine, The. Salt Lake City, Utah: The Deseret Press; published by the Genealogical Society of Utah.

Van Wagoner, Richard S. *Sidney Rigdon: A Portrait of Religious Excess.* Salt Lake City, Utah: Signature Books, 1994.

Van Wagoner, Richard S., and Steven C. Walker. *A Book of Mormons.* Salt Lake City, Utah: Signature Books, 1982.

Waite, Mrs. C. V. *The Mormon Prophet and His Harem: or, An Authentic History of Brigham Young, His Numerous Wives and Children.* Cambridge: Printed for the author and sold by subscription; C. F. Vent and Company, Cincinnati, Ohio, 1867.

Warsaw Signal. Weekly periodical edited by Thomas C. Sharp. Warsaw, Illinois.

Wasp, The. Weekly periodical edited by William Smith. Nauvoo, Illinois, 1842–1843.

Whitmer Historical Association Journal, The John. Lamoni, Iowa: John Whitmer Historical Association, 1990.

Wyl, Dr. W. [Wilhelm]. *Mormon Portraits or the Truth about the Mormon Leaders from 1830 to 1886.* Salt Lake City, Utah: Tribune Printing and Publishing Company, 1886.

INDEX

abortion, 138, 140, 164
Adam and Eve
    example of monogamy, 227
Adams, High Priest George J.
    consultant and advisor to Joseph Smith, 37
    missionary to England, 37
    polygamist, 37
    witness for Henry Cobb divorce, 37–38
adultery, 13
    Brigham with Elizabeth Mayer, 35
    Chauncey Higbee charged with, 142
    Cochran arraigned on, 13
    John C. Bennett, guilty of, 118
    shall not commit, 57, 163
affidavits
    Catharine Fuller Warren, 138
    denying seraglio, 197
    Hyrum Smith, 163–166
    Joseph Smith, 145–146
    Margaret J. Nyman, 135–136
    Matilda J. Nyman, 136–137
    Nauvoo City Council, 181
    Sarah Miller, 137–138
    William Law, 166–167
all things common, 11, 16
America, 41
Andrews, Captain, a Cochranite, 24
Angell, Mary Ann
    wife of Brigham Young, 209
apostles, 29, 41, 43–44, 61
arrest warrant
    for Chauncey Higbee, 146–147
article on Marriage
    adopted at Kirtland, 51
    deleted by Brigham Young's administration, 51

Babbitt, Almon
    elected president of the stake in Kirtland, 210
    followed Brigham Young, 211
    has contact with Isaac Sheen, 209, 214
    political career, 214
    polygamist, 211, 214
Babbitt, Drusilla, 211
Bailey, Mary
    married Samuel Smith, 29
Barker, Mary
    wife of John Bennett, 112–114
Bennett, James Gordon
    editor of the *New York Herald*, 190
Bennett, John C.
    abuses wife, 114
    accuses Joseph of treason, 183
    acknowledged own guilt, 127–128, 164–165
    acquainted with Church leaders, 63–65
    acquainted with Eliza Snow's family, 78–79
    acquainted with Sidney Rigdon, 78
    affair with Sarah Pratt, 133
    arrives at Nauvoo, 69, 79, 111
    attempts suicide, 114
    background, 77–78
    baptized, 64, 69
    begged forgiveness, 128, 165
    boards at Joseph's home, 79
    brought before Masonic Lodge, 167
    built house of ill fame, 128–129
    Campbellite preacher, 113
    candidate for Illinois House of Representatives, 175–176
    caused Oliver Snow to leave Nauvoo, 98
    character investigated, 114–115
    conduct of, 163–164
    criminal acts, 164
    dark side to personality, 111
    divorced wife, 86

drained swamps, 114
elected Brigadier General, 67
expelled from Church, 167, 173, 174
expelled from Masonic Lodge, 167
expelled from Nauvoo Legion, 167, 174
husband of Mary Barker, 112–113
Joseph's official statement concerning, 169–170
laid the foundation of polygamy at Nauvoo, 63
leaves Nauvoo, 173, 174
led youth to tread in his unhallowed steps, 133
letter from, 156
lies about meaning of Zion, 183–184
mayor of Nauvoo, 114
medical doctor, 65–66
meets Joseph, 64–65
minister in Christian Disciples Church, 63
moved to Fairfield, Illinois, 66
ordered to appear before High Council, 161
organized Masonic Lodge, 111
pact with editor of *Sangamo Journal*, 176–177
plausible tale, 134
professes Joseph to be virtuous, 168
Professor of Diseases of Women and Children, 65
Professor of Principles and Practices of Midwifery, 65
promoted schools, 114
quartermaster general, 68, 72
rejected Eliza Snow, 86
removed as mayor, 167
repented, but continued to practice spiritual wifery, 133, 164
requests interview with Joseph, 164–165
scheme, 71
Sidney Rigdon previously knew, 63–64
signs statement of Joseph's innocence, 165–166
six letters, 178, 184
statement of, 167–168
sworn statement of, 165–166
teaches false doctrine of spiritual wifery to young people, 72
to meet with Joseph and Sidney Rigdon, 64
to Missouri to promote prosecution of Joseph, 182
tries to poison a husband, 164
unfaithful to wife, 113
warning brought, 112
birth control, 96
Boggs, Joseph O.
brother of Lilburn W., 182
Boggs, Lilburn W.
Joseph implicated in shooting, 156
shot, 155–156, 182
Book of Mormon
condemns polygamy, 219
Boone County, Missouri, 68
Booneville, Missouri
Isaac Sheen takes family to, 211–212
Briggs, Apostle Edmund
statement against Isaac Sheen's position, 215–217
Briggs, Jason
editor of the *Messenger*, 34
Brodie, Fawn, 89–90
Brotherton, Elizabeth
first plural wife of Parley P. Pratt, 58
Brotherton, Martha
affair with John Bennett, 162
Bennett's charge, 186
claim of, against Brigham Young and Joseph, 133–134
English immigrant, 162
Bullock, Thomas
Joseph Smith's secretary, 231
Buxton, Maine, 4, 16

Carlin, Governor Thomas, 67, 156
Carthage, Illinois
 Bennett writes from, 182
 Joseph sued Chauncey Higbee in Circuit Court, 142, 143
Carthage Jail
 Joseph and Hyrum murdered in, 183
celestial marriage
 Alexander Smith writes on, 74–75
certificates, 203–205
Choir of Singers
 Joseph's speech to, condemned polygamy, 134
Christian Disciples Church, 63
chronology
 geographic movements of Church leaders and Bennett, 64–69
Church
 reproached with crime of polygamy, 18
Cincinnati, Ohio
 Isaac Sheen goes to, 211–212
Clark, General, 66
Clayton, William, 165
Cobb, Augusta
 baptized, 21, 35
 divorce case, 37–38
 plural wife of Brigham Young, 22, 32, 35–36
Cobb, Henry
 divorce case, 37–38
 husband of Augusta Cobb, 36
 sued for divorce, 37
Cochran Delusion
 book quoted, 1–7
Cochran, Jacob
 appeared before Supreme Judicial Court, 13–14
 arrested, 16–17
 brought before Justice Granger, 13
 court trial, 13–14
 established a community, 11–12
 goes to prison, 12, 17
 high priest of iniquity, 13
 introduced passover feast, 10
 introduced polygamy, 1
 mysteries of God basis for polygamous beliefs, 63
 power of life and death, 10
 Remich's testimony about, 12–14
 revelation to exchange wives, 3
 revelation to practice spiritual wifery, 2
 started Cochranism, 1
 started Garden of Eden ceremony, 3
Cochran, Mrs.
 wife of Jacob Cochran, 3
Cochranism
 compared with LDS Church, 8
 continued after founder's death, 17
 denomination, 1–6
 far-reaching, 5
 paved the way for Mormons, 6–7
 received death-blow, 17
 rise and spread, 14–17
Cochranism Delineated, 9–11
Cochranites
 against church organization, 7, 14
 allowed seven wives, 13
 Church exposed to polygamy by, 63
 converted by Latter Day Saints, 18
 converts moved to Manchester, New York, 7
 gather to Kirtland, Nauvoo, 18, 19, 24–25, 26, 27
 gather to Zion, 23, 24, 25, 26–27, 28
 missionaries attend Cochranite meeting, 22
 return to Saco, Maine, 17
 revival, 15
 secret meetings by oath, 10
Commerce, Illinois
 Saints settle at, 68
community of wives, 67
concubines, 16

conference
Maine, 1836, 32
Saco, Maine, June 1834, 32
conspiracy, 59, 76
Conway, New Hampshire, 9
Cook, Harriet Elizabeth
wife of Brigham Young, 209
Coolbrith, Agnes
married Don Carlos Smith, 29
Coolidge, Joseph W.
administrator of Joseph's estate, 234
Court Case–*People vs Higbee*
disposed of, 155
documents, 145–155
fate of Joseph's affidavit, 158
how found, 143–145
Covington, Kentucky
Isaac Sheen moves to, 211–212

Danites, 179–180
deaths, 69–70
Dennett, George, 26
Dennett, John
becomes leader of Cochranites, 19
Dennett, Lovey, 27
Derry, Charles
English convert, 48
gathered from England to Utah, 95
joined Reorganization, 48, 95–96
visited Joseph Smith III, 96
differences
between Church marriage law and Bennett's fabrication, 202
Dixon, William Hepworth
author of *Spiritual Wives*, 41–43
Doctrine and Covenants
on marriage, 200–201
section 42, LDS and RLDS, 163
Doniphan, General Alexander
attorney for Church leaders, 68
defended Orrin Porter Rockwell, 183
Douglas, Judge Steven A., 157
Downes, Elder Samuel

published book promoting polygamy, 45–47
England, 41
books published on polygamy in, 43
mission opened, 32–33
polygamy practiced in, 33
polygamy revealed to Brigham Young in, 33
Evening and the Morning Star, The,
report of June 1834 conference at Saco, Maine, 32
exchanging wives
revelation on, by Cochran, 3
ruins home life, 3–4, 5, 27–28
taught by Cochran, 3

Fairfield, Wayne County, Illinois
Bennett moves to, 66
Far West, Missouri
headquarters of Church, 66
Fielding, Joseph
gathered to Nauvoo, 55
letter to Parley P. Pratt, 55–56
Foster, Dr. Robert D.
quote of, 170
Surgeon General of Nauvoo Legion, 162
wrote letter naming women involved with Bennett, 162–163
Foster, Solon
interview of, by Joseph Smith III, 92–95
Joseph Smith's coachman, 89
testimony of, 89–90
Francis, Simeon
editor of *Sangamo Journal*, 176
enters into pact with Bennett, 177
Freeman, Solomon
charged with crime of polygamy, 51
Fuller, Catharine
affidavit of, 138–139
seduced by Chauncey Higbee, 134
stopped at home of, 135

Gallatin, Missouri
  Church leaders taken to, for trial, 68
Garden of Eden ceremony
  practiced by Cochran, 3
  practiced by LDS Church, 8
Gates, Susa Young
  comments on Eliza R. Snow, 106
  daughter of Brigham Young, 106
gathering
  Joseph and Hyrum forbade families being separated in, 56–58
  separating of spouses in, 55
Gee, Amanda
  subpoenaed to testify, 154
Governor Carlin of Illinois, 156
Governor Reynolds of Missouri, 156
Greenough, _____
  adultery with Brigham Young, 35

Ham, Timothy
  a Cochranite, 24
Harendeen, Elizabeth, 21
Harris, George W.
  Nauvoo alderman, 136, 137, 138
Herald, The True Latter Day Saints'
  article by Isaac Sheen causes controversy, 208–209
Higbee, Chauncey
  affidavit of, 141–142
  arrest warrant, 146–147
  bail set, 150
  brother of Francis M. Higbee, 134
  colonel in Nauvoo Legion, 134
  comments in regard to, by John Taylor, 139–140
  court case found, 143–145
  expelled from the Church, 142
  found guilty of spiritual wifery, 134, 141
  had five women subpoenaed to testify against Joseph, 154–155
  lawyer, 134
  People vs, *The*, 143, 158
  said Joseph taught him there was no harm in spiritual wifery, 137
  seduced Catharine Fuller, 134, 138–139
  seduced Margaret and Matilda Nyman, 134–137
  seduced Sarah Miller, 137–138
  son of Elias Higbee, 73
Higbee, Elias
  Church historian, 73
  member of Nauvoo High Council, 115
  personal friend of Joseph Smith, 115
  reported to Joseph, 157
Higbee, Francis
  brother of Chauncey Higbee, 134
  courted Nancy Rigdon, 115
  immorality of, 115–118, 127
  seduced Nancy Rigdon, 117
  seduced six or seven women, 127
  son of Elias Higbee, 115
Hiram, Ohio
  Bennett and Joseph meet for first time, 65
Hollis, Maine, 4
holy kiss, 15, 130
house of ill fame
  built by Bennett and others, 129–130
  Nauvoo city authorities order, to be destroyed, 129
Hyde, Apostle Orson
  adopts polygamy, 1, 19, 21
  knew John Bennett, 78
  lecture on marriage relations, 223
  married six wives, 48
  mission among Cochranites, 19, 21–29

Illinois
  polygamy a crime in the state of, 160
important events, 173–175
investigation of Bennett, 112–115
Invincible Dragoons, 67

Jackson, Sarah, 52
Jacob
   Book of Mormon prophet, 219
   correct interpretation of Jacob 2:39, 226
   gives inspired message forbidding polygamy, 220–222
   incorrect interpretation of Jacob 2:39, 226
jealousy
   among Masons, 111
Jefferson City, Missouri, 156
Johnson, John and Elsa
   Joseph and Bennett meet for first time at home of, 64–65
   provide room in home for work to be done on the Inspired Version translation, 65
Jordan, Ichabod
   filed charges against Cochran, 13
Journal of History
   case of Aaron Lyon, 52–53
   Charles Derry discusses polygamy with Joseph Smith III, 96
Journals
   Orson Hyde, 36
   Samuel Harrison Smith, 35–36
Judge Woodman, 11

Kennebunk, Maine, 10
Kimball, Apostle Heber C.
   adopts polygamy, 1
   married forty-three wives, 48
Kirtland High Council
   approval of, for general conference at Saco, Maine, 1834, 32
   decision of, to allow Brigham Young to travel alone, 32
Kirtland, Ohio, 63–64, 228

Ladies' Relief Society
   Bennett accuses, 184
   declaration by, 185
   public stand against polygamy, 103
Latter Day Saint missionaries
   arrive in Maine in 1832, 18
   baptized Cochranites, 18, 19, 21
law of marriage, 199–201
Law, William
   affidavit of, 166–167
   brought indictments against Joseph, 231
   counselor to Joseph, 161
   formed conspiracy, 231
   pleaded for Bennett, 161
   second counselor in First Presidency, 114
   sent to gather information on Bennett, 114
   testimony of, 161
   tried to persuade Bennett to go to Texas, 175
LDS (see Mormon Church)
Lehi
   example of monogamy, 227–228
Liberty Jail
   Joseph's letter from, denouncing polygamy, 67
Limington, Maine
   Cochranite meetings held at, 4
lust
   deny the faith if, 163
   if repents not, to be cast out, 163
   shall not have the Spirit if, 163
Lyon, High Priest Aaron
   priestcraft of, 52–53

Macedonia, Illinois, 211
Maine
   home of Cochranites, 1–29
   missionaries arrive in, 18
Maine Historical Society
   report on Cochran, 14–17
malaria
   at Nauvoo, 68
Manchester, England
   Brigham Young commits adultery in, 34–35
Manchester, New York
   Cochranites moved to, 7
Mansion House stairs
   diagram of stairs, 88

Eliza Snow was not pushed down, 89–100
Marks, Henry, 154
Marks, High Priest William
   Joseph and Marks conferred, 60
   Joseph asked Marks to help, 60
   Nauvoo Stake President, 50, 60
   testimony of, 60, 216
marriage
   dissolved at convenience, 13
   law of, 228–229
Marriage article, 51
Masonic fraternity
   Bennett requests interview with, 164
Masonic Lodge, 70, 111, 167, 189
Masons, 72, 189
Matthias, Robert
   appears in Kirtland in 1835, 190
   Bennett likens Joseph to, 190–191
   doctrine was of the devil, 191
Mayer, Elizabeth
   committed adultery with Brigham Young in England, 35
McLellin, Elder William
   agrees to take Bennett to meet Joseph and Sidney Rigdon, 64
   met Bennett while doing missionary work, 64
   takes Bennett to meet Joseph, 65
McRae, Alexander, 153, 154
Mercy, Sister, 4
Messenger and Advocate
   fifty-two members of Saco Branch attended Maine conference, 32
   seventies adopted resolution, 51
Messenger, The
   Brigham Young's vision on polygamy, 33
   Jason Briggs quoted in, 34
Miles, Joel S.
   testimony in Bennett-Higbee trial, 116
Millennial Star
   case of Aaron Lyon, 52–53
   Catharine Fuller Warren testimony, 138–139
   caution to the Church on gathering without spouse, 55–58
Miller, Bishop George
   sent to investigate Bennett's background, 112–113
   wrote letter to Joseph, 112
Miller, Sarah
   affidavit of, 137–138
   Chauncey Higbee's spiritual wife, 134
   confessed to Church authorities, 137–138
   heard Joseph speak against polygamy, 134
   one of Bennett's clique, 134
   subpoena to appear, 147–148, 153–154
Milliken, Arthur, 29
missionaries
   popularity of, 44
missionary spirit, 18
Mississippi River, 68
Missouri State Militia
   Church officials arrested by, 66
monogamy
   God uses, 226–228
Morley, Patriarch Isaac
   knew John Bennett, 78
   married plurally to Eliza Snow's sister, 98
   practiced polygamy, 98, 99
Morley Settlement, 98
Mormon Church (LDS)
   adopts polygamy, 31
   changed history, 107
   Chauncey Higbee case not in history of, 159
   compared to Cochranism, 7
   excluded details of court case from history, 143, 159
   mysteries of God basis for polygamy, 63
   polygamy document, 47

position based upon theory and false foundation, 108–109
proclaims Joseph a polygamist, 75
Section 101 removed from Doctrine and Covenants, 200
tampered with Doctrine and Covenants, 224–225
temple ceremonies, 8
unable to find descendants of Joseph from an alleged plural wife, 186–187
uses part of Bennett's seven steps to polygamy, 140

Mormon empire, 184

Muhammad
a polygamist Bennett compared Joseph to, 192
founder of Islamic religion, 192

Mulholland, James
death of, 69
Joseph's clerk, 69

mysteries of God
polygamy one of, 63, 163–164, 236

Nauvoo Choir
Joseph's speech to, 134

Nauvoo City Council
Joseph's report on expulsion of Bennett, 167–168
removed Bennett from office of mayor, 167–168
signed affidavit, 181

Nauvoo *Expositor*, 108

Nauvoo High Council
Catharine Fuller Warren appears before, 138–139
expels John C. Bennet, 167
investigates seductions, 135
Joseph brings Chauncey Higbee before, 141
those interrogated before, 162
voted to expel Chauncey Higbee, 142

Nauvoo, Illinois
adultery by Brigham Young in, 35–36
citizens of, voted Joseph innocent, 198
city charter, 70, 111
City Council, 121
deaths at, 69–70
Legion, 71, 111
Masonic Lodge, 71–72, 111
Municipal Court, 71, 111
name changed from Commerce, 68

Nauvoo Legion, 78, 111, 114, 167

Nauvoo Municipal Court
Joseph prefers charges against Chauncey Higbee in, 142

Nauvoo Neighbor
Catharine Fuller Warren's testimony, 138–139
seven steps to seduce a woman, 140
testimonies of four women appear in, 135

Newburyport Herald
report on Cochranites, 13

New Gloucester, Maine, 13

Noah
example of monogamy, 227

Nyman, Margaret J.
affidavit of, 135–136
repents, 136
seduced by Chauncey Higbee, 134, 135, 140
subpoena to appear, 147–148, 153–154

Nyman, Matilda J.
affidavit of, 136–137
repents, 136
seduced by Chauncey Higbee, 134
sister of Margaret J. Nyman, 134
subpoena to appear, 147–148, 153–154

Partridge, Bishop Edward
death of, 69

plausible tale, 134, 140, 171

plural marriage, 101, 199

plurality of wives
Joseph forbids, 107

poison
Bennett offers to, man, 164

Bennett takes, 114
polyandry, 36
polygamy
    abomination to God, 67
    among Cochranites, 1, 13, 25
    apostles involved in, 29, 41
    Bennett taught it was one of the mysteries of God, 63
    Book of Mormon condemns, 219–222
    books on, 43
    casts dark shadow over Church, 48
    Church reproached for, 18
    common subject of discussion in 1830, 41
    Eliza Snow supported, 100
    ex-Cochranites took beliefs to Kirtland and Nauvoo, 18
    false document on, 213, 215
    had in secret chambers, 49
    important events, 173–175
    in Church, 1, 18, 25
    in Morley Settlement, 98
    Joseph Smith's writings condemn, 31, 53–55, 103–104
    Ladies' Relief Society certificate against, 103
    law of the Church on, 59–60, 103–104
    no rule or law in Church permitting, 129
    Ridlon's account, 1–7
    secretly practiced in Nauvoo, 1
    seven basic steps to seduce women, 140
    seventies' action against, 51
    supposed purpose of, 171
    three cases of, 133–134
    warnings against, in Church, 31
Pratt, Orson
    introduced polygamy document, 213
    LDS apostle, 209
    published Lucy Mack Smith's manuscript, 214
    sermon on polygamy, 47
    ten wives, 47
    visited Isaac Sheen, 209, 213–214
Pratt, Parley P.
    adopts polygamy, 1
    disobeyed Joseph Smith's direction, 58–59
    Joseph Smith warns, 59
    married first plural wife, 58
    married twelve wives, 47–48
    president of English Mission, 55
    presides over conference in England, 46
    sent to York County, Maine, 6
Pratt, Sarah
    affair with Bennett, 72, 133
    brought before High Council, 162
    subpoenaed to testify, 154
    wife of Apostle Orson Pratt, 72–73, 186
Price, Richard and Pamela
    discover Chauncey Higbee case, 144–145
    Pamela's journal entry, 144–145
    return to Carthage Courthouse, 158
    Richard's journal entry, 144
    study of polygamy, 143–144

Quincy, Illinois
    Saints gather to, 68
Quincy Whig
    account of Cobb divorce case, 37–38

Ramus, Illinois, 211
Reformed Mormon Church
    conspirators organized, 231
Remich, Daniel
    testimony of, 12–14
rewards offered
    for Joseph, 156
    for Orrin P. Rockwell, 156
Reynolds, Governor, 156
Rich, Apostle Charles C.
    testimony of, 91, 95
Richards, Willard

Joseph's scribe, 106
journal entry says Joseph forbids polygamy, 106–107
personal records of Joseph in care of, 234
Richmond, Missouri
Church officials imprisoned at, 66
moved from, to Liberty, Missouri, 66
Ridlon, G. T., Sr.
described Cochranite polygamy, 1–7
tells how Cochranism continued, 17–18
Rigdon, Nancy
affair with Bennett, 72–73
daughter of Sidney Rigdon, 115, 186
seduced by Francis Higbee, 117
subpoenaed to testify, 154–155
Rigdon, Sidney, 63–64, 66, 96, 97
father of Nancy Rigdon, 115
in Carthage, 157
in Disciples of Christ Church with Bennett, 78
knew Bennett at Kirtland, 78
righteous seed
examples of, 227–229
through monogamy, 226–227
righteous seed theory
LDS Church principle of, 226
Roberts, Sidney
expelled from Church, 130
revelation on "holy kiss," 130
Robinson, Ebenezer
brother-in-law of Brigham Young, 159
··~e of the peace, 143, 145, 150, 6, 182,

headquarters of Cochranism, 1, 2, 14, 32
Saco River, 2
Saints Herald
Elbert A. Smith comments, 108–109
Heman C. Smith writes about Boggs shooting, 183
Joseph Smith III remembers Lorenzo Wasson brings the news of Joseph and Hyrum's deaths, 83
Joseph Smith III's account of interview with Solon Foster, 92–95
Young Joseph's memories of Bennett, 79
Sangamo Journal
article against Saints at Nauvoo, 176
Bennett writes letters to, 156, 170, 182, 189
Danites, 179
Sappho, 86
Satan
efforts to destroy Church through polygamy, 42
Scarborough, Maine
Cochran preaches at, 2
Schindle, Melissa
subpoenaed to testify, 154
Scriptures
condemn polygamy, 46
secrecy theory, 73–74
secret chambers
enemy in, 49
mystery had in, 49
polygamy had in, 49
secret wife system, 129
Section 42 (RLDS; LDS), 163
Section 132 (LDS), 60–61, 213, 223
seduce
seven steps used to, 140
Seely, Lucy Decker
first plural wife of Brigham Young, 36, 171, 209

wife of William Seely, 36, 58, 171
Seely, William, 36, 58, 171
Seer, The
    paper published by Orson Pratt, 214
    revelation on polygamy printed in, 215
separation of spouses
    forbidden by Joseph Smith, 55–58
seraglio (harem), 184
    Bennett describes, 191–195
    refuted by Church, 197
seven wives
    Cochranites allowed, 10, 13
    Joseph accused of having, 87, 233
seventies
    their action against polygamy, 51
Sheen, Isaac
    abolitionist, 210
    article causes controversy, 207–208
    associated with Almon Babbitt, 209
    baptized, 210
    believed Joseph had been in polygamy, 208
    early life, 209–210
    editor of the *True Latter Day Saints' Herald*, 207
    married Drusilla Babbitt, 211
    member of First Presidency in William Smith's organization, 212
    not a primary witness, 209
    sold Orson Pratt valuable manuscript, 213–214
    statement of, 208
    studied law of lineage, 212
    writes to William Smith, 212
Sheen, John Kirk
    son of Isaac Sheen, 212
Sherwood, H. J.
    testimony in John Bennett-Francis Higbee trial, 116

sin
    no, where no accuser, 135, 136
Sister Mercy
    a medium, 4
    immoral with Cochran, 4
Smith, Alexander
    challenged polygamous system in Utah, 101
    condemns secrecy theory, 74
    Joseph not a coward, 74
    responds to charges against father, 74–75
Smith, David
    challenged polygamous system in Utah, 101
    son of Joseph and Emma, 108
Smith, Don Carlos, 29
    brother of Joseph Smith, 65
    death of, 69
    editor of *Times and Seasons*, 65, 115
    married Agnes Coolbrith, 29
Smith, Elbert A.
    grandson of Joseph and Emma, 108
    wrote on Joseph's sermon, 108–109
Smith, Emma
    did not push Eliza Snow down Mansion House stairs, 87, 89–100
    named in Joseph's affidavit, 146
    president of Ladies' Relief Society, 103, 185
    was denied Joseph's personal papers, 234
    worked to eradicate Bennett's false teachings, 73
Smith, Heman C., 183
Smith, Hyrum
    affidavit of, 163–166
    arrested, 66
    directed teachers to report any who had more than one wife, including Bennett, 129
    forbade separation of spouses, 56–

58
  moved from Richmond Jail to Liberty, Missouri, 66
  presiding patriarch, 114
  sent to gather information on Bennett, 114
  testimony in Francis Higbee case, 127
  worked to eradicate Bennett's false teachings, 73
Smith, Joseph, Jr., 135, 136
  accused of revelation on polygamy, 1
  affidavit of, 146
  affidavit of, missing, 158
  arrested, 66
  condemned polygamy, 134
  forbade separation of spouses, 56–58
  forced into hiding, 155
  had Chauncey Higbee expelled, 143
  importance of his lawsuit against Chauncey Higbee, 160
  letter written from Liberty Jail, 67
  meets John C. Bennett, 65
  mentions Parley P. Pratt in sermon, 59
  moved family from Kirtland to Missouri, 66
  moved from Richmond Jail to Liberty, Missouri, 66
  official statement concerning Bennett, 169–170
  preached in the Grove at Nauvoo, 133
  published article against Bennett, 80–82
  published statement against polygamy, 54–55
  sermon against polygamy, 232–234
  sued Chauncey Higbee, 142, 143
  takes Chauncey Higbee before High Council, 142, 143
  waited for proof to file charges against Bennett, 133
  wanted charges brought against offenders, 31, 50
  worked to eradicate Bennett's false teachings, 73
  writings condemn polygamy, 31, 54–55
Smith, Joseph, Sr., 69
Smith, Joseph, III
  challenged polygamous system in Utah, 101
  disagrees with Isaac Sheen, 217
  interview with Solon Foster, 92–95
  responds to claims about father, 74
  takes editorial control of *Herald*, 217
  visits with Charles Derry, 95–96
Smith, Lucy
  her manuscript sold, 214
  tells of Bennett's "scheme," 71
Smith, Mary, 69
Smith, Samuel
  baptized Augusta Cobb, 21
  mission among Cochranites, 6, 21–29
Smith, William
  brother of Joseph, 212
  declares himself president of the Church, 212
  editor of the *Wasp*, 162
  Isaac Sheen wrote to, 212
  parts with mother's manuscript, 214
  published Robert D. Foster's letter, 162–163
Snow, Eliza, 77
  affidavits, 101
  article written by, 85
  bore no child at Nauvoo, 96
  did not bear Joseph's child, 95–96
  directs preparation of manuscript, 104–105
  knew John C. Bennett, 78–79

life and writings, 96–100
lived with the Rigdons, 97
not Joseph Smith's plural wife, 89
plural wife of Brigham Young, 100
produced book with Edward W. Tullidge, 105
rejected by Dr. Bennett, 86
secretary of Ladies' Relief Society, 103, 185
signed petition saying Joseph innocent, 103–104

Snow, Leonora
polygamous wife of Isaac Morley, 98
sister of Eliza Snow, 98–99

Snow, LeRoi C.
testimony of, 89–90

Snow, Lorenzo
brother of Eliza Snow, 44
friend of Sidney Rigdon, 96
statement of, 44

Snow, Oliver and Rosetta, 96, 97, 98
knew Bennett, 78
left Nauvoo and Church, 85

Spencer, Clarissa Young
comments on Eliza R. Snow, 105
daughter of Brigham Young, 105

spiritual matrimony
taught by Cochran, 16

spiritual wifery, 10, 11–12, 19
Alexander Hale Smith responds to, 74–75
book on, 41–42
Chauncey Higbee found guilty of, 141
Cochran's revelations on, 2
John C. Bennett claims repentance from, 133
John C. Bennett taught and practiced, 63, 72–73

Springfield *Sangamo Journal,* 66, 156

Stafford, Edwin
elder in Reorganized Church, 34
testified of Brigham Young's adultery, 43

Stafford, Thomas
seventy in Reorganized Church, 34
testimony of Brigham Young's adultery, 34–35
testimony of Joseph's innocence, 35

Stinchfield, Ephraim
hears Cochran preach, 9–10
published booklet on Cochran, 9

subpoena
for Joseph's witnesses, 147–148

Taylor, Apostle John
adopts polygamy, 1
comments of, regarding Chauncey Higbee, 139
comments of, regarding publishing of affidavits, 139–140
editor of *Times and Seasons,* 115, 139
married fifteen wives, 48

Taylor, Sally, 27

Taylor, Teacher John
followed Bennett to house of ill repute, 129
investigates Bennett, 128
testimony of, 128

Testament of the Twelve Patriarchs, the Sons of Jacob, The
book promoting polygamy, 45, 47
theme of, adopted by LDS Church, 46–47

time and eternity phrase
significance of, 196–197

Times and Seasons, 176
affidavit of Hyrum Smith, 163–166
article from St. Louis *Atlas,* 131
Bennett arrives in Nauvoo, 69
Bennett is Chancellor of the University, 134
Bennett led youth astray, 133
Bennett says Joseph is innocent, 173
Bennett's baptism, 111

Bennett's charge of duress, 180–181
bravery of Joseph, 76
Choir of Singers, 134
Danites, 180
Don Carlos Smith editor of, 65
Dr. Wilhelm Wyl implied Bennett seduced Eliza Snow by quoting article by her in, 85
Francis Higbee, 115, 116, 117, 118, 127
High Council meets at Kirtland, 32
house of ill fame, 130
Joseph confronts Bennett, 113
Joseph lays conduct of Bennett before Church, 80–82
Joseph member of the Board of Regents, 134
Joseph preached against polygamy, 131
Joseph published article detailing Bennett's sins, 174
Joseph published Church belief on polygamy, 104
Joseph sends William Law and Hyrum Smith to gather information, 114–115
Joseph writes of Bennett's case, 87
Joseph wrote of Bennett, 198
Joseph's letter from prison, 54–55, 67
Joseph's possessions, 131
Lorenzo Wasson offers help, 83
notice published in, hand of fellowship withdrawn from Bennett, 176
petition by Ladies' Relief Society, 185
proclamation to Saints scattered abroad, 70
Relief Society certificate, 103
seven basic steps to seduce women, 140
signed certificates, 203–205
warning about Bennett, 112–113
William Law's statement under oath, 161, 175

Townsend, James
a Cochranite converted by Mormons, 7
Trial of Bennett and Higbee, 116–118, 127
True Latter Day Saints' Herald, The,
Isaac Sheen's incorrect statement in, 215–217
truth and lies, 75–76
Tullidge, Edward W.
Eliza Snow's alleged marriage, 101
produced book with Eliza Snow, 105

venereal disease, 115–116, 127

Waite, Catharine V.
lawyer, 39
wife of Judge Charles B. Waite, 39
wrote a book about polygamy, 39
Waite, Judge Charles B.
justice appointed to Territory of Utah, 39
Wandell, Elder Charles
declared Joseph's history changed, 235
employed in Historian's office, 235
Warren, Catharine Fuller, 145
affidavit of, 138–139
allowed home to be used for seduction, 140–141
married William Warren, 141
Wasp, The
Nauvoo newspaper, 162, 163, 174, 181
Wasson, Lorenzo
brought news of martyrdom, 83
Emma Smith's nephew, 82
testimony of Joseph's innocence, 82–83
Webb, C. G., 90
Webster, Illinois, 211
Wells, Justice Daniel, 181

Wells, Seventy Gomer R., 34
Weymouth, Esther, 27
Weymouth, Simeon, 26, 27
White, Captain Hugh
 Joseph purchased Homestead from, 162
White, Emmeline
 affair with Bennett, 162
 ex-wife of Captain Hugh White, 162
 nonmember, 163, 186
 subpoenaed to testify, 154–155
Whitehead, High Priest James
 convert from England, 58
 joined Reorganization, 59
 moved to Alton, Illinois, 58
 secretary to Joseph Smith, 58
 testimony of, 59
Whitney, Newell K.
 became a polygamist, 78
 knew Bennett, 78
Wight, Lyman
 became a polygamist, 78
 knew Bennett, 78
Willoughby, Ohio, 63–64
Willoughby University
 Bennett on faculty of, 65
Winter Quarters, 58
Women of Mormondom, The, 105
Woodman, Judge, 11
Works, Angeline, 159
Works, Miriam, 159
Wyl, Dr. W. [Wilhelm], 90, 92
 implied Bennett seduced Eliza, 85–86, 87

York County, Maine
 Cochran fanaticism in, 14
 missionaries preach in, 6, 22
Young, Brigham
 adopts polygamy, 1, 19, 21
 adultery with Elizabeth Mayer, 35
 adultery with ____ Greenough, 35
 brings forth polygamous document, 235
 built upon Bennett's foundation, 63
 claimed vision from God, 32–33, 171
 Cochranite connections, 31–32
 deletes portion of Joseph Smith's journal, 107
 disobeyed Joseph Smith's direction, 58
 Ebenezer Robinson's brother-in-law, 159
 excludes court case from Church history, 143
 father of Mormon polygamy, 31
 fifty-six children born to, 31, 171
 great knowledge of polygamy, 41–42
 influence and power, 39
 introduced document on polygamy, 213
 judge in Bennett and Francis Higbee trials, 170
 learned to practice polygamy secretly, 170–171
 married Augusta Cobb, 32, 36
 married Harriet Elizabeth Cook, 209
 married Lucy Decker Seely, 36, 171, 209
 Mary Ann Angell, legal wife, 209
 ministered among the Cochranites, 6
 palmed a fraudulent polygamy revelation, 76
 polygamous revelations in England, 32–33
 rewrote Joseph's history, 235
 testimony in Francis Higbee case, 118, 127
Young, John R., 92

Zion
 Bennett lies about meaning of, 183–184